Metamorphosis and Identity

Metamorphosis and Identity

Caroline Walker Bynum

ZONE BOOKS · NEW YORK

2001

Printed in the United States of America.

Distributed by The MIT Press,
Cambridge, Massachusetts, and London, England

Library of Congress Cataloging-in-Publication Data

Bynum, Caroline Walker.
    Metamorphosis and identity / Caroline Walker
Bynum.
        p.   cm.
    Includes bibliographical references (p.) and index.
    ISBN 1-890951-22-6.
    1. Change. 2. Metamorphosis. 3. Identity
(Philosophical concept). I. Title.
BD373.B96 2001
126—dc21   00-047316

For Guenther Roth

Contents

Acknowledgments

Two of the essays in this volume first appeared as follows: "Wonder," in the *American Historical Review* 102.1 (1977), pp. 1–26, and "Metamorphosis, or Gerald and the Werewolf," in *Speculum* 73.4 (1998), pp. 987–1013. I am grateful to the editors of these journals for permission to publish revised versions of the original articles. The final essay was delivered as the Jefferson Lecture for 1999 and appeared on the internet through the National Endowment for the Humanities, which sponsored the lecture. Whereas the first essay is republished with only minor revisions, Chapters 2 and 4 have been substantially changed from their original versions.

Because the occasions and audiences for these essays were so diverse, my debts of gratitude are broad. Moreover, any book written in mid-career will have roots in questions and research, and hence in scholarly friendships, of many years' duration. I owe thanks to more people than I can name here. Nonetheless pride of place must go to Peter Jelavich and Pamela Smith, who shared with me the veritable orgy of operagoing in Berlin that led me to spend two weeks reading Ovid with riveted attention. I am also grateful to the scene of that passionate reading, the Wissenschaftskolleg zu Berlin, where I was a fellow in 1994–1995. All the fellows and staff there contributed to my work, but I would like to thank especially Arnold Davidson and Carolyn Abbate for sharing research that fed directly into my own. The staffs of the American Historical Association, the Medieval Academy of America, and the National Endowment for the Humanities helped with the duties that came along with the opportunities to deliver these addresses. The Warburg Haus in Hamburg provided a congenial setting in which to do the final work of revision on this book; my thanks to Marianne Pieper and Barbara Eggert for their assistance with both libraries and daily life in Hamburg. As always, I am grateful to the Columbia University Libraries and especially to Michael Stoller, whose boast that he can always find a book is one I constantly prove true (like any medieval collector of marvels and miracles) by experience. I am also grateful to Patricia Decker, a research assistant of extraordinary intelligence, perseverance, and imagination; to Peter Brown, Thomas E.A. Dale and Jeffrey Hamburger, who read portions of this book and offered detailed comments; to Philippe Buc and Philip Lyndon Reynolds for help in acquiring material; and to my friends at Zone Books, especially Meighan Gale, Ingrid Sterner, Victoria Velsor, and Amy Griffin, for technical and scholarly assistance. The following colleagues, friends, and family have helped in ways to which I pay only inadequate tribute by the alphabetical listing of names: Bruce Altshuler, Katisha Baldwin, Roberta Bondi, Giles Constable, Ann Douglas, Carmela Franklin, Martha Howell, Adam Kosto, Stephen P. Marrone, Katharine Park, Frederick Paxton, Edward Peters, J. Wim Smit, Robert Somerville, Tracey Strasser, Antonia Walker, and Stephen D. White. All my students have been part of the intellectual explorations recorded here, but I would especially like to mention Anne-Marie Bouché, Rachel Fulton, Manuele Gragnolati, Anna Harrison, Bruce Holsinger, Jacqueline Jung, Susan Kramer, and the late Claudia Rattazzi Papka, whose ideas have contributed directly to these essays and whose work makes me proud to be part of the pedagogical enterprise. Teodolinda Barolini, Kathy Eden, Joel Kaye, and Dorothea von Mücke have read and criticized and listened and argued until their ways of thinking are woven deeply into my own. I rely more than they know on their clear-sighted intelligence and generosity. I also thank Ramona Naddaff, friend and editor, for her uncanny ability to get to the heart of what I am trying to say. I dedicate the volume to my husband, Guenther Roth, who has never failed to find my ideas wonderful in all the senses of "wonderful" I explore below.

Change in the Middle Ages

The Ulster Werewolves

Sometime around 1187, a certain Gerald of Wales wrote an ethnography of Ireland, based in part on his travels there with an English expeditionary army two years before.[1] One of the stories he told has intrigued recent historians, as we know it did readers in Gerald's own day. It is the story of a priest traveling from Meath to Ulster who meets a talking he-wolf in the wild and must decide whether to accede to the wolf's request to give the Eucharist to his dying mate. In Gerald's first telling, the focus is squarely on the nature of the wolves (are they animal or human?) and on the attendant question of the legal status of the priest's decision to administer the sacrament. Gerald, however, spent much of the rest of his life revising his already lengthy account of Ireland, and it is interesting to see what he added to the tale of the Ulster werewolves in recensions two, three, and four. His additions are not what modern readers expect. Hence they have been ignored by recent critics in favor of the uncanny tales that seem relevant and appealing to a public prepared to find in the Middle Ages a combination of *Y2K the Movie*, *Ladyhawke*, and *Buffy the Vampire Slayer*.[2] But Gerald's further ruminations on the werewolf story were philosophical, not psychological or literary, and the subject

[margin note: Gerald added]

of these additions is the subject of my book. What, then, did Gerald insert as his own idea of the context necessary for understanding the werewolves of Ulster?

Part of what Gerald added was political. Into the he-wolf's mouth he put a prophecy that predicted English success in dominating Ireland unless and until the conquerors adopted the "depraved habits" of the conquered. Framed in reference to Leviticus and Ecclesiasticus, the prophecy almost but not quite suggests a pattern of repeated decline as nation replaces nation in world history. Hence even Gerald's first addition concerns change.

Almost three times as long is his second addition to the story, and that addition is an explicit and complex discussion of what it means for something to become something else. The titillating story of the wolf-humans and even the seemingly topical threat of political failure through moral decline are swamped by what appears to modern tastes a dry, even pedantic impulse to analyze the werewolves' metamorphosis as one type of transformation among many. Gerald begins with a rather dubious analogy between Christ and the werewolf: as divine nature assumed human nature for the salvation of the world, so "by no less a miracle" human nature here assumes the nature of a wolf. Since both the preceding account of the Ulster werewolves and the borrowings from Augustine and other writers that follow sometimes imply that skin or pelt or outer form is mere appearance, the parallel to the Incarnation is an odd one. It seems even odder when Gerald summarizes from Augustine the view that demons or wicked men perform elaborate shenanigans which God permits to deceive our senses into acceptance of illusion. Gerald does not, however, seem to mean either that the incarnate Christ is an illusion or that no change of what we would call species is possible. Without returning to the original Christological analogy, he now announces:

16

It is to be believed ... as an indubitable truth that Almighty God, just as he creates natures, can, when he wishes, change them into each other [*in se invicem permutare*] ... , either transferring one into the other completely [*penitus*], as Lot's wife, looking back against the Lord's command, became a pillar of salt, or water became wine [*in vinum mutatione*]; or as, the inner nature remaining the same [*interiore manente natura*], only the exterior is transformed [*transformare*], as is clear from the examples given before.

But I think it safest to skip over that change of the appearance of bread [*de illa vero speciali panis ... mutatione*] into Christ's body, which is not a change of appearance only but truly a change of substance [*substantiali*] because the appearance or species remains completely and only the substance is changed [*specie tota manente substantia sola mutatur*]. Comprehending it is arduous and very far beyond human understanding.

Hence Gerald has begun his discussion of change with a confused analogy that vacillates between taking Christ and werewolves as hybrids (the joining of two incompatibles) and taking the two very disparate figures as masquerades (changings of costume or skin, where nature endures). Both understandings are conceptualizations in some sense of non-change: either something is added to something else that perdures, or a something that perdures is overclothed or re-overclothed with something else. Gerald then, however, asserts that God can change one thing into another, as, for example, in the miracle at Cana or the transformation of Lot's wife into salt. Miracles can be metamorphoses. And Gerald ends, somewhat awkwardly, with an incoherent although orthodox statement that the Eucharist is transformation in which the metamorphosis occurs at the level of substance or nature while the appearance endures. Aware perhaps that he has failed to find a satisfactory classification for the werewolf with whom he began,

17

Gerald concludes with the warning that it is safest not to treat the Eucharist at all and turns his attention to wonders, such as the bearded woman or the ox-man, that are clearly cases of hybrids, not metamorphosis.[3]

Scholars have recently been interested in a number of aspects of Gerald's account: the emerging national or regional stereotyping, the evidence of cross-cultural encounter, the construction of the marvelous, the concern for documentation and verifiability, the fear of and fascination with the borderline between animal and human, the threat of the wild, the suggestion of gender-bending and human-animal sex, and above all the werewolves themselves.[4] But the lengthy theorizing of change has escaped notice. Nonetheless I want to argue that there is something paradigmatic about the particular discussion Gerald engages in here. Gerald's explicit, energetic, and confused efforts to understand change seem to me typical of the late twelfth century, and the terms in which he distinguishes varieties of *mutatio* (inner and outer, nature or substance and appearance, illusion and transformation, metamorphosis and hybrid) figure in major discussions by his contemporaries.[5] I shall argue in this book that intellectuals, religious leaders, and (insofar as we can glimpse them) ordinary people were fascinated by change as an ontological problem — not merely the birth and decay inherent in the life cycle, the economic and political opportunities attendant upon growth, the threat and promise posed by shifting gender relations and family structures, the efforts to position self engendered by cross-cultural contacts and emerging national identities — but also and preeminently change itself: the fundamental fact that something can become something else.

18

Change: The Concept

"Change" is a deceptively simple word. We use it constantly, and we all know what it means, or so we think. We change our shoes; we change addresses; we change partners; we change our minds. We say a color changes if we view it in sunlight and in shadow, that a memory changes from the distance of a week or a decade. A moment of reflection suggests, however, that these understandings of "change" are not all the same — that, for example, the change in color as I shift perspective is something quite different from the change of high heels for sneakers at the end of a work-day. To oversimplify a little, "change" can mean the substituting of one thing for another — sneakers for high heels — or it can mean that one thing alters its appearance or qualities or modes of being: my job evolves so that it is largely paper pushing and administration whereas before it was teaching; the peach paint sample changes to lavender in the moonlight; a traumatic event seems in hindsight benign.[6]

Change
1. Substitute
2. alters qualities of being

The question of change is, of course, the other side of the question of identity. If change is the replacement of one entity by another or the growth of an entity out of another entity in which it is implicit, we must be able to say how we know we have an entity in the first place. What gives it its identity — that is, makes it one thing? Whether or not the "job" I hold stays "the same" from week to week, why do I call this bundle of activities one "job" in the first place? To say peach changes to purple involves drawing a line between one set of light waves and another on what some would see to be a continuum.

How is it the one thing to begin w/?

In the current culture wars, "identity" tends to have divergent denotations. Nonetheless change is the test, the limit, of all denotations of the term "identity." I may, for example, test what constitutes my identity understood as personality by imagining what would have to change through a mental illness such as Alzheimer's

change all het of identity

19

in order for "me" to cease to be "me." I may also explore what constitutes an "identity position" such as heterosexual female by asking under what circumstances and whether it changes. And whatever identity-as-personality or identity-as-identity-position I claim, I can question how I survive as an entity at all if the physical stuff of my body is replaced completely every seven years and the stream of my memories is in such constant flux that I no longer know what I ate for lunch a week ago Saturday. Hence whether we think of change as, at one end of the spectrum, replacement or, at the other, an unfolding of an essence or core forever present, our conception of change is intrinsically tied to our conception of entity or identity. Evolution-change may or may not (but often does) assume an unfolding kernel or essence; hence identity, entity-ness, tends to perdure, but difference over time is hard to express. Replacement-change permits newness and difference but tends to make its appearance, no matter how well prepared for, arbitrary and ultimately inexplicable. Unless there is some connection, or nexus, between what was and what comes after, we tend to think we have not a change but merely two things.[7]

In our own popular culture as in the writing of other eras, different sorts of images tend to express these two very different understandings of change and identity. Replacement-change is frequently depicted in mechanical images where binaries are involved: the now-you-see-it-now-you-don't, on-and-off world of machines and human agents, making, remaking, substituting, and so on. For example, when we want to emphasize replacement rather than modification of roles, we say "I 'switched' jobs." Evolution-change is often illustrated or explained in images of unfolding or developing. Organic or biological or psychological images seem especially appropriate: seeds growing, the young maturing, an intention or plan being realized. Certain images tend, moreover, to express resistance to both sorts of change: for example, images of overclothing or accumulation in which radical difference is added to a core that is little if at all affected by the addition.

Almost any actual sequence of events can, of course, be described by both concepts and a wide variety of metaphors. The sprouting of an acorn can be perceived as the replacement of rotten nut-stuff by sprig and root or as the unfolding of a tiny tree carried in the seed and itself carrying future seed-stuff. Even taking off high heels and donning sneakers can — although this is harder — be seen as placing in a space that needs shoes one version after another of what that space needs and hence a condition of shoe-neediness met by different instances of shoe. What we encounter experientially and empirically does not seem alone to determine how we understand and describe change.

Thus we will learn a good deal about any cultural moment by asking what conception of change, whether implicit or explicit, tends to dominate its various discourses. We may indeed be able to ferret out which concepts different discourses favor by studying which metaphors for change they tend to choose. Moreover, it will matter greatly to our understanding of a period whether writers are explicit and self-conscious about questions of change and identity and whether the concepts are stable or themselves in flux. It is my contention, in the essays that follow, that many different discourse communities in the twelfth and thirteenth centuries were newly and explicitly concerned with the question of change, a question often understood quite technically and complexly. But there is more to my argument than this. I also propose that concepts of change themselves tended to change in the years around 1200 and that two images in particular, hybrid and metamorphosis — images prominent in imaginative literature, theology, the visual arts, and natural philosophy — were sites of these competing and changing understandings.

21

Change and the Twelfth Century

As the example of Gerald of Wales suggests, writers in the mid- to late twelfth century devoted energetic and complex speculation to the topic of change. But it was by no means only the marvelous or the peculiar that impelled such speculation. Questions such as the end of history, the nature of the universe, the purpose of humanity tended to be treated as questions about change, about coming to be and passing away. Devotional and secular literature tackled in a variety of forms the topic of self-transformation. Not only magic, monsters, and hybrids but also the elements, the process of digestion, and the growth of seeds received new attention.

Nonetheless the literature of mid-century tended to resist what I have above called replacement-change. In his influential treatise *On the Sacraments*, which is really a textbook of theology, Hugh of St. Victor (d. 1141) discussed creation itself as change. Enumerating six "modes of operating," Hugh concluded that, whereas God can make something from nothing, make something into nothing, make a greater new thing from a smaller and a smaller new thing from a larger, human beings can only divide a thing into parts or assemble parts into a whole. In such analysis, any change outside that effected by divine power is accumulation or separation of perduring particles, a version, it seems, of non-change.[8] Otto of Freising (d. 1158), in his world history, introduced technical discussion of ontology into his account of the end of time. Glossing Psalm 101.27 ("They [the heavens] shall perish but thou [God] remainest, and all of them shall grow old like a garment") and 1 Corinthians 7.31 ("For the fashion of this world passeth away"), Otto asserted that "to pass away" does not mean to go from being to nonbeing; nothing ever really disappears. Hence "there will be a new heaven not by destruction of substance but by a change of form [*non abolita substantia, sed mutata figura*]."[9] The poet Bernard Sylvestris (d. ca. 1160) posed the issue of survival through change when he

22

praised a nourishing and fertile universe in which sexual reproduction defeated death by perpetuating species. But the soul sur-
vives by immortality; the crucial preservation of identity is non-
change.[10]

In the mid-twelfth century, people producing a wide variety of
discourses tended to think of change not as replacement but as
evolution or development, as alteration of appearance or mode of
being. For example, heroes and heroines of twelfth-century literature tend to display an essential self. The biographer of a saint
who grew up to be a bishop might tell of the saintly child building
churches of sand on the beach while other boys, destined for
knightly careers, built sandcastles. Behavior revealed character or
type; a self was always what it was. The "end" or goal of development, if there was development, was to achieve the ideal version
of that type or self. The singers of epics described heroes who are
ever heroic, although the plot often turns around the villain's ability, at least for a while, to obscure the hero's virtue from the perception of his sovereign. When in the course of the century the
romance replaced the epic as the popular aristocratic and bour-
geois entertainment, heroes and heroines were understood to
develop psychologically but in order to fill a given social role and
become better versions of virtuous selves. Like the soul in devotional literature, created capable of (because like) God and hence
returning toward what it already is, the hero or heroine of secular
literature grows into or unfolds rather than replaces a self.[11]

In natural philosophy and theology also, technical discussions
of change piqued curiosity and raised anxiety. Grafting was examined; digestion and embryology discussed. But theologians held
nutrition and growth to occur by the self-multiplication of entities,
not by their assimilation of extraneous material; and even the natural philosophical tradition, which maintained real digestion to be
possible, tended to explain physical events by the rearrangement

23

of existing particles.[12] Moreover, the dominant model of explanation for what appeared to be evolution was a notion of seminal
reasons — that is, the idea that pattern was implanted in organisms
and species from the moment of creation so that all development
was the unfolding of an inner structure and plan (rather like
DNA). Thinking about entities was dominated by the classical
trope "like from like," understood to mean that like is generated
from like, like returns to like, like knows like via likeness. Mind
knows ideas because both mind and ideas are intelligible. Eye sees
objects via images or likenesses of those objects. Oak trees produce acorns that grow up to be oaks, not turnips. As did the idea
of seminal reasons, the idea of likeness figured even natural events
such as spontaneous generation, or miracles such as Christ's heal-
ing of the blind man, as the unfolding of an essence or the preservation of species or type.[13] Even in the case of eucharistic change
— an exception to natural processes and a clear replacement of
something by something else (bread by flesh) — theories of the
coexistence of two substances or the survival of substance were
considered tenable in the twelfth century, and the concept of
transubstantiation was elaborated as a way of expressing the necessary "going over" of one thing into another. A Sentence Gloss
from about 1160/65 asked why God converted bread into flesh
and wine into blood rather than vice versa and answered that
bread has more "similitude" to flesh than to blood.[14] The Boethian
principle that "every change occurs according to something in
common [aliquid commune]" still held sway.[15]

A final example of the tendency to think in terms of evolution
rather than replacement comes from the mid-twelfth-century
understanding of conversion. Ironically enough, in this age of
both missionizing activity and conquest, of the Crusades in Asia
Minor, the Reconquista in Spain, and the intensification of anti-
Semitism in Europe, "conversion" — which we might expect to

mean radical change, the replacement of one affiliation, even one self, by another — tended instead to mean development. Consider, for example, twelfth-century discussions of the conversion of Paul on the road to Damascus. In the biblical story, Saul, persecutor of Christians, is struck from his horse by a blinding light and transformed suddenly into a disciple of Christ. But mid-twelfth-century interpretations of this story do not stress sudden or radical transformation. Rather, the story is used to illustrate "vocation," or calling — the notion that God has a purpose for a person that is built into, and hence known by and in, his or her talents and virtues.[16]

Toward the end of the twelfth century, however, a new understanding — a new model — of change emerged. In a quite stunning shift of intellectual paradigms, people were increasingly fascinated by change of the first sort I sketched above — radical change, where an entity is replaced by something completely different. Concerning topics such as digestion and nutrition, for example, theologians now asserted that growth occurs because food really changes into blood and bile in our stomachs and rejected older notions that growth must be a mysterious expansion of a given physical stuff because basic particles and atoms cannot change their natures. Concomitantly, natural philosophers began to study and debate alchemy — a science learned from the Arab world that promised to change one metal into another (especially, of course, base metals into gold). In eucharistic theology, some theorists proposed that the previous substance, bread, was annihilated or dissolved into a sort of prime matter and the body of Christ then introduced into the same place. And, to give a fourth example: metamorphosis stories, popular in Antiquity but not in the early Middle Ages, revived. The proliferation of tales of vampires, fairies, and werewolves testifies not merely to an enthusiasm for alterity and escapism but also to a fascination with, and horror at,

the possibility that persons might, actually or symbolically, become beasts or angels, suddenly possessed by demons or inspired
to prophecy.[17]

The question for historians is why ways of conceptualizing
change might themselves change, why many people around 1200
might entertain, with fascination and fear, understandings of
change that were infrequent only fifty years before. Part of the
answer certainly lies (as scholars have long held) in the wealth
of new intellectual materials available.[18] For theologians, natural
philosophers, grammarians, chroniclers, and even poets, the newly
circulating works of Aristotle, especially the *On Generation and
Corruption*, not only provided tools for thinking about the process
of becoming but also forced to the fore the idea that change really
meant not just an unfolding of, or a tinkering with, existing things
but new being — being that followed upon the annihilation of what
was.[19] But (as historians have also long held) the existence of texts
cannot account for their (correct or incorrect) use. Texts are studied — indeed sought — because something about what they confront seems relevant.[20]

Changing social circumstances provided the context for such
relevance.[21] Agricultural, economic, and urban growth in the
course of the eleventh and twelfth centuries had led to transformations of familial and social structure that made it increasingly
possible (if still not easy) for people — especially privileged people
— to change their social roles. The rise of patrilineal inheritance
that left younger sons to fend for themselves, economic opportunities in towns that gave men and women a number of new
careers, proliferation of intellectual and religious vocations that
encouraged adult recruitment in place of childhood socialization, colonial wars and missionary activity that brought European
Christians into contact with radically different mores — these are
only a few of the trends that led individuals to a new sense of

choosing where they were socially and culturally situated.[22] Not
perhaps to actual choosing (for how can we ever know who is able
to choose?) but to a sense of making choices. And such awareness
of choice entails a sense of either-or, a sense, that is, of replacement-change — of a knightly patrimony renounced in order to
study rhetoric or theology, of a farm left behind in order to go
on a Crusade and kill for God, of painful self-doubt and illness
replaced by the trumpeting of divine prophecy through one's own
unworthy lips or pen. It also entails anxiety — a need for limits,
for knowing what is outside, other, different, as well as what is
home and self. Thus we find, in the years around 1200, a new fascination with the other and with images of change in which one
thing is, for better or worse, really replaced by something else.[23]

We also find fear — fear of new identities, fear of boundary
crossing. Misogyny and scapegoating of out-groups such as Jews
and lepers emerged in tandem with new enthusiasm for the glory
and the regularity of the world. Alarm at decay and spirit possession intensified alongside confidence in both intellectual and mystical approach to God. The basic threat of heresy was increasingly
conceptualized as assault not just on pious practice but on fundamental notions of the human as well. Dualists and antinomians
were criticized not merely for rejection of Church and sacraments
but also for denying the boundaries of things — for preaching
metempsychosis or a deification in which person was lost in
divinity. The point of Gerald's discussion of the werewolves of
Ulster was not only to titillate his readers with the possibility of
wolf-humans but also to contain the possibility within theoretical
discussion that denied it to be true metamorphosis. Did the priest
improperly give the Eucharist to a wolf or properly comfort a
dying if deformed "human"? In the indeterminacy and incon-
clusiveness of Gerald's account, we see delight and horror at
the story itself; in the incoherence of his theorizing, we see his

27

awareness that replacement-change is possible, categories can be breached, identities destroyed, yet we also see a fierce determination to hold such breaches at bay, either as illusions or as miracles done only by God.[24]

Hybrid and Metamorphosis

The essays that follow give a number of examples of the new fascination with radical change that characterized the years around 1200: wonder collections (Chapter 1), werewolf stories (Chapters 2 and 4), new theories of the nature of physical change and of miracle (Chapter 2). But they also describe a profound resistance to exactly the replacement-change that was increasingly theorized and explored. Whether theologies (such as Bernard of Clairvaux's) in which change is really addition to or subtraction from an inner core (Chapter 3), or understandings of miracle and marvel (such as Gerald's or Caesarius of Heisterbach's or Albert the Great's) in which even the violation of the natural order is limited by a principle of likeness (Chapter 2), or poetic images of metamorphosis (such as Marie de France's and Dante's) in which self is transformed but not lost (Chapter 4), medieval discussions struggled to retain the identity of things, both their entity-ness, or *unitas*, and their spatiotemporal continuity, despite physical or spiritual transformation.

But resistance to replacement-change raised conceptual problems, whether for those such as Bernard who did not fully conceive of its possibility or for those such as Albert who did, and feared it. For if such change is impossible, or possible but dangerous, how can one then image to oneself the natural change with which one is surrounded? And yet one must. Medieval thinkers were, at the level of ordinary, empirical observation, as aware as we are of species violation and radical transformation — of butterflies emerging from cocoons, of hysterical behavior erupting in

28

previously calm people, of monsters born from cows or humans.[25] They needed ways of conceptualizing such "midpoints" as mules (half horse, half donkey) or coral (half plant, half stone) while retaining species distinctness; they sought images with which to speak of sudden spiritual reorientation without relinquishing the idea of gradual edification. But given their resistance to, as well as titillation by, notions of radical replacement, they often spoke of such boundary violations, such personal or status reversals, not with metamorphosis stories but with a very different image: the image of the hybrid. For example, Gerald himself, fascinated by ruptures in nature's regularity, especially species transgressions, seems nonetheless to have been more comfortable with doubles (ox-men and bearded ladies) than with metamorphosis, so much so that his werewolf is really more a hybrid (man plus wolf) or an overclothing (man covered with wolf pelt) than a metamorphosis (man become wolf).

It seems, then, that hybridity and metamorphosis are very different images for the possibility we all face that a thing may be, or become, partly or totally something else. Nor are they mutually interchangeable, for if each in some sense addresses both the transformation and the continuity of natures, they do so to different extents and in different ways. These essays thus explore not only the evolving notions of change and identity in the high Middle Ages but also hybridity and metamorphosis as ways of thinking about them. Although scholars often assume that all marvels, miracles, and oddities belong together under the category "alterity" or "transgression," I suggest, rather, that hybrid and metamorphosis are fundamentally different images and occur in different cultural contexts.[26] They express different rhetorical strategies and different ontological visions; as the literary critics say, they do different "cultural work." The hybrid expresses a world of natures, essences, or substances (often diverse or contradictory to each

[margin handwritten notes: appear in different context]

29

other), encountered through paradox; it resists change. Metamorphosis expresses a labile world of flux and transformation, encountered through story.

In an obvious sense, the contrast is that metamorphosis is process and hybrid is not. But this observation is more complex than it first appears. For a hybrid is not just frozen metamorphosis; it is certainly not the end point or the interruption of metamorphosis. A hybrid is a double being, an entity of parts, two or more. It is an inherently visual form. We *see* what a hybrid is; it is a way of making two-ness, and the simultaneity of two-ness, visible. Metamorphosis goes from an entity that is one thing to an entity that is another. It is essentially narrative. There is, to be sure, a certain two-ness in metamorphosis; the transformation goes from one being to another, and the relative weight or presence of the two entities suggests where we are in the story. At the beginning and end, where there is no trace of the otherness from which and to which the process is going, there is no metamorphosis; there is metamorphosis only in between. Nonetheless metamorphosis is about process, *mutatio*, story — a constant series of replacement-changes, or, as Bernard of Clairvaux puts it, little deaths.[27] It is about a one-ness left behind or approached. In contrast, hybrid is spatial and visual, not temporal. It is inherently two. Its contraries are simultaneous, hence dialogic.[28] Forever in the present, the one plus one that we find together in the hybrid must be in conversation with each other; each is a comment on the other. Gerald's ox-man raises the issue of bestiality (animal-human sex) exactly because it itself depicts such encounter and conjoining.

Whether understood as literary genre or as image of the world, hybrid and metamorphosis are not, of course, completely different. Each can be understood both to destabilize and to reveal the world.[29] In other words, hybrid and metamorphosis can, on the one hand, be ways of suggesting that the reality they image is what the world really is; in this sense, they are revelations. The man who becomes a wolf (metamorphosis) can be seen as revealing his rapacity; satyrs, chimeras, or mermaids (hybrids) can be understood as depicting lust, hypocrisy, or the insubstantiality of love. On the other hand, both hybrid and metamorphosis can be destabilizings of expectation. Both can suggest that the world, either in process or in the instant, is disordered and fluid, with the horror and wonder of uncontrolled potency or violated boundaries. Both Gerald's werewolf and his bearded lady shake our assumptions about the boundaries between the sexes and between species. At an even deeper level, they shake our confidence in the structure of reality, in the basic synchrony between inner and outer we tend to assume.

Nonetheless hybrid and metamorphosis reveal or violate categories in different ways. Hybrid reveals a world of difference, a world that *is* and is multiple; metamorphosis reveals a world of stories, of things under way. Metamorphosis breaks down categories by breaching them; hybrid forces contradictory or incompatible categories to coexist and serve as commentary each on the other. It is, then, no surprise that thinkers who resist conceptualizing replacement-change tend to use images of hybrids and doubles, to employ rhetorical strategies that force confrontation with paradox or contradiction, and to see meaning in the simultaneity of opposites. Bernard of Clairvaux, for example, does not situate the figures that fascinate him — the monk-knights known as Templars, the administrator-monk-pope Eugene III, the vile yet believing human heart — in history. His hybrids have no stories. Indeed, they have entity-ness, identity, only because he asserts without explanation their *unitas*. What his rhetoric forces us to encounter is not change but contradiction. Although Bernard stresses that we approach God through likeness, his prose evokes

31

not development but paradox — an eternal moment in which the dissimilitude that we are is also like.[30] In contrast, thinkers such as Ovid or Marie de France, for whom metamorphosis provides the fundamental metaphor, tend to employ and find meaning in narrative and to plumb the possibilities and horrors of replacement-change — apotheosis, disappearance, or loss. Identity is explored via threats to it. Yet throughout the change of man to wolf, woman to tree, youth to nightingale, something perdures, carried by the changing shape that never completely loses physical or behavioral traces of what it was. Daphne becomes a laurel whose leaves flutter in eternal escape; Ovid's werewolf Lycaon and Marie's Bisclavret retain in (or under) wolfishness the rapaciousness or courtesy of human selves.[31]

Since the days of the pre-Socratics, change has been seen in the Western tradition as both horror and glory. If there is real replacement, we can after all both lose and transcend the self. And in writers of the Western mainstream, there has been a tendency to fear these two — loss and transcendence — as the same thing. There has thus been a tendency to resist replacement of self — in death, in mystical absorption, in psychosis, spirit possession, or pantheism. We see such resistance in the thirteenth-century Church's rejection both of metempsychosis and of antinomian or quietist teachings that the individual can become God. In the writers I consider here, images of hybridity and metamorphosis also express such resistance. They affirm, even while destabilizing, survival of self. If we compare the hybrids and transformations of Ovid, Bernard, Marie de France, or Dante, for example, with the chameleon shape-shifters of various Indian traditions, or even with stories of composites and tricksters found in European folklore, we see how strongly authors in Western high culture insist on identity.[32] For however counterintuitive it may seem, these images of lability, confusion, and transgression become in

32

their hands supports for the individual. Whether Bernard's sense of paradox, which asserts simultaneously the ontological similarity and dissimilarity of self and other, or Ovid's and Marie's experimentation with a transformation that carries self far into otherness while retaining in body traces of what was before, both hybrid and metamorphosis express a resistance to change that may be what we mean, for better or worse, by the "individualism" of the Western tradition.[33]

Some Methodological Considerations

The four essays collected here were written for different occasions and very different audiences. The first essay, delivered as my presidential address to the American Historical Association in January 1997, was composed not for medievalists but for historians and was intended to offer both a new interpretation of the activities of medieval intellectuals and a meditation on the task of writing history. Since I had become alarmed at a pervasive recent tendency among scholars to write about themselves rather than about their subjects, it was part of my agenda to discuss the historian's task only via research that was thickly documented and described. The last chapter, delivered as the Jefferson Lecture for 1999, was written for a large general audience in Washington, DC both as an exploration of a literary genre and as an unabashed defense of reading the classics (whose canon it sought slyly to revise by adding female authors, one of whom was a far from obvious choice). The second chapter, my presidential address for the Medieval Academy of America in 1998, was by definition intended for professional medievalists. Connected more closely than the others to my previous work, it was less a new interpretation than an effort to enrich, with a large amount of research, the picture of twelfth-century insistence on bodily continuity offered in my book on the resurrection of the body. But in the course of the new research, the old argument became a new topic. I came to see that the question of identity is also, as I explain above, the question of change. The third chapter was written especially for this volume. It grows out of the reading in Bernard of Clairvaux's sermons I did for the American Historical Association essay and complements Chapters 2 and 4 by exploring hybridity as contrast to metamorphosis. Although the focus on a single figure might suggest that its scope is smaller than that of the other chapters, it is in fact the most technical and conceptually complex piece in the collection.

The general themes discussed above should not give a false impression of unity. Despite their convergence, these essays were not originally intended to form a whole. Tying them together in an introduction inevitably neglects some topics — in particular, the exploration of wonder as emotion in Chapter 1 and the discussion of image theology in Chapter 3. I hope the four essays will be read independently and for themselves as much as for the connections between them or the common themes emphasized here. I also hope they will encourage further work. This introduction is more a prolegomenon to the full study of *mutatio* these articles adumbrate than any sort of summing up. It suggests several new questions to which the essays, partial as they are, should not be the only answers.

Because the origins, audiences, and agendas of these essays differ, the methods employed may seem different as well. Yet the essays share certain very simple methodological assumptions. All four audaciously relate current to past concerns yet argue paradoxically for embedding texts, painstakingly and obsessively, in their historical context. Although each essay in its own way allows the present to pose questions to the past, each interrogates those present questions to show their complexity before using them to consider anything else. Hence all four essays resist drawing analogies

34

between past and present until each is put in its own context. Just as current notions of change must be understood in their full social, philosophical, and semantic range before they are helpful as tools, so medieval understandings of *mutatio* should be explored across and among medieval discourses before comparisons are drawn to modern problems. It is unwise, for example, to relate Gerald's bearded lady to modern circuses or modern theories of gender-bending before we look, first, at the stories and concepts among which Gerald embeds his account and, second, at how words such as "monster" or "marvel" or even "beard" occur in other types of literature and discourse communities in Gerald's own day.[34] The suggestion I make in these essays about a twelfth-century context for Gerald's and Bernard's concern with hybrid and monster is *not* the application of some general theory of deprivation or status anxiety to an isolated medieval example but rather the conclusion of a long and careful process of tracing a topic or idea through specific metaphors and phrases in dozens of the authors' own writings.[35] Yet in each chapter, particular words and images (*admiratio*, for example, or *admiscere* or *unitas*) lead through and beyond their immediate contexts to the authors' worlds. So also the four essays themselves are *monstra* (indications or showings) in the medieval sense, gesturing toward the larger and more significant topic they do not fully encompass: change itself.[36]

It is not part of my agenda in this book to prefer hybrid or metamorphosis as rhetorical strategy or insight into ontology, although the careful reader will detect a preference for paradox in Chapter 3, for metamorphosis in Chapter 4. Nor is it my purpose to support (or denigrate) the resistance to change inherent in Western high culture. But we, like all peoples, must think with the concepts and images we have. Moreover, thinking about change is what historians do. Thus I suggest, in conclusion, that both hybrid and metamorphosis can serve as images for the historian's task.

The history we attempt to write is always metamorphosis — a flux to which we have access only through texts and objects that bear vestiges of past lives to us from across time. To historians as to poets, shapes carry stories. Potsherds, tympana, illuminated manuscripts, field patterns from long ago revealed by aerial photography, and the texts themselves — texts of romances, saints' lives, chronicles, land transfers, laws — bring stories to us, changing because they have traveled through time but conveying also important vestiges of what was there. Yet we, if we succeed in writing that past, are hybrids, monstrous combinations of past and present, paradoxically asserting through common, ordinary words such as "change" or "identity" a then and a now that may be incompatible, unknowable, inexpressible in those common, ordinary terms. Like the hybrid figures twelfth-century students used as memory aids and learning tools (see Figure 11), the history we write is less a synthesis and reconciliation than an assertion of opposites. The most profound evocations and analyses of the past tend, I think, to put us in contact with the contradictory aspirations of that past and to keep us ever aware of the contradiction inherent in the arrogant effort to understand something radically other than ourselves. In this sense, all history writing is not only comparative history but even paradoxical history. Perhaps, then, the best we can hope for as historians is to achieve what Bernard of Clairvaux called in another context a "marvelous mixture": a simultaneous assertion of past and present, self and other.

CHAPTER ONE

Wonder

Let him who does not know how to astonish go work
in the stables!
— Giambattista Marino (1569–1625)[1]

Unlikely though it may seem for a medievalist, I am a product
of the sixties. I submitted my dissertation in the spring of 1969
on the very day students occupied University Hall at Harvard to
protest military recruiting on campus and the war in Vietnam.
During the next tumultuous years, as I struggled to become a
teacher and a professional with the high (and admittedly somewhat naive) ideals of the sixties sounding in my brain, I kept on
my bulletin board a copy of a Paris wall slogan from the student
rebellion of 1968: "Toute vue des choses qui n'est pas étrange est
fausse" (Every view of things that is not strange [i.e., bizarre or
foreign] is false).[2] It seemed to me then that I was trying, both as
a scholar and as a teacher, to jolt my listeners and readers into encounter with a past that is unexpected and strange, a past whose
lineaments are not what we at first assume, whose traces in our
sources answer questions we haven't asked and deliver only si-
lence to our initial, self-referential queries. So when I began to
think about this address and about the intellectual challenges to
the historian's task that engage me most, I returned to this wall
slogan. Could a penchant for the strange help us avoid what Patricia

37

Limerick has identified as presentist flattening of the past,[3] or what John Toews has diagnosed as the danger of being trapped by the multiple readings of texts open to — but, we may fear, reflective only of — us after the linguistic turn?[4] In other words, could wonder be the special characteristic of the historian?

Those of you who are specialists in European history or literature may find this introduction to my subject somewhat disingenuous, for surely my question emerges from current scholarship as well as from out-of-date wall slogans. Wonder is at present a "hot topic." But not, it would appear, a medievalist's topic. Wonders and marvels have recently been the subject of a good deal of research on early modern Europe, some of it inspired by the cinquecentennial of 1492 and the welcome new sensitivities to its darker side.[5] Moreover, some influential literary theory — above all, the ideas of Tzvetan Todorov — suggests that the marvelous is a particular aesthetic that emerged in the seventeenth century (or perhaps later) and is predicated on an "implicit reader" hardly present in the simpler tales that amused medieval audiences.[6] Thus some of you may suspect that I am engaging in a version of that mid-twentieth-century "medievalists' revolt" in which historians earnestly asserted the claims of the Middle Ages, over against those of early modern Europe, to phenomena no one is quite sure about today — the Renaissance, for example, or the origins of the modern state.[7] Perhaps, then, I represent a rearguard action to claim back from early modernists the irrational and grotesque and to "re-enchant," if not the world, at least the historical profession. After all, much recent work has demonstrated that the period from about 1180 to 1320 saw a great increase in stories of marvels, monsters, miracles, and ghosts;[8] and the characterization of medieval Europe as "awash in wonders" has been employed by many of our century's greatest scholars.[9]

No revolt or reappropriation is, however, intended. I leave

"the marvelous" to literary theorists and "the age of marvels" to
the Renaissance. My topic is wonder, not wonders, and what I
want to do in this essay is to explore not only the different theories of wonder present in a variety of medieval discourses but
also (and this is, of course, quite tricky to determine) the circumstances under which medieval men and women felt wonder,
whether or not the sources use the term. In other words, I intend
to explore not only wonder-talk but also wonder-behavior.[10] Although I shall not come up with *a* medieval definition of wonder
or *a* medieval wonder experience, I shall delineate a complex set
of ideas and reactions very different from those recently studied by
early modernists. Medieval theorists, I shall argue, understood
wonder (*admiratio*) as cognitive, non-appropriative, perspectival,
and particular. Not merely a physiological response, wonder was a
recognition of the singularity and significance of the thing encountered. Only that which is really different from the knower
can trigger wonder; yet wonder will always be in a context and
from a particular point of view. To medieval thinkers, human
beings cannot wonder at what is not there; but neither can we
wonder at that which we fully understand. I shall thus suggest
that there are analogies (not correspondences) between medieval
discussions and those of late twentieth-century historians.[11] For
surely what characterizes historians above all else is the capacity
to be shocked by the singularity of events in a way that stimulates
the search for "significance" (a word that includes — but is not
limited to — cause or explanation). So my topic is, first, a set of
very sophisticated discourses produced by medieval thinkers and,
second, the web of horror and delight we can decipher in medieval texts. I describe these as an antidote to recent fears that
because it is impossible to know without in some sense appropri-
ating, it is therefore impossible to know. And as I proceed, I hope
to tell you some wonder-ful stories.

Recent Scholarship on Wonder and Wonders
Before I turn to the Middle Ages, I wish to say a bit more about recent scholarship on wonders in order to make clear how my emphasis will differ from it. This work has been characterized by three arguments. First, a great deal of research on the early modern European impulse to collect and explore — displayed in such phenomena as the origins of the museum in the *Wunderkammer*, voyages to the New World with their attendant goals of conquering and missionizing, and the use of inquisitors and questionnaires by government to assemble information for judicial proceedings and taxation — has stressed the enthusiasm for wonders as expropriative and appropriative. The collections of narwhal horns and jewels, deformed fetuses and human captives, made by rulers, missionaries, and naturalists have been understood as an early modern "Orientalism" — a projection of self or construction of "other" as self.[12] Columbus's "desire to know the secrets of the world" has been glossed with José de Acosta's praise of proselytizing curiosity: "And the high and eternal wisdom of the Creator uses this natural curiosity of men to communicate the light of His holy gospel to peoples who still live in the darkness of their errors."[13] In such interpretation, the rape of the New World seems implicit in wonder at it.

Second, natural philosophical discussions of wonders and wonder have been interpreted as moving in a more or less straight line from medieval Scholastics to the Enlightenment.[14] According to such analysis, philosophers between the thirteenth and eighteenth centuries developed from the opening of Aristotle's *Metaphysics*, which associated wonder with ignorance and doubt, the idea that the goal of *admiratio* was its own destruction: if wonder arose from the desire to seek causes it did not understand, wonder should lead to its own replacement by *scientia* or *philosophia*. This understanding of wonder then combined with the development of an ontological distinction between *miracula* and *mirabilia*, in which marvels were defined as natural effects we fail to understand, whereas miracles were "unusual and difficult" (*insolitum et arduum*) events, "produced by God's power alone on things that have a natural tendency to the opposite effect."[15] Thus, while preserving the possibility of objective verification of miracles as *contra naturam*, such definitions led to an ever-increasing sense that seemingly extraordinary events could be explained (that is, rationalized) as ruled by the laws of nature.[16]

Third, work on early modern marvels has tended to begin exploration of the wonder-reaction with Descartes's famous definition from 1649: "wonder is a sudden surprise of the soul which makes it tend to consider attentively those objects which seem to it rare and extraordinary."

> When the first encounter with some object surprises us . . . this makes us wonder and be astonished. . . . And since this can happen before we know in the least whether this object is suitable to us or not, it seems to me that Wonder is the first of all the passions. It has no opposite, because if the object presented has nothing in it that surprises us, we are not in the least moved by it and regard it without passion.[17]

Although in this discussion the cognitive element in wonder is in fact large,[18] Descartes has been treated, in the new field of the history of the emotions, as beginning the tendency to reduce emotion to physiology.[19] Such analysis has traced a unilinear development from Charles Le Brun's drawings of the passions, published forty-nine years after Descartes's treatise to illustrate his theories, through Burke and Kant, to Charles Darwin's *The Expression of the Emotions in Man and Animals* (1872), which equated wonder with raised eyebrows, opened and protruding lips, and a hand held up, palm out, with fingers open — reactions that, Darwin argued, increased the animal's chances of survival by making it see and breathe better in a crisis (Figures 1 and 2). The wealth of new psychological, anthropological, and historical discussion that assumes the emotions to be culturally constructed thus understands itself as in opposition to an early modern psychology for which the startle response of admiration or wonder was the paradigmatic emotion.[20]

It is not my purpose here to suggest that current arguments about the early modern "age of the marvelous" are correct or incorrect. It will, however, be clear that none of these interpretations, complex though they be, describes a wonder-talk or wonder-behavior that is empowering (or even relevant) to what historians do. A philosophical understanding of wonder as ignorance rationalized or erased by knowledge, a wondering desire that collects and appropriates what it endeavors to know or projects its self onto an imagined other, a passion that reduces to a startle response at the unfamiliar — whether or not such interpretations are correct understandings of early modern texts and events, they have little to do with the historian's vocation. But medieval wonder was not any of the above. I therefore turn to the conceptions of wonder current in the Middle Ages, confident that — although the past never provides answers or solutions — these ideas can nonetheless help us imagine the kind of non-appropriative, perspectival, and intensely cognitive response we must aspire to if we are to meet our responsibilities as teachers and historians.

The Many Wonder Discourses of the Middle Ages

Although medieval writers did not for the most part produce theories of wonder in the areas of psychology or poetics, where such theories would later figure so prominently, they certainly produced theoretical discussions of wonder.[21] As we might expect, we find not one but many discourses, although it is difficult — as always for the Middle Ages — to know how to characterize their differences.[22] I shall discuss three: a theological-philosophical understanding of wonder emanating from university intellectuals; a religious discourse about wonder found in sermons, devotional writing, and above all in the enormously popular genre of saints' lives; and a literature of entertainment, within which I include travel accounts, history writing, and the collections of odd stories called by one author "trifles for the court."[23] In each case, I shall explain what wonder meant by identifying what authors saw as its synonyms and opposites.[24] Thus for theologians and natural philosophers, the opposite of *admiratio* was in some sense the *scientia*, or knowledge, to which it led; but wonder was also associated with *diversitas*, and its opposite was *solitum*, the usual, or even in some sense the general.[25] In the religious discourse of sermon and hagiography, the most frequent opposite of *admiratio* was *imitatio*, less frequently *curiositas* or *disputatio*. Readers and audiences for saints' lives, whether Latin or vernacular, were urged to wonder at, not imitate, the power and extravagant asceticism of holy men and women. Wonder was moreover associated with paradox, coincidence of opposites; one finds *mira* (marvelous) again and again in the texts alongside *mixta* (mixed or composite things), a word that evokes the hybrids and monsters also found in the literature of entertainment. In this entertainment literature, which is the third discourse I treat, *admirari* (to wonder at) is sometimes contrasted to *rimari* (to pry into), although it is sometimes seen as an inducement to such prying. Above all, to the authors who collected stories to amuse, instruct, and move their (usually aristocratic) listeners, the opposite of wonder was, as John of Salisbury put it, *inductio exemplorum*, which really means in this context "generalizing."

43

Figure 1. Astonishment combined with admiration. Drawn by Charles Le Brun in *Méthode pour apprendre à dessiner les passions* (1698) to illustrate the theories of René Descartes. Some recent scholars have seen Descartes's idea that wonder is the most basic of all emotions as leading to the physiological reductionism of Charles Darwin.

Figure 2 (opposite). Astonishment and distress. Plate 7 from Charles Darwin, *The Expression of the Emotions in Man and Animals* (1872). Darwin used the photograph at the top of the plate to illustrate what he argued to be the basic physiological response of wonder, common to animals and humans. The lower figure shows a face being manipulated to alter wonder to distress.

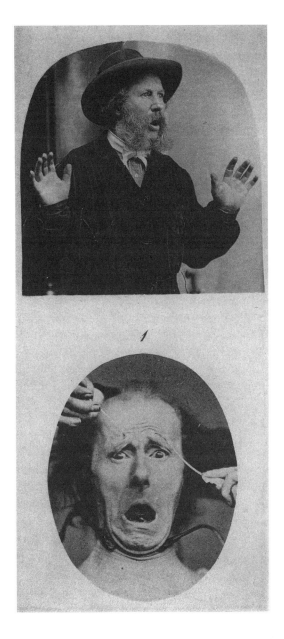

Figure 3. The Ascension of Christ. Fol. 75r of the *Evangeliary of Henry the Lion* from 1175 (Cod. Guelf 105 Noviss., Herzog August Bibliothek, Wolfenbüttel). In this, the lower register, a complex range of reactions and gestures accompanies the wonderful event. Medieval images do not employ a single, standard representation of wonder; rather, they suggest that *admiratio* is shaped by complicated cultural expectations and ranges from ecstasy to terror.

Figure 4. Nicolas Froment, *The Burning Bush* (1476). In the fifteenth century, expressions of astonishment begin to look more like the depictions in the works of early modern theorists of the emotions.

Theological and Philosophical Discussion
The theological-philosophical discourse produced in the schools and universities of the twelfth to fourteenth centuries drew on a tradition of understanding wonder as perspectival and psychological that went back to those twin authorities for the Middle Ages: Aristotle and Augustine. Aristotle had suggested, in the well-known opening of the *Metaphysics*, that

> all men begin ... by wondering that things are as they are ..., as in the case of marionettes or of the solstices or of the incommensurability of the diagonal of a square with respect to its side.... But we must end with the contrary ... for nothing would make a geometrician wonder so much as this, namely, if a diagonal were to be commensurable with the side of a square.[26]

Augustine had written that marvels are not "against nature" but "against what we know of nature"; and one of the examples he gave — that the behavior of lime in fire would seem miraculous to us if it occurred in India and we heard of it seldom — was quoted often in the Middle Ages.[27] Such a tradition, while implying that philosophy might replace wonder, also suggested that human beings wonder at the regularity, structure, and beauty of the universe and made wonder a situated response to what is unusual or "other" to a particular viewer. Augustine, however, also made statements that seemed to lodge the wonderfulness of things not in our reaction to them but in their ontological status. His *De utilitate credendi* described a miracle as "something difficult which seldom occurs, exceeding the faculty of nature and so far surpassing our hopes as to compel our astonishment."[28] Building on this contrast between nature and those wonder-inducing events that surpass it, Anselm of Canterbury in the early twelfth century distinguished between the marvelous, the natural, and the voluntary (by which

48

he meant what we would probably call the artificial — that is, that which is made by human will).[29] In the thirteenth century, these passages from Augustine and Anselm were used to argue that miracles are objectively wonderful (*habentia in se admirationis causam*) because produced by God's power alone.[30]

Although Latin texts in the early Middle Ages used *mirabilia* and *miracula* more or less interchangeably, university intellectuals by the thirteenth century distinguished the two in terms of ontological status.[31] Such theorizing might seem to flatten the impulse to marvel in two senses. First, it tends to separate out a small number of phenomena as objectively wonder-inducing, whereas all others — no matter how odd — are wonderful only to the ignorant; moreover, by accompanying such discussion with hairsplitting distinctions concerning ontological status, it embeds even the miraculous in a forest of ratiocination that allows little room for surprise or delight. Second, such theorizing suggests that most events have natural causes.[32] If philosophers are diligent enough, wonders will cease. Thus William of Auvergne observed around 1235 that people turn too quickly to God's power, calling things miracles, when it is merely the case that they do not know how to go about investigating the cause. A little over a century later, Nicole Oresme observed:

> People marvel at . . . things only because they rarely happen, but the causes for these are as apparent as for others. . . . For example, at night a fearful man who sees a wolf in the fields, or a cat in his room, will immediately . . . judge that it is an enemy or a devil . . . because he fixes his imagination on these and fears them. And a [devout] person . . . will judge that it is an angel. . . . A vigorous imagining of a retained species, then, together with a small external appearance or . . . an imbalance of some internal disposition . . . produces marvelous appearances in healthy as well as in sick people.

49

An anonymous thirteenth-century treatise, "On the Marvels of the World," falsely attributed to Albert the Great, went so far as to assert: "A great part of philosophers and physicians believes that all marvellousness of experiences and marvels [*tota mirabilitas experimentorum et mirabilium*] arises from natural things."[33] Such a tradition may indeed seem anti-wonder, as some modern scholars have alleged.

In considering the discussion of marvels found in theology and natural philosophy, we must not, however, be too quick to conclude that distinguishing miracle and marvel ontologically rather than psychologically and perspectivally, or attributing marvels to natural causes, entailed the eclipse of wonder. Even Nicole Oresme, who argued that it is possible to produce general arguments for the naturalness of almost all phenomena, showed himself fascinated and enchanted by the "marvelous properties" of animals and the *diversitas* of human experience, especially of tastes in food and in sexual positions and partners.[34] Roger Bacon attempted naturalistic explanations of saints who lived without eating and of the resurrection of the body, as well as of charms and amulets; but he spoke in remarkably heightened language of the terror and sweet wonder of the Eucharist, called the magnet one of the "miracles of nature" (*miracula naturae*), described the bending of cut twigs toward each other as "wonderful beyond all I have seen," and waxed lyrical over the infinite complexity of the common fly.[35] Albert the Great, like Oresme, described the physiological manifestations of *admiratio* as "a constriction and suspension of the heart" confronted with something "great and unusual."[36] Thomas Aquinas quoted Aristotle's *Rhetoric* to connect wonder with pleasure and drew on the *Metaphysics* to associate it with a desire that culminates not so much in knowledge as in encounter with majesty; he argued that the angel of the Annunciation shocked the Virgin because "wonder is the best way to grab the attention of the soul" and insisted that Christ's capacity to wonder was not an indication of discomfort but a proof of his humanity — a sign indeed that he was a teacher.[37] Thus wonder as a response was not devalued or dismissed, even in a philosophical and theological tradition that (as Katharine Park has aptly put it) "de-wondered" anomalies by insisting on an increasingly ordered world whose laws were decipherable by the wise.[38]

Admiratio *in Devotional Literature*

If we turn from the discourse of university intellectuals to the homiletic and hagiographic tradition, we find that the wonder-ful was contrasted not with the known, the knowable, or the usual but with the imitable.[39] The phrase *non imitandum sed admirandum* (not to be imitated but to be marveled at) had been used since the early Church to express the distance between heroes and martyrs, on the one hand, and the ordinary faithful, on the other.[40] Augustine had written of the female martyrs Perpetua and Felicity: "People [are able to] wonder at sooner than imitate [their courage]."[41] In the *exempla* collections, sermons, and saints' lives of the high Middle Ages, the contrast was sometimes a kind of humility topos intended to express an author's conviction that the miracle-working charisma of a saint was far beyond the capacity of author and reader alike; sometimes, it was frankly an effort to channel the attention of the faithful away from miracles and marvels and toward emulation of the ordinary virtues — that is, to control credulity, extravagant asceticism, and straining after flamboyant religiosity. Thus James of Vitry wrote of the piety of an extraordinary group of thirteenth-century women ascetics, which included Christina, known as Mirabilis (that is, the Marvelous or Astonishing): "When we read what certain saints did ... we should wonder at rather than imitate their deeds." Bonaventure repeated the injunction in his life of Francis of Assisi.[42] Caesarius

51

of Heisterbach's *exempla* collection underscores repeatedly that works of piety are to be preferred to the miracles that follow one after the other in his flat — even boring — prose and that the true *admirandum* is God's patience and forgiveness.[43] What we should also note, however, is the way in which elaborate wordplays on the *imitatio/admiratio* contrast stress the non-appropriative nature of wonder.

I illustrate this from the sermons of Bernard of Clairvaux. A master of rhetoric, Bernard made much use of opposition: thus he contrasted wonder with curiosity (prying into the affairs of others or the secrets of the universe) and even fulminated against the *mira quaedam deformis formositas* (wonderful, deformed beauty) of Romanesque sculpture — a beauty to which he was, as many historians have noticed, seductively drawn.[44] But Bernard's most complex rhetorical contrast is *admiratio/imitatio*, and he meant something more subtle than the standard message that the saints were to be imitated in their virtues rather than wondered at in their miracles, although he says this, too.

Imitatio, to Bernard, is appropriation; it is, he says, "being in society with," "experiencing," "learning," "taking into oneself," "consuming."[45] Its semantic field includes words such as "pattern," "mirror," "example," "model," "image," and "nourishment." In order to understand fully what such imitation means, we must remember that in medieval piety, *imitatio* could be as literal as Henry Suso's carving of Jesus' name into his chest with a stylus or Saint Francis's stigmata; it could be as inner and invisible as the approach to God expressed by Hugh of St. Victor when he said:

> [T]he shape of the seal presents to the present matter another consideration.... For the figure that is raised in the seal, when imprinted appears concave ... and that which appears sculpted inward in the seal is ... shaped convexly in the wax.... Therefore ... we,

when we take the deeds [of others] for imitation, ought to make the
lofty things hidden and the humble ones manifest.[46]

What is encountered in such imitation is an "other," of course,
but the encounter is made possible because an ontological similarity to that other (expressed by monastic writers in the biblical
phrase "image and likeness") is built into the experiencing self.[47]

To all this, *admiratio* was in emphatic contrast. As Bernard
explained: when we are offered a golden goblet, we consume,
absorb, incorporate the drink (that is, imitate the virtues), but we
give back (that is, we wonder at) the goblet.[48] Thus we wonder at
what we cannot in any sense incorporate, or consume, or encompass in our mental categories; we wonder at mystery, at paradox,
at *admirabiles mixturae*. The ecstasy and stupor Bernard calls
admiratio is triggered above all, he says, by three hybrids beyond
nature and comprehension: the mixture of God and man, of
woman and virgin, of belief with falsity in our hearts.[49]

The Marvelous in Literature of Entertainment

The third group of texts that provide a medieval theory of wonder are the history writing, travel accounts, and story collections
I have called the literature of entertainment. Such literature drew
on the encyclopedic tradition of the ancient world known as
paradoxology — the collection of oddities (including monsters or
hybrids, distant races, marvelous lands) — and on antique notions
of portents or omens, that is, unusual events that foreshadowed
the (usually catastrophic) future and were accompanied by a
vague sense of dread.

This entertainment literature sometimes includes what came
to be the separate ontological category of "miracle," about which
authors tended to be increasingly skeptical, even cynical. For
example, Walter Map concluded an account of a failed exorcism

by Bernard of Clairvaux with the following story, placed in the mouth of a twelfth-century contemporary:

> "[A] certain man from the borders of Burgundy asked him to come and heal his son; . . . so Bernard ordered that the body be carried into a private room, and after sending everybody out he lay upon the boy, and arose again after praying; but the boy did not arise, for he lay there dead." Thereupon I [Walter] remarked: "This was surely the most unlucky of monks; for never have I heard of a monk lying down upon a boy without the boy rising up immediately after him." The abbot [who was listening] blushed, and many people went outside for a laugh.[50]

Such literature also included *fabulae* (stories), which came increasingly to be contrasted to *historia* and told without claims to their ontological status.[51]

When we consider not the categories of events but the theory of wonder itself found in such writings, we note that wonder here has three characteristics: it is a response to facticity; it is a response to the singular; it is deeply perspectival. Although William of Newburgh, for example, tends to contrast *rimari* (to probe or pry into) with *admirari* (to wonder at), most such literature tends to assume that some sort of *probatio* (testing or evidence) is the basis for *admiratio*.[52] Gervais of Tilbury, for instance, groups marvels with *res gestae* (deeds or historical accounts) and opposes them to stories (*fabulae*) or lies. He asserts that only facts can induce wonder: although you will wonder only at what you cannot explain, you cannot be amazed by what you don't believe.[53] Gervais recounts as "marvelous" not only stories of ghosts and vampires but also details of the migration of quail and the flight of squirrels. He explains in detail how he "proved from his own experience" the "marvel" of a refectory in Arles in which no fly could survive:

54

I made myself an assiduous investigator to see if the flies would light, as they are accustomed to, on bowls smeared with honey and grease. Discovering that the truth actually went beyond what was rumored, I wanted to uncover by force this ruse by which the mind was tricked. I made myself into a hunter of flies and placed a prize of honey and grease and milk in the refectory. My amazement [*admiratio*] grew the more I saw that the effort of mind and the physical constraint I tried were in vain. [The flies did not light.] So my stupefaction [*stupor*] grew with the proof I made of what I had heard.[54]

If *admiratio* is a response to credible though deeply unusual events, it is also a response to singular events, what John of Salisbury calls "marvelous singularity." In his collection of advice for courtiers and princes, John tends to naturalize miracles (arguing that many — for example, changing water into wine — are only a speedup of natural processes) and states explicitly that reason (in the sense of understanding cause) removes wonder. But John also sees wonder as a response to "majesty," to "hidden wisdom" or significance, and contrasts the activity of generalizing or moralizing (*inductio exemplorum* — that is, the citing of instructive general cases) with the emotion or experience of wonder.[55]

In such tales and accounts, wonder is, moreover, deeply perspectival. It is a reaction of a particular "us" to an "other" that is "other" only *relative to* the particular "us." James of Vitry commented, shortly after 1200: "perhaps the Cyclopes, who all have one eye, marvel as much at those who have two eyes as we marvel at them"; and similar statements are found in the later and immensely popular works of Gosswin of Metz and John Mandeville.[56] Moreover, medieval authors were capable of turning such perspectivalism into gently ironic comments on themselves. The thirteenth-century Franciscan missionary William of Rubruck wrote, in what many scholars consider the most informed of early travel accounts, "the men [at the Chan's dwelling] surrounded us and gazed at us as if we were monsters [*tam quam monstra*], especially because we were bare-foot, and [inquired] if we had no need of our feet since they supposed we should lose them straightaway."[57] Thus William suggests that the barefoot travel through harsh terrain and climate required by Franciscan asceticism seems as monstrous a practice in the East as certain Eastern customs appear when reported "back home."

The Range of Wonder Responses

When we turn from the theoretical statements about wonder made by historians and travelers, theologians and philosophers, preachers and devotional writers, to the behavior of medieval men and women, what do we find? The question is an extremely difficult one. We cannot simply study medieval emotion. The traces of emotion that survive are mediated through texts, pictures, and artifacts; we are not entitled either to assume a sort of Darwinian universal emotion that we might find simply by looking for depictions of people with open mouths and raised eyebrows or to think that emotion-behavior is so culturally constructed as to exist only where we find words for it.[58] Indeed, in European texts from the ancient and medieval past, emotion-terms (particularly terms for negative emotions, such as anger, pride, or fear) are more likely to occur in discussions of how to regulate or erase the phenomenon in question than in places where it seems clearly to occur. (For example, a keyword search for "anger" will tend to turn up set pieces on how to control it — that is, discussions of where it is *not*.) Moreover, reactions such as wonder, delight, or terror do not simply occur; they are evoked, sometimes even staged; we can explore what evokes them. Thus texts may give us access to reactions less through adjectives attached to nouns (that is, by calling something "wonderful," "dreadful," and so on) than by indicating the responses of an implicit reader or viewer or by describing acts and objects intended to provoke responses. Finding wonder-words is easy; finding wonder is far more complicated. Neverthe-less, basing my conclusions on broad reading in chronicles, saints' lives, Scholastic treatises, entertainment literature, and sermons, I should like to venture some suggestions about where medieval texts give us access to wonder-reactions and about what the components of such reactions are.

The question of what components constitute the wonder-response is the easier one, and I begin with it. Examination of the complex semantic fields for "wonder" and "the wonderful" suggests that the wonder-reaction ranges from terror and disgust to solemn astonishment and playful delight. Wonder often has a mischievous quality in medieval accounts. Bernard of Clairvaux refers to it as a "spice" for stories;[59] an eleventh-century miracle collection regularly calls the deeds of its impish girl saint "jokes."[60] Gerald of Wales speaks of "nature's pranks" when discussing the geography of twelfth-century Ireland and says of the bearded woman he describes that she "makes people laugh." Clearly using a moralizing bestiary tradition, Gerald makes his analogies between animals and humans anything but solemn and didactic: when he draws parallels between the incorruptible flesh of king-fishers and of holy men, between grasshoppers who sing after their heads are cut off and the holy martyrs, between storks and resurrection, he appears to take more pleasure in the animal tales than in the theology.[61]

But wonder was also dread. When the early fourteenth-century rhetorician Robert of Basevorn came, in his treatise on preaching, to the topic of winning over the audience, he used Gerald of Wales as an example, but not an example of amusement or delight. Robert wrote:

[handwritten margin note: Wonder = terror, disgust, solemn astonishment, playful delight]

The preacher ... ought to attract the mind of the listeners. ... This can be done in many ways. One ... is to place at the beginning something subtle and interesting, as some authentic marvel. ... For instance, suppose that the theme is concerned with the Ascension or the Assumption [and the text is]: *a spring rose from the earth*. One could adduce that marvel which Gerald narrates in his book ... about the spring in Scicilia [where] if anyone approaches it dressed in red clothing, immediately water gushes forth. ... That spring is Christ ... to Whom he "approaches dressed in red" who ... finds living water, viz. graces, because His blood was of such virtue that, when it was shed, the earth quaked and the rocks were torn asunder. Much more ought our hearts to quake and be torn by the cry of God's word. ...

Another way is to frighten them by some terrifying tale or example, in the way that Jacques de Vitry talks about someone who never willingly wanted to hear the word of God; finally when he died and was brought to the church ... [the crucifix] pulled His hands from the nails ... and plugged His ears.[62]

Gerald himself expresses dread. Recounting some of the earliest werewolf stories to survive in European literature, he repeatedly glosses the *admiratio* felt by those inside the story as *stupor*, *timor*, and *horror*. The question of whether and how shape-changing violates natures is highly charged for Gerald, as for others among his contemporaries; and it is surely no accident that his tales of metamorphosis are embedded in a complex discussion where the limiting cases are, on the one side, the real change of substance in the Eucharist and, on the other, the (to him) terrifying possibility that sexual intercourse between humans and animals might produce monsters.[63] Whether amusement or horror, wonder was not — to Gerald, Robert, and their contemporaries — a response to the trivial or the merely odd.

I return, then, to the first and more difficult question I raised above. What in medieval accounts or artistic representations tends to trigger wonder (understood in its full range of awe and dread)? Or, to pose the question more precisely: Where do the surviving sources give us access either to intensely heightened reactions or to events and objects calculated to evoke or stage such reactions?

The thing that strikes us first when we ask the question this way is where wonder is *not*. Miracles, for example — though routinely referred to as "marvelous" — are seldom presented as evoking or intended to evoke wonder. Indeed, the didactic purposes to which miracle collections were directed and the hairsplitting distinctions about ontological status indulged in by theologians seem to have reduced miracle accounts to rather dull enumerations of events. Arguments, such as William of Auvergne's and Nicole Oresme's, that natural causes can be found for marvels tend to flatten the language of some accounts of the natural world as well. Although chronicles and annals sometimes couch their descriptions of unusual natural events such as eclipses, earthquakes, and famines in terms of dread and a kind of hovering significance, these events are also sometimes merely listed in clipped, matter-of-fact prose. Thus miracles, portents, and oddities are sites and stagings of wonder less often than we might suppose.

Nonetheless narrative accounts from the twelfth to the fourteenth century tell us of objects and events carefully constructed to elicit awe, delight, and dread. Rulers, both secular and ecclesiastical, competed in displays of power and splendor, which included intricate tricks and automata, calculated to amaze and tantalize (see Figures 5 and 6). From the later thirteenth century, for example, we have evidence of a count of Artois who built an elaborate fun house with distorting mirrors, rooms that simulated thunderstorms, and hidden pipes for wetting unsuspecting visitors and covering them with flour. Banquets were elegant entertainments,

Figure 5. A flamethrower in the form of a youth holding his heart (from which fire would spurt forth when the body of the statue was filled with turpentine or distilled spirits and the wick lit) illustrates the medieval love of automata. From Conrad Kyeser, *Bellifortis* (before 1405), fol. 95v.

60

Figure 6. A flying dragon inflated by a bellows and crank. From Kyeser, *Bellifortis*, fol. 105r.

which featured entire puppet shows in pastry (called "sotelties" in Middle English). Indeed, cookbooks make it clear that food was often planned as an illusion or trick for the eye: for example, imitation meat concocted from fish, roast fowl sewn back into its plumage in order to appear alive, pies (like that in the nursery rhyme) with living birds inside.[64] Changes in church architecture, in liturgy, and in the fabrication of monstrances all tended to define the moment in the Mass when the consecrated Host was elevated as a sudden revelation of the unexpected and paradoxical: the divine installed in food (or flesh or matter) in the twinkling of an eye.[65] Although collections of relics and their elaborate containers, or reliquaries, are not exactly the *Wunderkammern* of early modern princes, there was both a similarity and a historical connection (see Figures 7 and 8). Theologians and many of the ordinary faithful continued to value the supernatural power mediated through bone chips or dust more than the intricate workmanship or sheer novelty of the container — that is, to understand the object more as a means of access to an other (whether God or saint) than as a singularity, fascinating in itself. But some medieval prelates added natural marvels such as shells and ostrich eggs to their church treasuries; early modern rulers included reliquaries in the "wonder collections" they assembled; relic cabinets and cabinets of novelties came to resemble each other in form, suggesting that an impulse to collect underlay both.[66] The twelfth-century abbot Suger of St.-Denis, writing in extravagant language of the beautiful materials and workmanship used in refurbishing the reliquaries of his church, shows both the parallels and the differences between medieval and early modern accounts. In one sense far more desperate to touch, possess, and appropriate than any later collector, the crowd Suger describes is frantic over access to a power not only *beyond* but also in its nature *other than* what contains it (other because it is God and other because it is God lodged in body — decayed body, manifested and hidden behind the crystal and gold). Suger speaks of frenzied hands grasping to touch caskets until the king himself finally holds the martyrs and "mirabile visu!... No greater joy in the world could ever have exalted [those who beheld this]!"[67]

As this example from Suger makes clear, narrative accounts not only described objects and events that were staged or constructed to produce wonder, they also teemed with complex wonder-reactions. Hagiographers, for example, detailed in emotional, even sensual, language the extravagant asceticism and para-mystical manifestations holy women experienced and the amazement such manifestations engendered in others. Beauty — natural, human, and artistic — was not merely referred to as wonderful, it was also described, in loving and lyrical language, as signaling a deeper pattern or purpose.[68] Drawing on the old Augustinian idea that the world itself is a miracle, the great Anglo-Saxon homilist Aelfric, like Bernard of Clairvaux more than a hundred years later, spoke of the *wundra* (marvels) of God, who has set all creation in measure, number, and weight; thus it requires no sorcery that the moon waxes and wanes, that the sea agrees with it, that the earth greens in response to its power.[69] Recounting the migration of salmon upstream to spawn, Gerald of Wales said: "They leap from bottom to top with a leap that is marvelous and, except that it is proper to the nature of fish, miraculous."[70] Marco Polo, whose rather limited vocabulary for describing marvels does not seem to have undercut the popularity of his descriptions, called the peacocks of the East "larger and more beautiful," asserted that ostriches there were "as big as donkeys" and chickens "the most beautiful in the world," and concluded enthusiastically, "in fact everything is different!"[71]

Travelers' tales also recounted as wonderful the fearsome and the ugly. To Marco Polo, almost every animal he met (the

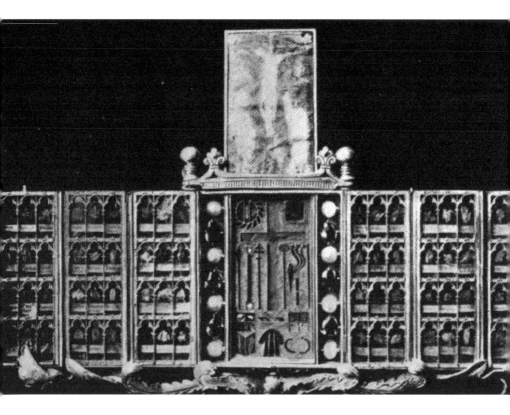

Figure 7. A fifteenth-century reliquary triptych from the Baptistery in Florence displays many powerful holy fragments. Although the impulse to collect is expressed in medieval relic cult, the fragments are assembled not for their intrinsic diversity and oddness but for the power beyond to which they give access.

Figure 8 (opposite). A cabinet of fossils from Michele Mercati, *Metallotheca* (published in Rome in 1717), illustrates the early modern mania for collecting unusual natural specimens. The form of such "wonder cabinets" is quite like that of late medieval reliquary cabinets.

Figure 9. These monsters belong to a long tradition going back to Herodotus and Pliny. Fol. 29v illustrating the *Travels* of Marco Polo, one of the texts in manuscript Fr. 2810 of the Bibliothèque nationale (late fourteenth or early fifteenth century), known as the *Livre des merveilles*.

Figure 10. Men carrying a Western marvel, the barnacle goose born from trees, meet wise men from the East bearing their comparable marvel, the vegetable lamb. The depiction suggests the perspectivalism of medieval marvel literature, which includes the ironic awareness that even "we" are "other" to someone. Fol. 210v illustrating the *Travels* of Sir John Mandeville, one of the texts in the *Livre des merveilles*.

"horrible" crocodile as well as the "beautiful" giraffe) was a marvel, described with an earnest and urgent facticity. Indeed, in the
later Middle Ages, stories abounded of fabulous places, of stones
with marvelous powers, of monsters, mermaids, and fairies,
of bizarre races with eyes in their chests or enormous umbrella
feet. Strangeness appealed. Fantastical travelers' accounts far out-
stripped in popularity the soberer versions.[72] But even through
awkward and impoverished prose such as Marco Polo's, or credu-
lous tale-telling such as Mandeville's, there gleams a powerful
sense that what is wonderful is not chickens and peacocks — even
Cyclopes and cannibals — per se but a world that encompasses
such staggering diversity. Moreover, the impulse to chronicle such
things could also be a critique of the impulse to possess them. For
example, Walter of Châtillon's epic, the *Alexandreis*, drawn from
one of the great storehouses of medieval marvel material, puts the
following speech into the mouth of the Scythians:

> If you [Alexander the Great] had a body that matched your
> greedy mind and heart that know no bounds in their desires, or if
> your body equaled your great cupidity, the great world itself would
> not suffice to contain you.... Your right hand would hold the East,
> the left the West. Not content with this, in all your prayers you
> would be consumed with desire to investigate and find out where
> that amazing light hid itself, and would dare to climb into the sun's
> chariot and...control its wandering beams. So, too, you desire
> much that you cannot possess. Having subdued the world and con-
> quered the human race, delighting in blood, you will wage war
> against trees, wild beasts, rocks and mountain snows. You will
> not allow the strange creatures that lurk in the caves to be un-
> touched. Even senseless elements will be compelled to experience
> your rages.[73]

Although the Alexander material on which Walter draws is centuries old, this passage is not merely a medieval retelling of traditional and titillating stories. Whether or not Walter sides with the Scythians, his powerful prose understands that marveling at diversity can be the prelude to appropriation.

Marveling →
appropr.

Wonder and Significance

Hence in the chronicles, lives, and stories I have studied, wonder is induced by the beautiful, the horrible, and the skillfully made, by the bizarre and rare, by that which challenges or suddenly illuminates our expectations, by the range of difference, even the order and regularity, found in the world. But marveling and astonishment as reactions seem to be triggered most frequently and violently by what Bernard of Clairvaux called *admirabiles mixturae*: events or phenomena in which ontological and moral boundaries are crossed, confused, or erased. Singularity per se, or the absence of a "cause," is not enough. When Roger Bacon, for example, writes in heightened language of the horror and wonder of the Eucharist, while accepting without surprise the resurrection of the body, the difference in reaction seems owing to his sense that living again is not remarkable for a human body but appearing as meat to be masticated is an awe-ful condescension (in worldly terms, an assuming of an inappropriate nature) for God. Caesarius of Heisterbach, flat-footedly recounting what to a modern reader seems a mind-dulling succession of totally improbable events, suddenly expresses genuine wonder that God does not take revenge at an insult as men would. Peter the Venerable, whose twelfth-century collection of miracle stories was intended to inspire (he said) both pleasure and fear, penned his most emotionally heightened paragraphs about those who returned from the dead, "revenants." Peter framed one account in direct discourse in order to intensify the horror; the first-person

Marveling = when ontological and moral boundaries crossed, confused, erased

69

narrator he inserted describes himself as "almost driven to madness by excessive fear." In the other incident, recounted as Peter's own experience, a monk who has been poisoned appears in a dream while the murder is under investigation:

> When I saw him [the murdered monk], I got up full of joy and began to embrace and kiss him with much affection. Although a deep stupor [*sopor*] took the place of my outward senses ... I was not unaware that I was sleeping.... And what is more wonderful [*mirum*], it occurred to me immediately ... that the dead could not remain long with the living.... So I decided to question him quickly, for the vision seemed not a phantasm but true [*non fantastica sed verax*]. [The monk attests his faith and affirms that he has been murdered; then he disappears.]
>
> I wondered greatly ... then rested my head again ... and immediately he reappeared.... I rushed toward him and ... began to kiss him as before.... I heard the same answers as above concerning his state, his vision of God, the certitude of the Christian faith, and his death.... [Then] I woke up ... and found my eyes wet and my cheeks warmed by fresh tears.[74]

Peter's intense emotional and physical encounter with the dead man is triggered by his moral dilemma over how the perpetrator of the crime is to be punished.

The often cynical Walter Map provides another, and unexpected, example of the conjunction of wonder with moral significance. Although given to a rather arch framing (and literary distancing) of some of his more improbable tales, Walter speaks simply and movingly of an occasion on which Peter of Tarentaise, confronted with a deformed man, questioned him closely and sent him away unhealed but with a new sense of self-worth. It is the moral reaction that is described in heightened emotion-language:

70

hearing of the man's psychological suffering, "Archbishop Peter leaped back as if from a blow and gazed at him with wonder."[75] Walter does not simply inform his readers that the archbishop's perception is a marvelous one; rather, we see the response enacted inside the story. Two hundred years later, Julian of Norwich uses her most wonder-filled language not for the "myracles" of the saints but for those "merveyles" impossible to encompass in human categories but having profound implications for salvation: first, the fact that God cannot be angry and, second, the paradox that — because of the Incarnation — we are a marvelous mixture ("medle so mervelous") of sin and grace.[76]

It is when phenomena such as eclipses or double suns are recounted in conjunction with troubled and human events such as war, crime, or corruption that they are given heightened emotion-language. Describing the "unheard-of prodigy" of green children born from the earth, the chronicler William of Newburgh finds himself forced to marvel (*mirari*) at what he cannot grasp (*attingere* or *rimari*). But William assumes that there must be a "reason" for the strange occurrence — by which he means not a cause but a significance or moral use (*utilitas*). Writing of other "marvelous, terrifying, and terrible things" (such as springs that portend scarcity, a mysterious dog discovered in a stone, a crucifix in the sky), William explains: "We call these things marvels and prodigies [*mira et prodigiosa*] not so much because of their rarity as because they have a secret reason [*occultam rationem*]."[77] Thus the wonder-reaction is a significance-reaction — which is only another way of expressing the tautology that things are signs or portents not because of their natures or their causes but because they indicate or point. As every medieval schoolboy knew, monsters are named from the verb *monstrare* (to show) — that is, not from their ontology but from their utility.[78] If to theologians, chroniclers, and preachers, the wonderful was indeed often the

71

strange, the rare, and the inexplicable, it was never the merely strange or the simply inexplicable. It was a strange that mattered, that pointed beyond itself to meaning.

Wonder as Cognitive, Perspectival, and Non-appropriative
The medieval theories and reactions I have discussed were quite different from the wonder described recently by early modern historians. Of course, not all medieval statements about wonder were synonymous or compatible, any more than early modern theories were. Nor was what we can learn about how people acted and reacted necessarily in very close synchrony with the definitions they gave or the platitudes they propounded. Nonetheless the wonder we find in medieval texts was not an increasingly rare exception to an Enlightenment sense of unbreachable laws of nature. Neither was it the startle reflex of early modern psychology nor the appropriation practiced by early modern rulers, explorers, and conquistadores.[79]

Although by the late fifteenth century medieval artists had begun to paint wondering faces with the startle reflex later drawn by Le Brun, it is more difficult to be sure in earlier depictions whether a figure confronted with stupendous or bizarre or dread-filled news is amazed or not (see Figures 1, 3, and 4).[80] No medieval theorist reduced wonder to the physiological reaction of the wonderer. The amazement discussed by philosophers, chroniclers, and travelers had a strong cognitive component; you could wonder only where you knew that you failed to understand. Thus wonder entailed a passionate desire for the *scientia* it lacked; it was a stimulus and incentive to investigation.

Nor was wonder reducible to the nature per se of the marvel that triggered it. To the Scholastics, who sometimes aimed to de-wonder the rest of the world, only miracles were, objectively speaking, wonder-causing; but no one thought men and women felt *stupor* or *admiratio* only, or even primarily, at miracles. All theories of wonder saw it as a significance-reaction: a flooding with awe, pleasure, or dread owing to something deeper, lurking in the phenomenon. The wonderer was situated; wonder was perspectival (even if miracles were not). What is remarkable to one may be expected to another; as Mandeville observed, to the one-eyed, those with two eyes will seem deformed, and to those of other religions, Christians will be the cannibals. Wonder was a response to something novel and bizarre that seemed both to exceed explanation and to indicate that there might be reason (significance — not necessarily cause) behind it.

Thus medieval theories of wonder made the point that wonder is non-appropriative yet based in facticity and singularity. The opposite of *admiratio* is not only to investigate; it is also to imitate and to generalize. To wonder is emphatically *not* to consume and incorporate; it is, as Bernard of Clairvaux said, to give back the goblet after draining the potion. But, as Gervais of Tilbury also said, if you do not believe the event, you will not marvel at it. You can marvel only at something that is, at least in some sense, there. Marveling responds to the there-ness of the event, to its concreteness and specificity. Amazement is suppressed by the citing of too many cases, the formulation of general laws, the *inductio exemplorum*. Wonder is at the singular — both its significance and its particularity.

Wonder and the Modern Historian

Am I then wrong to suggest that wonder is the special characteristic of the historian? I think not — if we understand *admiratio* in its medieval sense, as cognitive, perspectival, non-appropriative, and deeply respectful of the specificity of the world. There is something old-fashioned, almost absurd, in such an assertion, of course. Medieval philosophers and theologians emphasized wonder as a first step toward knowledge; we, in our postmodern anxiety, tend rather to emphasize how hard it is to know. Medieval devotional writers and hagiographers stressed wonder as the opposite of imitation or possession; we are aware that any response involves some appropriation. Medieval travelers and collectors of marvels argued that awe and dread are situated, perspectival; we share this perception and give credit to feminism and postcolonial theory for it, but we suspect that such awareness shatters the possibility of writing any coherent account of the world. Medieval chroniclers and occasional writers stressed the uniqueness of events rather than the trends they illustrated, their moral significance rather than their temporal causes; we fear that the particular is the trivial and that significance is merely the projection of our own values onto the past.

Nonetheless, I would argue, we write the best history when the specificity, the novelty, the awe-fulness, of what our sources render up bowls us over with its complexity and its significance. Our research is better when we move only cautiously to understanding, when fear that we may appropriate the "other" leads us not so much to writing about ourselves and our fears as to crafting our stories with attentive, wondering care. At our best, we strive for the "strange view of things" — not least because, as Thomas Aquinas understood, *admiratio* has to do with teaching. I am certain my students sometimes feel that I speak to them of things as bizarre and unheard of as William of Newburgh's green children or the barnacle geese born from trees that some medieval authors alleged they had seen.[81] But surely our job as teachers is to puzzle, confuse, and amaze. We must rear a new generation of students who will gaze in wonder at texts and artifacts, quick to puzzle over a translation, slow to project or to appropriate, quick to assume there is a significance, slow to generalize about it. Not only as scholars, then, but also as teachers, we must astonish and be astonished. For the flat, generalizing, presentist view of the past encapsulates it and makes it boring, whereas amazement yearns toward an understanding, a significance, that is always just a little beyond both our theories and our fears.

Every view of things that is not wonderful is false.

CHAPTER TWO

Metamorphosis, or

Gerald and the Werewolf[1]

It is now more than twenty years since a conference at Harvard University, organized by Robert Benson and Giles Constable, undertook to assess and situate Charles Homer Haskins's influential *The Renaissance of the Twelfth Century* (1927) on its fiftieth anniversary. The celebration of 1977 broadened Haskins's renaissance, which was, by implication if not by definition, a Latin movement in which science, philosophy, history, and law were central,[2] and added considerable attention to the flowering of religious movements and vernacular literature.[3] The optimistic and even triumphalist tone of Haskins's treatment continued. Since then, however, views of the "long" twelfth century (a period understood to run from ca. 1050 to ca. 1230) have darkened. The many twelfth-century references to reforming, burgeoning, developing, and unfolding, studied by Gerhard Ladner and taken by many scholars in the middle years of our century to characterize the period,[4] have recently given way to a sense that growth, optimism, and opportunity may be the mirror images of closure, suspicion, and condemnation. New choices and new awareness of choices produce self-definition, always achieved partly by the exclusion of other possible selves; exploration and increasing precision in ideas lead not only to creativity but also to condemnation of (and new mechanisms for the condemnation of) alternatives.

77

In the context of recent interest in the high Middle Ages as the locus of the disturbing and the "other" as well as in the late twelfth century as a "persecuting society,"[5] it seems time to reconsider medieval ideas of *mutatio* themselves. Ladner and subsequent scholars were certainly right to stress twelfth-century notions of personal *renovatio* and *reformatio* (returning to likeness with God) and extrapolations from this to ideas that *transformatio* of persons and institutions can be improvement as well as newness.[6] But recent attention to the role of the body in natural philosophy and in theological anthropology and to the specific problems twelfth-century thinkers had in understanding how the human person as a body-soul combination achieves and retains identity suggests that change was problematic in many areas of twelfth-century thought.

I have contributed recently to "darker" views of the twelfth century, both by stressing a concern for the monstrous, the marvelous, and the peculiar in writers of the late 1100s and by emphasizing the literalism and materialism of theological views of the body.[7] Neither emphasis need, of course, be negative. The monstrous can be — and was — treated playfully as well as fearfully.[8] A new attention to the human person as embodied can carry with it new curiosity about natural laws, increasingly positive evaluation of the senses as means of access to the world, and awakening awareness of the diversity body tends to signal. Nonetheless my work has, for better or worse, tended to stress the somatic as both expression of and limitation of the spiritual. And my study of bodily resurrection conjured up a twelfth century whose anthropology strained not only to account for body but also to interpret that body as starkly physical — bits of flesh and bones.[9] In this paper, written for the sort of occasion that is calculated to impel self-assessment, I want to return to that interpretation and ask whether I was right.

78

Again the Question of Bodily Change

In *The Resurrection of the Body in Western Christianity*, I connected
the extreme literalism and materialism of twelfth-century notions
of resurrection at the end of time with a fear of metempsychosis,
of loss of self through loss of body, or — to put it another way —
with a pervasive conviction, underlying many genres and divergent discourses of the period, that the human person is a psychosomatic unit whose survival necessitates bodily continuity.[10]
I pointed to the anxiety, found in condemnations of groups as
different as the antinomian Amauricians and the dualist Cathars,
that these dissident traditions neglected proper care of cadavers
in burial, erased differences of rank and gender carried by body
when they erased bodily elements in survival, and told fables of
body-hopping. Whatever the truth or subtlety of actual Cathar or
Amaurician positions, those Catholic clerics who opposed them —
and, I argued, projected onto them their own fears — interpreted
heretical doctrine as equating self with soul.[11]

    Orthodox attacks on heretics for metempsychosis — that is,
body-hopping, body-exchange, or body-erasure — came, I argued,
at the height of Western understanding of resurrection as materi-
alist and literal. Scholastic and monastic discussions of the twelfth
and early thirteenth centuries saw an embodied self as locus of
identity and connected this identity with triumph over change,
over physical process and decay.[12] Bodily resurrection was thus
both supernatural and natural. It is natural for the human person
to have a body, and survival of soul alone is hence an aberration
that cannot be perpetual; but divine power is necessary, for in
the natural order biological entities give birth only to like, but
numerically separate, individuals (additional instances of the
species).[13] Only God can sustain the "same" body through death,
decay, and resurrection. In analyzing all this, I saw significance
in the Schoolmen's fondness for Matthew 15.17 ("whatsoever

79

entereth into the mouth, goeth into the belly and is cast out into the privy"), which seemed to them to protect body from turning into food, and I cited as proof text Peter Lombard's use of the doctrine of bodily continuity in resurrection to limit the change involved in growth:

> A boy who dies immediately after being born will be resurrected in that stature that he would have had if he had lived to the age of thirty, impeded by no defect of body. From whence therefore would that substance [*substantia*], which was small in birth, be so big in resurrection, unless of itself in itself it multiplied? From which it appears that even if he had lived, the substance would not have come from another source but it would have augmented itself, just as the rib [of Adam] from which woman was made and as the loaves of the gospel story [were multiplied].[14]

I sensed in such discussions a fear of process that lay even deeper than the fear of loss of social and sexual differentiation also entailed in eclipsing body. And I quoted a number of monastic and Scholastic texts that took change as evil, stasis or immutability as good.[15]

Support for these arguments can indeed be found in work I did not cite in 1995. As Giles Constable has pointed out, twelfth-century historians and preachers had a new awareness of historical change and made complex, sometimes contradictory, use of the mutability topos. Nonetheless change was usually seen as for the worse, even if it might be the basis for later improvement, and writers such as Bruno of Segni, who spoke of the Incarnation as God's descent into mutability, saw man's constant changing (his failure to preserve *figura,* or form) as that from which redemption was necessary.[16]

In addition, I might have quoted from the numerous poets for

80

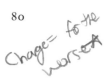

whom a sense of the changeability of the world led to ruminations on perishing. Walter of Châtillon, for example, wrote, in one of his satires:

The appearances [*species*] of the world are vanity.
Everything that is lit by the sun is as movable as
   the sun itself.
Every day all things alter.
. . . .
When error rages everywhere,
When everywhere the fool has precedence over the wise,
When insane disorder unshapes the four quadrants of
   the circle
With what chains can I bind and hold the ever-
   changing Proteus?
. . . .
Death is certain; what is not certain is when his
   sword falls.[17]

Milo, a minor disciple of Bernard Sylvestris, whose poem *De mundi philosophia* has something of Bernard's sense of flux as fertility, power, and promise, nonetheless also laments mutability and holds out heaven as the promise of stasis:

The creatures of the mire are not perpetual:
earth, mire of the elements, is their mother,
she absorbs all that decays . . .
takes back what she brought forth, gives new and takes
   the old.
. . . .
Heaven is for spirits, earth for mutable things. . . .
. . . .

Each man is born, flows by, ends in the sea of
death.
...justly [men] joy in their escape
...reaching their heaven-haven.[18]

Moreover, it is a commonplace in scholarship to emphasize a
medieval commitment to species immutability, tracing a straight
line from Augustine and Ambrose to modern creationism; and the
generalization seems to survive, although as Barbara Obrist has
pointed out, there is a great deal of evidence that it is not accu-
rate.[19] Nonetheless a more nuanced interpretation, which admits
medieval fascination with spontaneous generation and hybridization, suggests that there was concern to delimit species-crossing
very carefully. Church lawyers continued to employ the famous
Canon episcopi of ca. 900 that prohibited as blasphemy the belief in
metamorphosis or body-exchange. Theologians repeated Augustine's statement that humans do not become animals, although
demons may utilize extremely complex strategies to make it appear that they do.[20] An obscure early Irish text expressed the anxieties of many missionaries and preachers when it asserted:

> ...if it is granted that all things which are made of earth can be
> changed back and forth into one another,...say, that an animal can
> be turned into a piece of wood, bread into a stone, or a man into a
> bird, then none of these can remain firmly within the boundaries of
> its nature and we would be seen to assent to the ridiculous tales of
> magicians who say that their ancestors were flying about in the sub-
> stance of birds.[21]

Nor was the opposition to hybridization and metempsychosis
limited to theologians. Natural philosophers also used the principle "like begets like" to impose order on the world and hold indi-

viduals in mostly immutable categories. For example, Marius's *De elementis*, probably from the 1160s, gave a keen and fully Aristotelian analysis of physical change in which the elements come together to make a new entity (not just a crude mixture of previously existing particles).[22] But Marius saw the principle "like generates like" as a power God plants in things to preserve species and maintained that there are three basic categories of beings (animal, vegetable, and mineral) that cannot be changed into each other.[23] Early alchemical writing in the West drew on Avicenna's *De congelatione et conglutinatione*, which stated explicitly, "Let alchemists know that they cannot transmute the species of things" (although Latin translations added the phrase "unless [that species] be resolved to prime matter").[24] Albert the Great, who saw fossils as real species change (from plant to stone) and argued that alchemists could in theory change metal, nonetheless thought hybrids were rare, possible only between very closely related species, and held that species is not just that which defines a thing but also that which endures.[25]

Thus it seems that poets, theologians, and natural philosophers in the twelfth and thirteenth centuries — unwilling to deny what was to them empirical evidence of monstrous combinations, hybridization, grafting, and spontaneous generation — struggled to contain the natural world in categories of unalterable, or not-easily-alterable, species.[26] Scholars such as Leonard Barkan, Denyse Delcourt, Dennis Kratz, and Joyce Salisbury root this resistance to species-crossing and metamorphosis in an insistence on hierarchy that privileges the human person as rational, at the top of the ladder of corporeal beings.[27] Dyan Elliott connects it to pollution anxieties, based in a deep-seated fear of the female.[28] In my 1995 work on resurrection, I saw it as a fundamental ontological anxiety, grounded in the human experience of death and decay itself.[29]

Yet I remained uneasy with my own conclusions. After all, the work that had influenced me most during my graduate school years was Marie-Dominique Chenu's *La Théologie au douzième siècle*. How could anyone weaned on Chenu's wonderful essays, calling attention as they did to the twelfth-century sense of labile, percolating, fertile nature with all its internal orderliness and power, see such a dark idea of mutability as threat at the century's close?[30] These were the years of the revival of Ovid, of marvel-collecting, of theological exploration of shape-shifting and body-borrowing, of new kinds of transformation miracles and alchemy — in short, the era of greenmen and werewolves, stigmata and eucharistic miracles, and dreams of turning copper into gold. Clearly I needed to probe more widely and deeply into conceptions of change in the years around 1200.

I cannot treat here — nor have I been able to explore — all twelfth- and thirteenth-century discourses on *mutabilitas, mutatio*, and the related terms *transformatio, diversitas, alteritas*, and so on.[31] Change is too large a concept for a single study, nor is it clear that everything we might translate, or denominate, as "change" is the same, or even particularly closely related. Even if we concentrate on "metamorphosis" — change of one body into another or change of species — we find that the relatively few uses of the term we turn up with a keyword computer search or creative use of indices are hardly univocal.[32] For example, Thomas the Cistercian uses "metamorphosis" metaphorically when he glosses Song of Songs 2.9. The term can, he says, refer to deformation of the image of God (*imaginem Dei*) in man, making him "like the horse and ass which have no understanding [Ps. 31.9]"; it can also refer to man's rise to ecstasy.[33] The philosopher William of Conches uses *metamorphoseos* to refer to Plato's account of the actual transformation of the elements at the origin of the universe and *mutatio* (glossed explicitly as passing from one body to

84

another) to describe a moral transformation in which the soul, returning to God, changes not its essence but its likeness (*similitudo*).[34] Conrad of Hirsau, in an often-cited passage that echoes the *Canon episcopi*, takes metamorphosis to mean "transformation of substance" and forbids the reading of tales in which man's reason (the image of God) is obscured in his mutation into beasts or stones.[35] A Middle Irish text from the late eleventh or early twelfth century classifies types of change and emphasizes the impossibility of "*revolutio* or transmigration of souls" and "*metaformatio*, that is, transfiguration after the example of werewolves" — both of which it contrasts explicitly to *resurrectio*.[36] Still other texts take metamorphosis as normal biological process, although they usually employ the terms *transformatio* or *mutatio* for the change. Vincent of Beauvais's vast encyclopedia repeats Isidore of Seville's discussion, reminding us that "many things do experience mutation [*mutationem recipiunt*] and corrupt things are transformed into diverse species [*diversas species*] as bees from the putrid flesh of calves, beetles from horses, locusts from mules, and scorpions from crabs."[37] Gervais of Tilbury gives us a whiff of the schoolroom when he comments that scholars actually debate whether the biblical account of Nebuchadnezzar's transformation to an ass (Daniel 4.33) is a real metamorphosis or just a moral statement.[38]

Hence even the relatively rare word "metamorphosis" and its usual definition "transformation of substance" are not mere technical terms with precise delimited meanings and contexts. They do not denote simply species-crossing, body-hopping, or metempsychosis; sometimes they denote moral growth or deterioration, the unfolding rather than the transgressing of a nature. Nor can we say that they occur primarily in moralizing and Neoplatonic contexts (as metaphor) or in scientific and biological ones (as fact). Rather, such language appears to tap into many complex

85

and highly charged conversations about the moral and philosophical nature of things. What modern scholars denominate by metamorphosis (body-swapping, transformation from one species to another) is clearly worth exploring, but there are no shortcuts through the material via keyword searches, and collecting random quotations from twelfth-century authors does not get us very far.

I have therefore decided to explore — not all discussions of mutability, development, or process in the years around 1200 — but a number of discourses or genres that explicitly treat change from one thing to another and seem at first glance to contradict my earlier intuition that much of the religious and intellectual concern of the period was devoted to containing and countering a mutability seen as dark threat to survival and identity. In this essay I shall look at three such discourses: Ovidian poetry, theological discussions of miraculous change, and collections of marvels, especially marvels of species transformation. We shall find there passionate interest, even delight, in mutability: an enthusiasm for Lady Nature, a new curiosity about the creation story (whether in the version from Genesis or Plato), widespread appropriation of cultural material from the past (such as Ovid's *Metamorphoses* or myths of shape-shifting) that seems to encourage belief in species mutation, and a compulsion among university intellectuals to treat topics such as magic and the bodies of demons. But we shall also find, even in discourses that focus on the bizarre, the transgressive, and the transformed, a profound resistance to metamorphosis and metempsychosis (whether as metaphor or as fact) that appears to be the other side of the fascination they exerted.

Ovidian Poetry as Fascination with Change

I turn first to the revival of Ovid, for the new attention paid to his *Metamorphoses* in the late twelfth century seems the most obvious place to look for evidence that radical change of being was em-

86

braced as fascinating and wondrous, not (as I argued earlier) fled and suppressed.[39] Here the most important point to be made is one noticed by many scholars, above all by Simone Viarre: the parts of Ovid's poem that are influential in the twelfth and early thirteenth centuries are books 1 and 15. [40] The twelfth-century Ovid is a scientific, cosmological, philosophical Ovid, the Ovid who sings "of bodies changed into new forms" as the cosmos emerges (*Metamorphoses* 1.1–2), who promises in the mouth of Pythagoras that "all things are changing, nothing dies"; "what we call birth is but a beginning to be other than what one was before" (*Metamorphoses* 15.164 and 256).[41] Moreover, the part of book 15 that is used, echoed, and absorbed by twelfth-century poets and grammarians is not the doctrine of metempsychosis but the celebration of fertility. Although sometimes interpreted to mean by "metamorphosis" a Neoplatonic return of the soul to its Exemplar, this Ovid is usually seen as the story of form ordering, fructifying, and impregnating chaos.[42] Indeed, it is frequently read as natural philosophy. For example, early commentators take the story of Deucalion and Pyrrha, told to cast stones after the flood, as an account of the respective contributions of male and female seed in the act of reproduction (*Metamorphoses* 1.315–415), relate the sex change of Tiresias to the seasons and the germination of seeds (*Metamorphoses* 3.323–38), and interpret the story of Phaëthon driving the horses of the sun as a description of the role of sunlight in the ripening of the harvest (*Metamorphoses* 1.751–79 and 2.1–400).[43] Hence the twelfth-century Ovid expresses what many philosophers have come to see as Aristotle's basic insight: that the most remarkable thing about the world is change — the fact that things come to be.[44]

Even more important for my purposes than the marked preference for cosmological and biological readings is the profound influence of an Ovidian sense of mutability as fertility, sexuality, and vitality that floods much of the poetry of the twelfth century, particularly that of the group we used to call the Chartrains. In such poetry, biological change or growth is sometimes allegorized as the unfolding of a nature, less the transformation than the revelation of what is. Moreover, such poetry frequently contrasts nature's ever-flowing fertility or process, which defeats death through procreation, with the limited life span of the human being, who must inevitably die. Nonetheless these poets make new and explicit use of Ovid to celebrate diversity as wondrous, sex as a kind of immortality. For example, the poem *Profuit ignaris*, written by a cleric for a group of nuns and explicitly based on Ovid's *Metamorphoses*, sees Ovid's Nature as seduced, dragged down into mutable species and crime.[45] But as a whole, the poem reflects less the Platonic idea that fall into mutability is a fall from the real than a sense that the elements work in the sensible world to produce, under the influence of the heavenly spheres, a fascinating variety:

> ... whatever has influence on [things], from which we see every created form established, whatever you know and feel, whatever is begotten and exists by virtue of these elements — all this men saw in the sexual unions of these gods![46]

Or, to take another example, Bernard Sylvestris's *Cosmographia* gives an account of creation in which, as Brian Stock remarks, matter is the heroine.[47] Sometimes the chaos of primitive and warring elements longing to be reborn, sometimes a more abstract and indefinable substratum, this matter is the rough and teeming mass of Ovid's book 1. But it is also the perduring reality of book 15. In those much-analyzed passages *Cosmographia* 2.8 and 2.14, Bernard takes up, in Ovidian, even Pythagorean terms, the crucial question of individual survival and identity. Framing his description with references to Jove descending into the lap of his spouse and Ceres discovering her lost daughter, Bernard writes of a universe that contains the seeds of its own continuity; ever-flowing *silva* (matter) lurks beneath.[48] Procreation fights death by perpetuating species. As semen is reabsorbed by the brain if not used, so nature remains unchanged and flows into herself, nourished by her own flux. Bernard even strains to see the survival of the individual as guaranteed by a kind of Platonic-Pythagorean outflow and return. Although the whole person (*totus homo*) inhabits a body doomed to die, reabsorption of semen by the brain is, he writes, parallel to the return of the soul to heaven.[49] The throbbing rhythm of the cosmos becomes, albeit somewhat ambiguously and inconsistently, a kind of immortality.

Theological Speculation on Growth and Change
When we turn to my second topic — theological texts — we find, as I suggested in *The Resurrection of the Body*, a similarly ambiguous fascination with fertility and change. But I am now inclined to find in these texts less disquiet than I earlier sensed, more wonder, and, above all, more intellectual control. To explain what I mean, I return to the passage from Peter Lombard I quoted above. When Peter argues that instant growth to adult stature at the resurrection is like ordinary growth through life, he is of course arguing that the human body comes not from the addition of particles of food (the change of foodstuff into flesh-stuff) but from the expansion "of itself in itself" of a core of human nature. He appears to be opposing change, to be making organic process in some sense illusory. But three other aspects of the passage are worth noting — aspects that I did not previously emphasize. First, the Lombard is using resurrection doctrine to explain nature, not the other way round. Rather like the Ovid commentators, he marshals his intellectual inheritance to shed light on the natural

world. Second, his idea of internally expanding and self-explaining substances undercuts the distinction between natural and supernatural. It makes growth seem almost miraculous, and miracle (the creation of Eve, the multiplication of loaves and fishes, and so on) almost natural. It diminishes the impact of one thing on another, but it also suggests a world in which biological entities have built-in dynamisms, potencies to become either more themselves or something else entirely. Third, it is not in fact change, or growth, or organic process per se that disturbs Peter; growth, as Hugh of St. Victor said, is natural.[50] What disturbs Peter is the changing of something's nature or essence or *veritas* (for example, our particular human nature) into something else (for example, food).[51] Peter's idea that the essence or substance of something is accounted for by seeds (Augustine's "seminal reasons") unfolding within it gives him both an understanding of nature as mutability and a determination to ferret out its laws.

What strikes me when I return now to theological texts is the fascination with rules of change that permeates twelfth- and thirteenth-century discussions of the natural world. Theologians were intrigued by the (apparent) fact of spontaneous generation and argued about whether hybrids or new species could occur.[52] Moreover, as is clear from Peter Lombard, this search for the rules of change was carried right into discussions of the miraculous, where it was not *any* change or development but rather species change, especially change of body, that fascinated. The fullest Scholastic treatments of the miraculous come in discussions of the assaults of demons, especially in considerations of the question whether demons (or angels) use bodies or change the bodies of others;[53] the paradigmatic Scholastic miracles were not cures (by far the most common miracle in actual miracle collections) but species transformations, especially Exodus 7 (the changing of rods into serpents by Moses, Aaron, and the magicians of Pharaoh) and the wedding at Cana (the transformation of water into wine).[54]

By the thirteenth century, theologians and natural philosophers agreed that *mirabilia* included all things at which we might feel wonder because we did not understand but that *miracula* included only those things which were beyond nature and hence performed only by God.[55] Such categorization of course admits that the order of nature can be violated; but it also ipso facto emphasizes that order and provides an incentive for its discovery. If only God (and, with his permission, the angels and saints) breaks the regularity of nature, then magic must be natural — as must much at which we feel *terror* or *admiratio*. By about 1250, an anonymous master could remark that most philosophers and physicians held astonishing events and entities — monsters, unexpected cures, explosions, giants, mermen, magnets, fossils, and coral — to be *mirabilia*, explained entirely "from natural things."[56] Hence natural explanation was increasingly the first resort: a ghost was likely to be the product of bad digestion and insomnia, a double sun an illusion like the bent appearance of a stick in water.[57]

Nonetheless theologians could not deny magic. Peter Lombard wished to argue that we should feel more wonder at the failure of Pharaoh's magicians to make stinging gnats than at their conjuring of serpents from rods and frogs from mud (Exodus 7–8); but he asserted the change to be real and gave a naturalistic explanation. The serpents and frogs come from seeds "hidden by God in the elements of the world" and manipulated by conjurers.[58] A decade later, John of Salisbury argued that magicians really shake the elements (*elementa concutiunt*) and take away the species of things (*rebus adimunt species suas*).[59] In the mid-thirteenth century, Thomas Aquinas insisted in several works that Pharaoh's magicians produced real frogs and serpents (*vera facta*) but these were not miracles in a strict sense because they came by natural causes; Moses' frogs were, however, a miracle.[60]

It is thus easy to see how what we might think of as rational, naturalistic explanations of change appeared even at the heart of the discussion of miracles. Both John of Salisbury and Rupert of Deutz, for example, argued that there are seminal reasons in things that unfold in preordained time. Trees draw up water into grapes and make wine; if God speeds this up and turns water into wine without the intervening steps, we call it a miracle.[61] Peter the Venerable used the speedup argument to explain change of substance in the Eucharist: transformation of wine to blood is possible, he argues, because it happens in our own bodies.[62] In the thirteenth century, Albert the Great claimed that both Aaron and the magicians made serpents by speedup of the seeds in things. Although he differentiated *miracula*, done by God and the saints, from *mirabilia*, done by demons and magicians, Albert saw both as effecting real transmutation and stated explicitly: "the method of miracles is this: the transformation of matter."[63] At the heart of theological discussion of the miraculous is a discussion of the nature of change itself, especially change in which a thing becomes, radically and shockingly, something else.

Werewolf Stories as Testing of Boundaries

Hence the schools of the twelfth century produced not only a learned poetry that celebrated nature as fertile, mutable, and filled with possibility; they also produced theological and philosophical curiosity about the emergence of an ordered world from chaos and about actual species change. What has fascinated recent historians most, however, is another discourse concerning change, produced by intellectuals but borrowed from folktale as well as from classical paradoxology: a literature of entertainment, which often includes extensive collections of marvels.[64] Written by aspiring bureaucrats, most of them connected in some way with the court of Henry the Young in late twelfth-century England, this literature includes miracles (about which some of the authors are quite cynical) and *fabulae,* or stories (often contrasted to *historia* and told without claims to their ontological status). But above all it gathers tales of wonders, which range from salamanders, magnets, and volcanoes to vampires, werewolves, and islands on which no one can die.[65] As Jacques Le Goff has argued, such literature destabilizes reality, making boundaries fluid, categories and interpretations problematic.[66] It lodges at the heart of the world (not just on its margins) events that seem to make all identity labile, threatening, and threatened. Here we find not only serpents born from rods, flies from carcasses, wine from water, and bleeding flesh from consecrated bread. We also find two of Europe's first ethnographers — Gerald of Wales and Gervais of Tilbury — reporting as fact lycanthropy, or the change of men into wolves.

It is well not to be misled by the recent enthusiasm of scholars for the bizarre, the transgressive, and the disgusting.[67] Several of these histories and story collections evidence reserve and confusion about the marvels they recount.[68] Tales of fairies, vampires, ghosts, and oddities are told with relish, to be sure, but there are fewer hybrids and metamorphoses (that is, cases of real category transgression, not just "otherness") than we might expect from the secondary literature.[69] Moreover, certain of the authors who recount them seem concerned to sort out their ontological status so as to deny species violation. Walter Map reports about a seaman (*homo equoreus*) that he is *verus homo*; he has "nothing inhuman in his limbs."[70] The children born to fairy women are, in Walter's account, fully human, not hybrids, and they are rarely happy; the production of such children is an "injury to nature."[71] William of Newburgh, fiercely skeptical about reports of miracles, feels compelled by eyewitness accounts to accept the story of green children born from the earth, but he is decidedly uncomfortable in doing

93

so.[72] Gervais of Tilbury gives several lengthy discussions (drawn ultimately from Augustine) of demons using bodies and argues that these bodies are tricks or illusions, not real people.[73] Gerald of Wales worries about human-animal hybrids that result from human-animal sex, a practice he thinks "barbarous" and particularly Irish.[74] Such turgid and over-interpreted discussion suggests anxiety about controlling the material (and the world it describes) more than lighthearted escape into alterity.

Nonetheless these authors did speak, albeit anxiously and occasionally, of animal-human hybrids and evidenced a near obsession with fairy-human or demon-human sex. Moreover, Gerald and Gervais recount stories of lycanthropy, carefully glossed with explicit discussions of metamorphosis, and such stories are part of what we might call the "werewolf renaissance of the twelfth century."[75] Indeed, the revival of the werewolf motif in both imaginative literature and marvel collections is perhaps the most blatant piece of evidence to counter my earlier argument that rejection of metempsychosis was a leitmotif in much early thirteenth-century writing.

Werewolf stories have, of course, a long tradition in Europe. But the ancient werewolf, like the modern, is very different from the werewolf of medieval romances and entertainment literature.[76] Ferocious, hairy, dripping with blood, a devourer of human beings, the werewolf of Pliny, Ovid and Petronius is, like the werewolf of modern TV and folk story, an emblem of the periodic eruption of the bestial from within the human. In contrast, the werewolves that emerge quite suddenly and numerously around 1200 in entertainment literature (especially the works of Gervais and Gerald), in theological discussion (especially William of Auvergne's *De universo*), and in romance (*Bisclavret, Mélion, Guillaume de Palerne, Arthur and Gorlagon*) are what scholars have called "sympathetic" werewolves — victims who are changed into

94

wolves, usually by evil women, but who retain the "intelligence and memory" of rational human beings.[77] Hence several modern scholars see these werewolves as "fake" werewolves and argue that the earlier werewolf tradition of a constitutionally double being (that is, a being alternately human, then animal, by its very nature) remains as only a vestige in the two brief stories told by Gervais of Tilbury and the opening lines of Marie de France's *Bisclavret*.[78]

Recent scholarship has tended to see the tamed werewolf as a warping or repression of the idea of metamorphosis.[79] And it is certainly true that these stories stress the werewolf as a rational soul trapped in an animal body. Marie de France's shape-shifter serves as an example of civility to the court; in *Guillaume de Palerne*, a witty werewolf teaches naive lovers to survive and triumph by employing animal disguises.[80] The author of *Arthur and Gorlagon* underlines the full humanity of the werewolf by explaining that there was a mistake at the moment of magical transformation; the formula used erroneously was "be a wolf, have the reason of a man."[81] The stress on the rationality and civility of the wolf in some ways attenuates the horror of metamorphosis, although shape-shifting is real in these romances. The fact that the heroes in *Bisclavret*, *Mélion*, and *Guillaume de Palerne* all need to undergo reverse metamorphosis in privacy seems to be not merely (as critics have argued) a comment on their "civilized" anxiety about nakedness but also a comment on the horror of shape-changing itself. Indeed Bisclavret, changed back to his human form offstage, is then found asleep in the king's bed (a detail that echoes in reverse his exclusion from his wife's bed when she learns he is a werewolf). His metamorphosis from animal to human is bracketed and contained in a metamorphosis from sleep to wakefulness that perhaps reflects theological explanations of shape-shifting as dream or illusion.[82]

95

Most scholars have seen in these tales a conflict between Christian opposition to metamorphosis and folk enthusiasm for it, assuming that the power and horror of genuine change has been sanitized by clerical opposition to such assault on rational man's special place in the cosmos.[83] And as we have seen, it is true that clerical writing (usually based directly or indirectly on Augustine's *City of God*) opposed belief in shape-shifting. Writing in the 1230s, William of Auvergne, for example, told of a complex case in which demons committed lupine ravages in aerial bodies while a man slept, himself brought by the demons to believe that he was a werewolf.[84] But it is important to note, first, that even such stories make the ravages of phantom wolves quite real; the phantasms slip toward a horrible reality. Second, stories such as those of Marie de France or Gerald of Wales about wolves with the souls of men are different from what William imagines or rationalizes: Marie's werewolf, like Gerald's, undergoes real, not illusory, shape change. Third, resistance to loss of identity in such stories is not especially Christian or clerical. In Teutonic traditions, the soul (and hence the eyes) of the changed creature remains human under an animal skin; Eastern tales of shape-shifting, well known from the *Arabian Nights*, see the victims as humans in beast form;[85] Ovid himself says of Lycaon "he becomes a wolf and yet retains vestiges of his old form [*veteris . . . vestigia formae*]" (*Metamorphoses* 1.237). The accounts of the romance writers and marvel collectors do indeed, as all scholars have noticed, resist the suggestion that a human self slips into complete bestiality when its shape or skin or *species* changes, but it is not clear that this is owing to Christian ideas of the rational human soul as *imago Dei*. Resistance to complete transformation from human to animal hardly sanitizes the story; depiction of human eyes gleaming from a wolfface, if anything, only increases the heterodox overtones. For what scholars have not noticed is that the shape-shifting of these stories is metempsychosis. Gervais of Tilbury's account of a man who goes mad at the changes of the moon and becomes a wolf is a story of real body-hopping, not illusion. Just as in Ovid, shape is changed and carries with it story. In *Mélion*, for example, the ferocity of the wolf shape contaminates the man within and leads him, for all his "intelligence and memory," to kill human beings.

When Bisclavret awakens as a man after sleep, we may perhaps be reminded of an otherworld voyager waking after a trip to hell in a medieval vision; but Bisclavret has been a wolf. Whether the voyager has been to a physical or a metaphysical hell, he has gone in a body (aerial or physical) that is his own. The metempsychosis condemned by theologians in the years around 1200 was practiced by the werewolves for whose reality Gerald of Wales attests. The fact that a human soul can be said to be within hardly makes the shape-shifter less fearsome or more orthodox.

Thus we find in the later twelfth and early thirteenth centuries an Ovidian sense of mutability as power and possibility, a fascination with marvels in which species boundaries are crossed, and a theological interpretation of magic and miracle that emphasizes the reality of transformation. Yet the years around 1200 also saw strident insistence on resurrection of exactly the same physical particles that lay in the grave. The high point of literalist interpretation of bodily survival, of fear of an eschatology that severs soul from body, coincided with the revival of myths of shape-shifting, with literary challenges to a unitary psychosomatic self. How are we to understand this? Does the enthusiasm for werewolf stories and for Ovid, the increased theological discussion of demonic bodies and transformation miracles, suggest that the soul-body nexus was loosening, not tightening, in the years around 1200?

Careful review of the three areas I have just examined convinces me that this is not so. The late twelfth century does show, in many genres and discourses, an enthusiasm for fertile, labile nature carrying its own rules within, and those rules were increasingly formulated in Aristotelian terms that make substantial change the absolute replacing of a thing by something else. Resistance to any change or loss of physical stuff (as in alchemical manipulation or hybridization) lessened. Indeed, as I pointed out in *The Resurrection of the Body*, theologians and philosophers had by the late thirteenth century new (and Aristotelian) ways of guaranteeing survival of an individual and identical body without necessitating the survival of every physical particle.[86] But for all the new sense of mutability as possibility and vitality, we find deep resistance to severing of body and soul, to metempsychosis, at the heart of exactly that literature that might seem to encourage or propagate it. Body-hopping remained fascinating yet suspicious in widely divergent discourses. To theologians no less than collectors of marvels and tellers of tales, titillation and horror went together.

The Ovid Reception as Enthusiasm for Order

To make this point I turn again to the three topics I treated earlier. First, the Ovid reception. If we look closely at the poetry I spoke of above, what we find is either a Neoplatonizing interpretation that takes metamorphosis to mean return of soul to Exemplar — that is, of like to like — or an enthusiasm for natural change, for fertility and generation.[87] The Ovidian poetry of Bernard Sylvestris and his followers does not appropriate shape-shifting, species violation, or metempsychosis, either as metaphor or as fact. Moreover, when we look at early commentaries on Ovid's text, we find that metamorphosis is not metamorphosis at all.

Although Arnulf of Orleans and John of Garland, two of the earliest Ovid commentators, preface their glosses with discussions

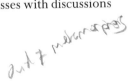

of types of *mutationes*, they do not in fact use the categories they develop.[88] Arnulf lists three kinds of change—natural (as in the development of chicken from egg), magical (as in the change of woman into cow), and spiritual (as in the appearance of health after insanity)—and argues that Ovid's *intentio* is to speak of change in the soul that leads to the creator, not of extrinsic changes in corporeal things. Nonetheless Arnulf speaks little of magical or spiritual change. Indeed, he rarely gives extended moral readings at all, and when he does, they almost never involve the soul's return to God. In a rare example of a moral reading, the woman Io is said to be changed into a cow because she falls into vice.[89]

Arnulf and John are interested, above all, in what we would see as scientific readings. They most often naturalize or euhemerize episodes. For example, Arnulf interprets the story of Ciparissus, changed into a tree with horrible leaves, as a description of the aging of a beautiful adolescent into a rough and hairy old man.[90] In glossing the rape of Europa, both John and Arnulf explain Jove's transformation into a bull as a reference to the picture of a bull carried on the prow of his ship.[91]

Hence, despite the occasional gesture in an *accessus* toward philosophical or moral analysis, these early commentaries evidence neither horror at nor even special interest in physical metamorphosis or species violation. Their fascination with change is a kind of cataloging impulse, found so often in the twelfth-century schools. Both John and Arnulf strain to find as many types of *mutatio* as possible and as many examples of each type.[92] But changes that are not in any sense shape-shifting ("Eurydice from life to death, from dead again to life, from life again to death" or "Io from chaste woman to adulteress") are cataloged as *mutationes* alongside transgressions of species ("Io to cow, then god").[93] And when episodes are glossed with moral rather than scientific interpretation, the thrust is often to attenuate or suppress the physical change rather than to explore the moral one. John of Garland, for example, insists on taking Lycaon's *mutatio* not as change into a wolf but as moral decline into wolfishness.[94] Myrrha, driven by lust for her father and changed into a myrrh tree, is discussed by Arnulf as an example not of incest but of incense.[95] *Mutatio* is thus reduced to a simple statement of something's nature or moral character with little or no attention to development, entrapment, or desire. Arnulf and John show no frisson of horror, no gasp of delight, at the diminution or liberation of self that may result from metamorphosis.

All this is not to deny that something important is going on. Arnulf and John skillfully dissociate and regroup elements of Ovid's text in order to treat what they wish to treat: the variety and complexity of the natural and moral world. As both Ralph Hexter and Paule Demats have noted, allegory is being born.[96] Ovid is evidence and evocation of the fearful fullness of nature: there is *admiratio* and *terror* in Myrrha, once woman, now tree, but it is the wonder of moral failure and biological multiplicity, not of physical metamorphosis. Hence Ovid is not used in the twelfth and thirteenth centuries to explore the relationship between shape, story, and identity so emphasized in modern Ovid criticism.[97] And since Ovid was not read as being about body and identity, we cannot take the enthusiasm for him as enthusiasm for probing the possibility of escape from the nexus of shape and self. The revival of Ovid was a revival of interest in mutability and flux, in the complexity of the moral and natural world, and in interpretation; it was not a revival of interest in metamorphosis.[98] Just as the poets' and commentators' attention to books 1 and 15 suggests a profound enthusiasm for the fertility and promise of the natural world, their avoidance of the topic of physical metamorphosis masks a deep disquietude at the possibility of slippage of the human body away from soul. By the early fourteenth century, allegorical explication had explicitly replaced *mutatio* as the focus of commentary, and Ovidian shape-shifting was labeled heretical.[99]

Learned Theology and Miracle Stories as Ontological Control

Nor when we come to discussion of the miraculous do we find that the theologians' fascination with change becomes an invitation to severing or attenuating the connection of body to self. Indeed, the theological discussion of marvel, magic, and miracle I considered above can be interpreted as straining to keep change within very precise limits. Not only were magic and marvel explained as natural or artificial manipulations of the natural order; miracles, especially the miracles of transmutation that interested the theologians most, were also understood as manipulations, simply unnatural or divine ones. Albert the Great even went so far as to use the notion of likeness, familiar from the biological principle "like generates like," to describe miracles. While discussing the complex senses in which we both can and cannot say that seeds or causes of miracles are planted in things from the beginning, Albert observes that there is a "potency to similar species" in things. Miracle may produce *mutatio* of matter, but "every miracle ... tends to some similar species of nature."[100] What the blind man receives is eyes, not an extra ear. Hence, in Albert's analysis, the category "like" tames and flattens, draws the astonishing toward the ordinary. Even in the realm of the miraculous we have not a topsy-turvy world but a very ordered one.

Behind the fascination with change in Scholastic writing (necessitated by the fact of miracle and magic), there seems thus to lie a determination — almost an obsession — to maintain matter and body. Hugh of St. Victor, discussing the creation of light and sun, uses the miracle at Cana counterintuitively to stress continuity. Perhaps God made sun from light as Jesus made wine from water "not so that something else should be made but so that it might be made from the same thing that was lowlier before."[101] Discussing the multiplication of loaves, Thomas Aquinas insists that Christ does not create new bread matter but rather adds extraneous preexisting matter to the loaves, as grains grow into a harvest.[102] Roger Bacon, using conventional arguments that entities give birth only to like but separate instances, not to the same instance, maintains that bodily resurrection (return of the same instance) is possible because God reduces body to prime or first matter and induces the same form in it again.[103] In all three of these examples, we find a good deal of technical terminology and complex reasoning employed to make a case of material change involve as little change as possible.

Such insistence on the importance and non-changeability of body appears especially in the treatment of demons, the place above all where Schoolmen discussed what we would call metamorphosis. As is well known, Augustine had taught that metamorphosis of human beings into animals is impossible.[104] What people experience, he argued, is either illusion, produced by demons working on the imagination, or a double (a phantasm), made by demons.[105] Twelfth- and thirteenth-century theologians have often been seen as merely repeating Augustine.[106] Close reading, however, makes it clear that these theologians actually tipped the discussion to emphasize angelic or demonic use of bodies (a topic that clearly titillated and horrified them) while continuing to deny metamorphosis. Peter Lombard, for example, makes heavy work of material he borrows from Augustine's *De Trinitate* about angelic apparitions. But what is important to Peter is not (as it was to Augustine) the psychological complexity of illusion but rather the demonstration that angels can be "overclothed" with corporeal bodies.[107] Thomas Aquinas merely repeats Augustine's two options to explain metamorphosis; but he is willing to choose among explanations when he deals with the bodies of good and bad angels.[108] Angels do not just produce forms in our imagination; they assume real bodies. This conclusion makes clear the importance of body to Thomas, but it might seem to suggest that he supports metamorphosis, at least of angels (good or fallen). The context shows, however, that the opposite is the case: the whole discussion resists rather than aids species-crossing or violation. Thomas's question is how angels or demons can exercise the functions of a living body (which we know from Scripture they do). His answer is that if the function is a transformation such as generation, then it can be produced only through a real body; hence demons can impregnate women but only with real seeds collected from human beings.[109] Angels do not become human, although they may take on human bodies to have the sort of relations only bodies can have.[110] Thus overclothing of demons with body maintains the distinction between human and demon, preventing hybridization or metamorphosis.

These theological discussions took place in the rarefied atmosphere of school and university; the miracles they considered were for the most part biblical events or thought experiments. But accounts of actual miracles also suggest horrified fascination with physical change. As numerous recent studies have shown, the miracle stories that circulated in the twelfth century contained relatively few transformation miracles.[111] In the earliest collections, most stories of genuine shape-shifting occur in dreams or visions.[112] But by the 1220s, when Caesarius of Heisterbach produced his *Dialogue on Miracles*, transformations and boundary crossings were, if not common, at least a noticeable part of the collection.[113]

Occasionally Caesarius's stories of transmutation are quite casual: the entrails of a hen, for example, turn into a toad.[114] But his tales of the devil as trickster, taking on shapes to seduce the weak, are stories of shifting apparitions, not of metamorphosis. Moreover, Caesarius struggles (as Thomas and Albert do later) to protect the embodied human person from invasion by, or change into, other bodies. He asks how demons can generate humans from real human seed and insists that people thus produced are fully human (not hybrids) and will rise at the end of time. He explains that demons cannot pass into the substance of the human soul but merely occupy empty cavities in the bowels. He gives an elaborate description of the glorified human body at the resurrection, explaining how parts from each of the four elements will go into one of the four gifts of glory. The final immutability of the body in heaven is presented as the result of what seems almost a natural development.[115] Most important, Caesarius gives a lengthy diatribe against Albigensian and antinomian heretics in which metempsychosis figures prominently.[116] Both groups are said to deny resurrection and Eucharist. The dualists are castigated for preaching transmigration of souls not only into the bodies of the poor and wretched but even into animals and reptiles. The antinomian heretics are accused of teaching that God spoke through Ovid! It is hard to imagine a clearer reflection of both fascination and horror at the prospect of species-crossing and metamorphosis.

The one transformation miracle that became truly prominent in the years around 1200 was the eucharistic miracle, in which the reality of Christ's body and blood — as baby, as beautiful young man, as lacerated flesh — broke through the bread and wine. Caesarius gives numerous examples, as does Gerald of Wales. But two points need to be made about this transformation. First, it was, as Benedicta Ward remarks, an inverted (or counter) miracle: it was not so much a metamorphosis as a restoring of the normal relationship between interior and exterior.[117] For the bread and wine had already changed to flesh and blood at the consecration, the metamorphosis had already happened. What the miracle did, then, was reveal what was already there: the body of Christ. Just as Ovid's commentators could read Io's bestiality as a revelation of her adulterous state (hence she did not change into a cow but became more herself), so eucharistic miracles could be understood as revealing the substance beneath by bringing accidents into accord with substance.[118]

Second, what made the Eucharist special was that it itself *was* a true metamorphosis, with or without counter-miracle. Exactly the change Peter Lombard feared (from food into body) really occurred. The struggle of theologians and commentators to control change by ordering it into intellectual categories left the true metamorphosis of eucharistic consecration rare and astounding. Roger Bacon could speak of bodily resurrection (the quintessential victory over change — that is, the return of precisely the same individual) in almost naturalistic language. But he spoke of the Eucharist with terror. God shows his goodness in veiling the sacrament, said Roger; if he did not, "we could not sustain it from horror and loathing. . . ."[119] The Eucharist was not a paradigm or a model, even for miracles; ordinary miracles, as Albert taught, tended not to metamorphosis but to likeness.

Were Medieval Werewolves Really Metempsychosis?

When we return to my third topic, entertainment literature, we find that it, too, maintains and indeed obsessively tightens, rather than attenuates, the link of self and body. Sometimes impudently hostile to miracles, collectors of *mirabilia* are far from dismissive of fairy visitors, inexplicable events, or uncanny objects. Yet the few cases of real metamorphosis in their collections are framed in ways that cast doubt upon the tale being told. Walter Map, Gervais of Tilbury, Gerald of Wales, and William of Newburgh tend to gloss their wonders with labored theorizing about aerial bodies, demons, and phantoms. Gervais — openly enthusiastic about marvels, which he explicitly connects to *mutatio* — nonetheless brackets his werewolves between two standard examples of transmutation taken allegorically: Nebuchadnezzar and the chimera.[120] Gerald of Wales, the most cheerfully confident of the marvel purveyors, seems to suppress transmutation even where he defends it. In his first preface to the *Conquest of Ireland*, he writes:

> ...someone...objects to [distinction 2 of the *Topography of Ireland*], hoping that by convicting me of lies in this part he will discredit the whole. And he objects to a wolf talking with a priest, bovine extremities on a human body, a bearded woman, and a goat and a lion as lovers. Let him, however, if he abhors these stories so, read in the Book of Numbers how Balaam's ass spoke.... Let him read the lives of the Fathers and find there Anthony talking with a faun and Paul given bread in the desert by a ministering raven.... Let him read Augustine's *City of God*, especially books 16 and 21, full of prodigies ...and the eleventh book of Isidore's *Etymologies*....[121]

The careful modern reader notes the fact of the criticism as much as the defense and observes as well that there is, even in the criticism, no reference to metamorphosis. Animal-human sex, yes, and one creature (the human with ox extremities) that may or may not be a hybrid; but even in the charges Gerald summarizes for answering, the wolf, although it speaks, is described as a wolf.

Yet what of the "werewolf renaissance" and my claim that at least these creatures seem to be examples of metempsychosis? To make my final point, I must recount the story of Gerald and the werewolf.

Gerald writes in the *Topography of Ireland* (first recension):

> About three years before the coming of Lord John into Ireland [1182 or 1183], it happened that a priest, journeying from Ulster towards

Meath, spent the night in a wood on the borders of Meath. He was staying up beside a fire . . . and had for company only a little boy, when a wolf came up to them and immediately broke into these words: "Do not be afraid. . . ."

They were completely astounded and in great consternation. The wolf then said some things about God that seemed reasonable . . . [and took them to his companion] a she-wolf groaning and grieving like a human being, even though her appearance was that of a beast. [She requested the sacrament, and] to remove all doubt [the he-wolf] pulled all the skin off the she-wolf from the head down to the navel, folding it back with his paw as if it were a hand [*quasi pro manu*]. And immediately the shape [*forma*] of an old woman, clear to be seen, appeared. . . . [122]

In later recensions of the story, Gerald has the wolf give an account of the curse of Saint Natalis that condemned two natives of Ossory to become wolves every seven years. He refers to classical stories of metamorphosis, especially Apuleius's golden ass; cites Augustine's *City of God* to argue that such changes are not real (*veraciter*) but only apparent (*specietenus*), done by the magic of demons; and explores at length the question whether one who slays such animals commits homicide, concluding that any creature that descends from humans (no matter how monstrous its appearance) answers to the definition of man as a rational animal. Gerald then becomes rather lost in an effort to categorize types of change. Magicians only deceive the senses of men or conjure up fictitious forms, he writes. God can, however, change one nature into another (as Lot's wife became salt), or change only the exterior while the "nature" remains, or (in the Eucharist) alter the substance while the accidents endure. But Gerald cannot locate his werewolves among the tricks of magicians, for they were transformed by a saint, and he evidences considerable confusion about exactly what kind of transformation they are.[123] The length of his discussion and the number of authorities cited are indications of the anxiety caused by the question of the wolves' status. But the description of the he-wolf as himself volunteering rational and orthodox analysis of his own situation makes it clear that the creature is throughout fully human.[124]

Thus Gerald's werewolves are certainly the "fake" or "sympathetic" werewolves studied by recent scholarship. But, as attentive readers will already have noticed, Gerald's werewolves are not souls trapped in alien bodies, cases of metempsychosis. A human being with a body and soul, a psychosomatic entity, a person, is underneath.

> ...to remove all doubt [the he-wolf] pulled all the skin off the she-wolf from the head down to the navel, folding it back with his paw as if it were a hand. And immediately the shape of an old woman... appeared....

The wolf worn by this werewolf is a skin or garment overclothing the human; it is not an essence, not even a body, unless one can (like the angels) assume several. The body is with the soul in the person underneath. Unlike the werewolves of European tradition before and after, Gerald's story — the fullest werewolf story of the twelfth-century revival — is not a case of metempsychosis at all.[125]

Recognizing this sheds new light on the theme of clothing in the werewolf romances.[126] The story of *Guillaume de Palerne* is particularly instructive here. In this romance, the witty werewolf Alphonse helps the lovers William and Meliors escape from danger first sewn up in bear skins, then in the skins of freshly slain deer. The queen of Sicily dons a deer skin herself in order to meet the lovers, whom she has seen from the window with their human clothes showing through cracks in the skins. Scholars have sometimes suggested that the explanation for the use of disguise (particularly for the queen's disguise, seemingly unnecessary since she knows she is meeting humans) is an earlier folk story in which the figures really turn into animals in order to obtain speed and stealth in their escape.[127] This may be so, but surely the whole romance plays with the idea that an appearance is a skin put on over, that bodies lurk under skins. The queen knows William and Meliors are human not because she sees something naked gleaming through the cracked deer skins but because she sees clothes, the normal covering for the human body. Small wonder that Alphonse's restoration is bathing and receiving new clothes; it's as if the human body were there under the wolf skin all along.

The enthusiasm for werewolf stories suggests both the attraction and the terror of shape-shifting, of exactly that metempsychosis feared by authorities as heretical. Francis Dubost may go too far when he suggests that such stories are about the "permanence of nature," but there is an element of truth in the claim.[128] For the way in which medieval romances and marvel collections use the theme insists on exactly what the theme seems to deny: the embodied nature of self. Thus it appears that the exploration of body-hopping and metamorphosis found in marvel collections and miracle stories, in theological discussion and commentary by grammarians, reflects less a desire to shed body than an effort to understand how it perdures, less an escape into alterity than a search for the rules that govern change.

Conclusion

What, then, have I learned by turning again to the theme of metamorphosis suggested by my study of bodily resurrection? I have found that the sense of mutability and multiplicity in the years around 1200 was less dark than I thought before, but I have also

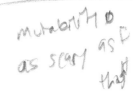

learned that the obsession with accounting for change was even greater than I suspected. The fertile, percolating natural world M.-D. Chenu celebrated was inhabited by Schoolmen and poets, not wonders and werewolves. But it seems to me that his description was not incorrect. Theologians devoted little attention to popular religious manifestations such as cures but expended much ink and parchment over Pharaoh's magicians and the appearance of worms from slime; grammarians saw Ovid's great poem, like Plato's *Timaeus* and the Book of Genesis, as an account of the emergence of an ordered world from primordial chaos; the enthusiasm for wonders was less an impulse to collect the odd than an effort to organize things into the more or less explicable. Natural, biological change fascinated; sex, fertility, generation were wonderful — a form even of immortality. But change of the human body frightened. Whatever we suspect behind these discussions — folk story, classical paradoxology, a growing philosophical sophistication owing to the recovery of Aristotelian categories, or theological tradition — what we find is writers returning again and again to worry, as one might a sore tooth, the possiblity of species-crossing, body-hopping, metamorphosis. Surely the tremendous intellectual effort devoted to categorizing types of change, to ferreting out its rules, to limiting while not denying species-crossing, to preventing contact with animals and angels from changing the human body suggests the importance of understanding person as psychosomatic unity.

And so, for all the new questions asked, the new texts explored, I have perhaps not departed very far from my earlier ideas. But as Ovid's Pythagoras reminds us, we live in a flux that perpetually clothes the old in new forms:

...and so the whole round of motion is gone through again.
(*Metamorphoses* 15.185)

... nothing perishes in the whole universe; it does but vary and renew its form. (*Metamorphoses* 15.254–55)

After all, it should not be such a surprise if one peels back the skin of a new study — as the he-wolf peeled back the skin of his mate — and finds underneath the same Bynum.

CHAPTER THREE

Monsters, Medians, and Marvelous Mixtures: Hybrids in the Spirituality of Bernard of Clairvaux

No matter how radically our perceptions of twelfth-century religion and culture alter from one scholarly generation to the next, Bernard of Clairvaux (1090–1153) seems to retain a central place in our interpretations. The majestic and cantankerous abbot of Clairvaux — famous for preaching the Second Crusade but opposing pogroms, for attacking Abelard and backsliding monks but also for penning one of the greatest paeans of love for a brother in the history of literature — has seemed emblematic both of the optimistic and psychologically astute twelfth century so admired in earlier scholarship and of the darker, more repressive period understood in recent historiography to have ushered in bureaucracy, clerical control, and persecution.

In the 1960s and 1970s, when historians tended to stress, under the rubric "the discovery of the individual," a new emphasis in spirituality on process and development and on the psychological complexity of the "inner person," Bernard's *De gradibus humilitatis et superbiae* and *De diligendo Deo* were proof texts for the twelfth-century sense of a developing self.[1] As the very title of Robert Javelet's *Image et ressemblance* suggests, such interpretation located at the heart of twelfth-century understandings of person an ontological similarity to (a *capax* for) God that seemed magisterially expressed in Bernard's sermons on the Song of Songs. When in the 1970s and 1980s the work of André Vauchez on hagiography and lay piety called attention to changing concepts of *imitatio* between the twelfth and thirteenth centuries, Bernard's injunction that we should imitate virtues, not miracles, seemed to indicate a turning away from older heroic notions of sanctity to a new sense of the accessibility of Christ and the saints through *mimesis*.[2] And indeed considerations of what *imitatio* meant to twelfth-century Cistercians have continued to challenge our understanding of medieval religiosity, the latest creative interventions in the discussion being Marsha Dutton's and Mary Carruthers's salutary reminders that *imitatio* was often more mnemonic than literally mimetic.[3]

Alongside emphasis on Bernard's sense of spiritual growth as the progress of like toward like, the 1970s and 1980s also saw a new emphasis on themes of mediation and "three-ness" in Cistercian religiosity. Whether in the form of Bernard McGinn's influential interpretation of Isaac of Stella's version of the chain of being, Jacques Le Goff's vast synthetic study of purgatory as a third place whose "thirdness" emerged in the later twelfth century as part of an explosion of "three-fold" or "mid-point" thinking fostered by the development of groups (preeminently the bourgeoisie) that were self-consciously "middle," or Steven Kruger's study of dreaming as a third kind of *visio* that linked body and soul, the emphasis on mediation central to many recent interpretations of twelfth-century religiosity draws heavily on Cistercian sources.[4] To these themes of development, likeness, and three-ness, or mediation, the 1990s have added their own concerns. The "otherness" or "alterity" now touted as characteristic of the twelfth century and of our interest in it also finds support in a Bernard whose articulated self-doubts and abhorrence of (attraction to?) the monstrous give him an important place in the plethora of scholarly work on gargoyles, monsters, and transgressive imagery.[5]

I do not wish to argue that any of these interpretations of Bernard's spirituality is wrong. The Bernard I shall discuss here is a Bernard concerned with monsters and mediation, with likeness and otherness, and with a sense of inner development that involves psychological and spiritual return far more than literal mimesis.[6] But I wish to pay closer attention than is usually done to some specific aspects of Bernard's use of language, to words he does and (more importantly) does not use, and thereby to argue that his particular understandings of what we would call "change" and of what we would denominate a "mixture" or a "hybrid" differentiate him not only from later thinkers but even from some of his Cistercian contemporaries. Thus it is less a sense of otherness, of three-ness or mediation, of development or likeness that characterizes Bernard's spirituality than his struggles with two-ness, or doubleness. I hope to use Bernard's sense of doubleness to illuminate what I have elsewhere argued to be a profound twelfth-century resistance to ideas of metamorphosis and to argue that Bernard's anxiety, which is both personal and ontological, was at the root not only of his rhetorical and spiritual power but also of what he could not express.

To raise the question of Bernard's understanding of change, of mixture, of two-ness, returns us to a number of much-discussed passages in his work: his description of himself as chimera, a passage so famous it has sometimes served to characterize the entire twelfth century or to sum up Bernard's career;[7] the notorious criticism of Romanesque art in the *Apologia*, to which a thoughtful and convincing monograph has recently been devoted;[8] the paradoxical and forceful rhetoric of the *De consideratione*, taken by scholars such as Elizabeth Kennan, John Sommerfeldt, Karl Morrison, and Jeannine Quillet as a key to Bernard's understanding of both spirituality and social roles;[9] and the lovely description from the early work the *De diligendo Deo* of union with God as the diffusion of water in wine, a description used by Etienne Gilson in what remains one of the most sensitive and moving accounts of Bernard's theology.[10] I wish, however, to put these familiar passages in a wider context. I shall, for example, place the discussion of a moral mean, or midpoint, in *De consideratione*, book 3, in the context of the theory of *unitas* and *mixtio* in book 5. I shall relate the denunciation of the monstrous in the *Apologia* not only to the similar denunciation of Stephen of Garland as a soldier-cleric hybrid in Bernard's letter to Suger of St.-Denis but also to the absence of such description in Bernard's praise of what we would call a new hybrid order, the Templars. I shall put Bernard's agonized self-denigration as chimera in the context of his obsessive tendency to allude to role conflicts when exegesis draws him into discussions of two-ness and shall also note that Bernard does not, for all his analysis of biblical passages about Mary and Martha, develop an explicit concept of the "mixed life." And I shall argue for the key role of a sermon not hitherto particularly noticed: Bernard's third sermon for Christmas Eve.

Christianity is, of course, a religion of paradoxes and dyads as well as of trinities: Christ is God and human, human beings are soul and body, God is three in one. Moreover, the problem of the One and the Many is at least as old as Platonism; the ontological scandal of change at least as old as Heraclitus; the notion of an ethical mean between extremes at least as old as Aristotle. Hence we expect any well-educated Christian theologian or rhetorician (and Bernard was certainly well educated, both in the Bible and in classically derived grammar and rhetoric) to make use of dyads, triads, midpoints, paradoxes, and oppositions and to wrestle with diversity in unity as well as the union of opposites.[11] Nonetheless not all Christian thinkers treat these topics in the same way.[12] I thus begin with Bernard's use of what we might expect to be a key term for ontological, psychological, and spiritual combinations: *mixtio* (and related terms such as *mixtura, miscere, admiscere*).

Mixture and Monster

Immediately we notice a fascinating pattern. *Mixtio*, to Bernard, is usually negative — the opposite of *pura*. A *mixtura* is a monster (*monstrum*), a boundary or category violation, the addition of one species to another. Or a mixture (still in such cases a violation of species boundaries or an addition of unlike to radically unlike) can be marvelous or miraculous — the *mira mixta* of Bernard's third sermon for Christmas Eve. Mixtures are objects of *stupor* or *admiratio*, unusual occurrences at which we feel terror or wonder.[13] In the realm of spiritual progress toward God, where like knows like and knows by like — the realm of *imitatio* in contrast to *admiratio* — Bernard uses not *mixtura* but rather a plethora of words with *con-* as a prefix, such as *conversio, conformare, consocio, convenio*.

The significance of this pattern becomes clear if we look at some specific passages. I begin with Bernard's discussion of Romanesque art in the *Apologia*.[14] In what is basically, as Conrad Rudolph has argued, an attack on the potential of elaborate figurative art to divert the attention of monks from prayer and to squander wealth better spent in care of the poor, Bernard fulminates against "the ridiculous monstrosity, the amazing deformed beauty and beautiful deformity . . . of an astonishing variety of diverse forms . . . [*ridicula monstruositas, mira quaedam deformis formositas ac formosa deformitas? . . . mira diversarum formarum . . . ibique varietas . . .*]" and lists among the offensive figures "unclean apes, . . . monstrous centaurs, creatures part man and part beast, tigers, warriors, . . . many bodies with one head and many heads with one body, tail of serpent on quadruped, head of quadruped on fish, horse with goat combined, horse with horn."[15] Eight of the thirteen figures to which Bernard objects are monsters, and of these, seven are hybrids that violate nature by crossing species, although only one (the centaur) is a figure familiar from classical mythology. Many reasons have been proposed by scholars for Bernard's fear of, and attraction to, such beautiful horrors, including Thomas Dale's perceptive observation (which can be supported from Bernard's own account of a brother's dream) that such art represented the frightening and tempting distortions seen in late twelfth-century Cistercian vision collections.[16] What I would stress is the doubleness or hybridity of these distortions. It is not merely the fascinating or the sensuously ugly that draws Bernard here but the hybrid, and a hybrid so dual that (except in the case of the centaur) there is no name for the combination; it has not really become a new entity. Each depicted object thus remains an "astonishing variety of diverse forms."

Many scholars have noticed that such discussion is connected to Bernard's persistent concern with *curiositas* as distraction or, worse, as descent into "likeness" to the "unlikeness" of beasts.[17] Less attention has been paid to the central role of mixture in Bernard's polemic. Yet it is worth noting that Bernard fulminates not only against hybrids in art but also against "mixings" and "adulterations" of "pure" foods created by God. (The rampant variety of recipes for eggs comes in for special mention.) And the monastic reader himself is described as "mixed" (*commixti*) with the Gentile when he is drawn to the "feces" of worldly beauty through any of the five senses.[18] "Wonder" (*admiratio*), which is elsewhere for Bernard a term for our reaction to those marvels and miracles beyond nature that we should venerate but not attempt to imitate, is here also a reaction to the *mira varietas* of the monstrous that draws us so dangerously. And Bernard slips easily from a discussion of such disorder into admonition against striving to rise from lesser to greater things or to pass rashly to a stricter order (that is, religious role). Thus in several places in this treatise on monastic practice, "mixed" is the opposite of "pure." Moreover, monsters — mixed things with no names — tend to crop up in passages or, we might say, to share a semantic field with two other concerns: first, a sense of wonder as a reaction both above and below faithful *imitatio*, or the progression of like toward like; and, second, discussions of where an individual should be located in a hierarchy of social roles.

Monsters and mixtures figure elsewhere in Bernard's descriptions of social roles and ambivalence about them. In addition to his description of his own "monstrous life," "I am a sort of modern chimaera, neither cleric nor layman,"[19] Bernard describes the dissident Arnold of Brescia not only as a bestial confusion of inner and outer (a wolf in sheep's clothing) but also explicitly as a hybrid: "the man whose life is as sweet as honey and whose doctrine is as bitter as poison, the man with the head of a dove and the tail of a scorpion."[20] And in Bernard's letter praising Abbot Suger for his reform of life, the powerful noble Stephen of Garland (seneschal to Louis VI and archdeacon of Notre Dame) is described as a monster (*monstrum*), an abuse (*abusio*), and a confusion of orders (*confundit penitus ordines*), because he wishes to be at once cleric and knight (*clericus et miles simul videri velit ... neutrum sit*).[21] Bernard's reference to Stephen as monster is no mere rhetorical flourish or expression of generalized disgust at opportunism but a comment on social roles. For Bernard points out that there are hybrids (possible to God) where both elements gain, hybrids where one element gains through the lowering of another, as when a noblewoman marries beneath her and "raises the man's dignity while she lessens her own," and combinations such as Stephen, "the loss of both to the advantage of neither." The implication is clear: crossing of role boundaries, like crossing of species boundaries, is dangerous and invariably involves loss, except in the realm of the marvelous hybrids of God. Bernard concludes by exhorting Suger to bring his friend Stephen to truth, since "true friendship is only possible between two who are united in the love of truth. And if he will not yield to you in this, do you hold fast to what you have got and join the head to the tail of the offering [*hostiaeque caudam junge capiti*]." The somewhat obscure reference to Exodus 29 conjures up not only an appropriate joining of body parts that belong together (truth with friendship) but also avoidance of the inappropriate hybridizing of roles (military with clerical) the monstrous Stephen has been accused of perpetrating.[22]

A similar sense of the monstrous occurs in Bernard's *De consideratione*, an important and complex exploration of hybrids and midpoints to which I shall return below. Here I wish simply to point out that Bernard repeatedly and casually uses the term "monstrous" to refer to clerics around Pope Eugene or to Eugene himself as coincidence of opposites or violation of hierarchy or social order.[23] What is at stake, however — what disturbs Bernard so deeply — is not merely reordering or disordering high and low but *confusio*.[24] Combining separate entities creates a monster, an incoherence with no name, a nothing. There is no way of mixing or grafting parts together to create a new being; the hybrid or confusion *neutrum sit*. The disturbing and graphic ugliness of Bernard's images suggests an anxiety about both the social violation he depicts and the bodily deformity he uses as analogy:

And just as those whom God has joined together must not be separated (Matt. 19.6) so those whom God has made subordinate must not be made equal. You create a monster [*monstrum facis*] if you remove a finger from a hand and make it hang from the head, above the hand and on the level with the arm. So it is in the body of Christ if you put members in places other than where he arranged them. [For Christ placed] "some in the church as apostles, some as prophets, some as evangelists, others as teachers and pastors.. (Eph. 4.11–12)."[25]

In Bernard's sermons, *mixtio* and *monstrum* are often synonymous. The opposite is *pura*, and *pura* means *nil admixtum*.[26] Such imagery is prominent in the seventeen sermons on Psalm 90, for example, in part because of the reference to asps, lions, and dragons in verse 13. Sermon 7 actually identifies the monsters we fear with nocturnal phantasms.[27] The most complex understanding of *mixtio* occurs, however, in sermon 9. As always, the movement of Bernard's rhetoric is subtle and complex. In a discussion of the reward offered by God to even the brother who gives as little as one cup of cold water, Bernard describes the reward as "an inebriating chalice of true wine well mixed [*plenus mixto*]." Jesus alone has pure, unmixed wine, says Bernard, because he alone is pure. Even the martyrs are "mixed"; for, as Isaiah says, "*Vinum tuum mixtum aqua* (Is. 1.22)." Mixed because no one is free from sin in this life, mixed because all must die, mixed because they must purchase immortality by death, mixed because they make only a poor return for Christ's love, the martyrs are not disdained by Christ. For he who is without mixture (*qui sine mixtura est*) does not disdain the mixture they are (*hoc mixtum*); he fills up what is lacking. As star differs from star in glory, so is the resurrection of the dead; in one house there are many mansions (1 Cor. 15.41; John 14.2). In this sermon addressed to his monastic brothers, Bernard's sense of mixture is more complex (we might say more tolerant) than in his advice to the monk-pope Eugene, trapped in the temptations of the curia. "Mixed" remains the opposite of "pure," something whose lack must be filled; but even Christianity's greatest heroes are mixtures, as we are mixtures. The absences Christ fills up are differences (not greater or lesser but different things). Star differs from star as mansion from mansion, but all are stars, as all are resurrected. Mixture, whatever the connotations of absence and negation, is what we *are*.[28]

If *mixtio* is often, for Bernard, a confusion that induces regret or even horror (*stupor*), it has a strikingly different semantic field as well. The greatest mysteries of Christianity are also, for Bernard, mixtures, but miraculous or marvelous ones. In this sense of a mixture beyond reason and understanding, Christ is a _mixtio_, the Virgin's womb the place of _mixtura_, and our potential for God a _capax miscere._[29] In the third sermon for Christmas Eve, which begins with a reference to Christ as redeemer and physician, Bernard writes:

> Oh who can presume to speak aloud or even to think of [the heavenly Sabbath].... In the meantime, however, brothers, we must strengthen our faith so that if we cannot see the marvels [_mirabilia_] reserved for us [in the life to come] we can at least contemplate a little the marvels [_mirabilia_] done for us on earth. And there are three works, three mixtures [_tria opera, tres mixturas_], that the all-powerful majesty did in assuming our flesh — so singularly marvelous and marvelously singular [_mirabiliter singularia et singulariter mirabilia_] that nothing like them has been or will ever be done on earth. For joined to each other [_coniuncta_] are God and human, mother and virgin, faith and the human heart. Wonderful are these mixtures, and more marvelous than any miracle, for so diverse and even so opposed to each other, they were joined together [_tam diversa, tamque divisea ab invicem, invicem potuere coniungi_].
>
> And indeed consider the creation, the ordering of its parts! God mixes the vile slime of earth with vital force [_limo terreno vim vitalem miscuit_].... And to honor [man] more, he united in his person God and slime, majesty and lowliness, such vileness and such sublimity.... This is the first and most excellent mixture [_mixtura_].... So remember, oh human, that you are dust but you are also joined [_iunctus_] with God....
>
> The second union... is marvelous and singular... and the third is ... no less strong. For it is marvelous [_mirum est_] what the heart can accomplish in yielding to faith, how it can believe God became man and Mary gave birth and remained a virgin. Just as iron and clay can-

not be joined [*iungi*] so these two cannot be mixed [*commisceri*] if the glue of the Holy Spirit does not mix them [*si non misceat glutinum Spiritus Dei*]. Who can believe that he who was laid in a manger, wept in a cradle,... died between thieves, is also God, majestic and immense?... But a multitude believes...

And the first mixture is a poultice [*cataplasma confectum est*] to cure infirmities. The two species are ground and mixed [*commixtae*] in the Virgin's womb as in a mortar, with the Holy Spirit the pestle sweetly mixing them [*illas suaviter commiscente*].... The first union is the remedy but only in the second does the help truly come, for God wills that we gain nothing unless it passes through the hands of Mary.[30]

With its suggestion that Bernard may have medical or physical models for *mixtio* in mind, its (for Bernard) quite unusual reference to a glue or third element joining two things, and its radical sense of the wonderful joining of opposites (slime and God, majesty and vileness, and so on), this is a complex passage.[31] The language is, even for Bernard, extraordinarily lyrical and heightened. It is *mira mixta*, not *similitudo*, that elicits our response, not our likeness to God or his closeness and accessibility to us but rather the hybridity of the God-man, the vast distances between earth/flesh/us and God. The response is not *imitatio* or even love but *admiratio*, a reaction that to Bernard conjures up distance and strangeness, the word for what we feel when we cannot approach or be like.[32]

These themes are also reflected in the fourth sermon for Christmas Eve, where Bernard, again referring to Christ as physician, connects the miraculous mixture of the virgin mother, fertile yet uncontaminated, breached yet intact, with the fertility of the world and the hope of resurrection.[33] Thus for Bernard, the mixture — whether hybrid or marvel — is double, twofold, a joining of contrarieties. At the lowest rung of the scheme of things, it is a disorder that cannot be a new entity, a horrid head with its dangling, inappropriate finger, a dove with a scorpion's tail. At the heights of *mysterium* beyond miracle, it is still a radical two-ness that promises to us believers the salvation that seems impossible: the return and survival as entity of that which is intrinsically and ontologically forever two — body and soul.

If the gargoyles on churches, ambitious courtiers such as Stephen of Garland, and Bernard himself, no less than Christ and his virgin mother, are *mixtura*, then we might expect Bernard to deploy the concept of mixture, hybrid, monster, or marvel in other places where his concern is clearly with the union of opposites. The most obvious place to look is his treatise on the Templars, that new religious order of knight-clerics or monastic warriors so similar in role to the despised Stephen of Garland.[34] The later Cistercian Isaac of Stella did, after all, call the Templars a "monster."[35] But they are not, to Bernard, either monster or mixture.

To be sure, Bernard's powerful rhetoric stresses the incompatibility of the two roles, the doubleness, the union of opposites (*ceterum cum uterque*). Those he praises here are metaphorically hybrids, "in a manner marvelous and singular [*miro ... ac singulari modo*], mild as lambs and ferocious as lions." [36] But he leaves the beast without a name:

> I would hesitate before the name that is best for you, *monachos* or *milites*, if it did not appear to me more adequate to give you one or the other as appropriate, to whom neither is known to be missing, neither the gentleness of the monk nor the fortitude of the soldier.... And what can we say of this except that the work of the Savior is a marvel [*mirabile*] in our eyes (Ps. 117.23)....[37]

Indeed Bernard does not call the Templars by any name, not even hybrid or monster, that denotes an entity but rather refers to them as engaged in "double" or "twin" (*geminus*) combat.[38] He can name them only by the alternation or combination of opposing roles. And his rhetoric repeatedly lifts them toward the *mira mixtura* of his Christmas sermon. The nameless hybrid of monk and soldier is a "marvel," "worthy of *admiratio*," the double role bringing "double good and double joy." [39] It is as if, ever anxious before role confusion, Bernard can render it acceptable only as a mystery or marvel; hence his language lifts it toward the ultimate marvel, the "role confusion" at the heart of the divine. It is also as if Bernard cannot quite conceive of two incompatibles becoming a new entity — cannot conceive, that is, of a genuine *mixtio* unless it be a monster or the marvelous mixture of ultimate paradox.

The other obvious place in Bernard's work to look for deployment of the concept of mixture or mixed is, of course, in his discussion of what scholars call "the mixed life." As Giles Constable's recent survey of medieval discussions of Mary and Martha has demonstrated, twelfth-century exegesis tended to move toward an understanding of monastic and/or Christian life as containing or alternating between the so-called active and contemplative lives.[40] And students of Bernard have long connected his agony over his own divided life, patched together like a chimera from preaching tours and monastic withdrawal, political meddling and asceticism, with his discussions of service and contemplation.[41] Almost all those who have written recently on the topic have noticed how nuanced is Bernard's sense of role difference; his understanding of the conflict or balance between activity, service, life in the world, on the one hand, and prayer, withdrawal, contemplation, on the other, depends on the audience for which he writes.[42] For example, Bernard exhorts monks to be vessels or wells, not conduits, whereas he advises the monk-pope Eugene to find a mean between extremes of administrative burdens and unworldliness.[43] And with characteristic rhetorical elegance and ambivalence, he warns monks not to undervalue bishops: "It is wrong to find fault with those whose burdens we have fled — wrong for women at home spinning to criticize men at battle. You do the womanly thing. . . ."[44] Indeed this is a passage in which one may genuinely ask which role is higher, for Bernard shares assumptions of his day about female inferiority yet shares as well a deep commitment to reversal as lying at the heart of Christian vocation ("many that are first shall be last" [Mark 10.31]; "hath not God made foolish the wisdom of this world?" [1 Cor. 1.20]).[45]

Nonetheless, for all the complexity and variety of his discussion of the "two lives," it is striking that Bernard does not in fact have a concept of the "mixed life." Carolingian writers before him speak of Mary (or Rachel or *contemplatio*) and Martha (or Leah or *actio*) as joined *mixtim*. (The contrast is with *separatim*.) Thirteenth-century theorists develop the technical notion of *vita mixta*.[46] But Bernard does not use such terms. Occasionally he asserts the two lives to be one, as when he unites Mary and Martha in the Virgin Mary (*in hac una et summa invenitur*).[47] In one of his most complex discussions, the third sermon for the Assumption, he associates the Mary-Martha contrast with the soul-body duality, treats Martha as a mediatrix, a midpoint or joining, who works for self and others, and adds a third figure (Lazarus or penitence) to the two sisters, asserting all three to be present at once (*simul*) in the perfect soul. (Note that Lazarus is not a combination or mean of the other two.)[48] Repeatedly, in the sermons on the Song of Songs, he speaks of alternations between two (or occasionally three) occupations, interruptions that make the soul uneasy; and he considers, only to reject, the notion that such interruptions are a deformity: "To aim at something other than God for the sake of God is not the repose of Mary but the activity of Martha. But never let it be said that I have called this deformed [*deforme*]. . . . [It] sprinkles the soul with dust. . . , [which] can be washed away easily at least in the hour of a holy death."[49] Hence Bernard's sense is of a variety of vocations or activities or roles, either loosely joined within a community or alternating in a life. Although some twelfth-century writers have a clear sense of a third life as mean between the other two, Bernard does not.[50] The combination or alternation with which he agonizes remains a nameless hybrid, not a new entity. Bernard's discussion of action and contemplation is not a theory of a third life, a third way, or a third place at all.

It thus seems as if, to Bernard, role confusion and the defilement of sin are monsters to which we respond with *stupor*; saving paradoxes are marvels to which we respond with *admiratio*. Both are *mixturas*, and mixtures seem, for Bernard, to be insistently drawn into the semantic field of "wonder." As the passages I quoted above demonstrate, Bernard seldom uses words such as *miscere* without hammering home "*mirum est....*" Yet even in "mixtures," Bernard stresses two-ness, not the appearance of a new thing or entity. The monsters he fears have no name, or two; the marvels beyond human comprehension are paradoxes. The shock of such things, the wonder, appears to lie in the fact that two (cleric and soldier, beauty and deformity, divinity and slime, virgin and birthing, and so on) approach so closely. But the two-ness remains.

Similitude and Doubleness

What, then, of the self between monster and God? Another of Bernard's recurrent binaries is the contrast *admiratio/imitatio*, the exhortation to admire (feel wonder or terror before) the miracles of the saints but imitate their virtues. As he likes to put it, we should drain (imitate or appropriate) the wine but give back in wonder the golden goblet.[51] How then does Bernard speak of the self between monster and marvelous mixture, a self created in God's image and striving to return to likeness, a self in the realm of *imitatio*, not *admiratio*?

127

It is here that Bernard's words for the relationship of self and God are repeatedly and insistently *con-* words: *conformare, consociare, conjungere,* and so on. When Christ became man he "conformed" to us; we are "conformed" to him in our inner likeness.[52] Insisting on the barriers between species and between entities — between humans and animals, humans and angels, one human self and another — Bernard nonetheless insists on the radical congruency (*congruentia*) of self and God.[53] Although, as is well known, his exegesis of the crucial phrase "image and likeness" differs between the *De gratia* and the sermons on the Song of Songs, he everywhere in his writings locates our God-capacity in our ontological likeness to God, our image-ness.[54] Operating with the classical assumption, which he repeats frequently, that one knows via likeness and by becoming like, he sees us as God-oriented because "like God" — that is, we are God-oriented because we are created that way.[55] (The statement is tautological or biblical, whichever way you prefer to phrase it.) Because we begin image-capable or image-oriented (as *imago* or *ad imaginem*), we can grow by the addition of bits of likeness. God is in a sense closer to us than we are to the divided and dissimilar self of our sinful, earthly present. Hence in his fifth sermon on the Song of Songs, Bernard writes that only with God is direct encounter possible, only God is poured into us as he is, fully himself (*infunditur per se*). We are between animals and angels, writes Bernard, but closer to God than to either. The Fathers differed over the bodies of angels, debating whether these spirits have natural bodies whose forms they change at will or assume, when needed, bodies that otherwise dissolve into the elements from which they came. But of whatever nature their bodies, angels (like animals) cannot act directly on our minds, cannot mix with or flow into us (*nobis immisceatur vel infundatur*); nor can angels join with each other. "I am not capable of angel or animal, for nothing angel or animal is

128

in this way accessible to me." *Mixtio* with other beings is not possible. Only with God am I congruent; only he pours in.[56]

Hence it might seem that to Bernard the self is an unfolding toward God, a likeness moving toward like, or a midpoint in the chain of being between animal and angel. But Bernard, unlike other Cistercians such as William of St.-Thierry and Isaac of Stella, has actually little sense of midpoint or median. This may seem an odd assertion in view of the importance of the notion of mean in the *De consideratione*, a treatise to which students of Bernard have recently given much attention. But the idea of an ethical mean between extremes, which almost becomes in the *De consideratione* a definition of Eugene III's role, is quite exceptional in Bernard, as of course is the actual role of the monk-pope whom Bernard addresses.[57] To be sure, Isaac of Stella argued for a complex anthropology in which the human person is a combination of soul and body joined at a midpoint by the meeting of a bodily part of the soul (imagination) and a spiritual part of the body (the senses); and the later (almost certainly) Cistercian *De spiritu et anima* actually posited a third part of the person where body and soul are connected.[58] But Bernard remarks explicitly: "there is no third part of man."[59] Contrasts (Bernard's favorite example is black and white) are to him useful for understanding divergence and difference. Although he very occasionally (as in the third sermon for Christmas Eve) refers to a "glue" holding binaries together, Bernard's concern is with doubles, not threes.[60] His typical rhetorical move is to heighten and exacerbate oppositions and incompatibilities, then force them together by assertion, then wrench them apart again.[61]

For example, in one of his most powerful pieces of rhetoric, the *De conversione*, Bernard repeatedly castigates the flesh as hindrance to — even extraneous to — the spirit, only to have body assert: "I am your body, your very self." Shining white with leprosy,

129

the body is, at one moment, a garment put on. At the next, Bernard insists: no one hates his own body, for body and soul are one; "If you tear your flesh, it is your mind you damage; if you look to the stomach or below, you bring ulcers on your soul."[62] Bernard sometimes speaks of body as flesh (caro) in the Pauline sense, as something in which sin and temptation lodge;[63] body is, however, often that through which we have access to experience and hence to the possibility of repentance;[64] it is our necessary companion in the ultimate joy of heaven.[65] Hence even Bernard's notion of flesh is dual; and his understanding of person alternates between affirming it as psychosomatic unity and glorying in, or agonizing over, its dividedness.

My point is not merely that Bernard speaks of the self both as a hybrid of incompatibles (even a hybrid of hybrids) and as a unity whose parts transfer qualities each to the other; the point is that his soaring, searing prose moves over and over again from asserting unity to asserting contradiction, drumming home what we might call the fundamental opposition between opposition and its opposite. Hence, despite his lyricism and his repeated exhortations to reform of self, Bernard's sense of process, development, unfolding, is often undercut by the way his language actually moves.[66]

> Oh lowliness! Oh sublimity! At the same time a tent of Cedar and a sanctuary of God, an earthly habitation and a celestial palace, a house of clay and a royal apartment (Wis. 9.15; Job 4.19), a body of death and a temple of light (Rom. 7.24), an object of scorn to the proud (Ps. 122.4) but the bride of Christ. She is black but beautiful, daughters of Jerusalem (Song of Songs 1.4).... And thus, both these things [i.e., lowliness and sublimity], though in contradiction each to the other [cum ad invicem contrarie sint], cooperate [cooperantur] for the good of the spouse and serve her salvation.[67]

Bernard of course employs standard Christian ideas of the Virgin as mediatrix and of human beings as between animals and angels. But midpoints and means are noticeably absent in the basic structure of his thought. The self is, to Bernard, both radically double and radically "like."[68] So like God that it is forever already "with" him (con- + verb), it is also the coexistence of two radical opposites, body and soul, each of which is a coincidence of filth and glory. For the person is not the *imago*, to Bernard; the *imago* is the soul or the will. To Bernard, the person is soul and body; and the glorified body of the resurrection is essential to the self for all eternity.[69] Therefore likeness is only part of the story. The self that comes so close to oneness is also eternal doubleness — slime and spirit.

Change and Unitas

Thus, as the *De conversione* makes clear, the human being is not really a middle position in the chain of being; rather, it is zenith and abyss. Nor is it primarily a *viator* on the way to God. Forever *dispars*, it is also forever already there. The movement from self to God, chronicled with such psychological perceptiveness in the *De gradibus humilitatis* and the *De diligendo Deo*, is not really a move from self to other at all; it is a discovery of what is.[70] Already an *imago* (or created *ad imaginem*), the person does not really change; dissimilitude is something extraneous added on.[71] Hence Bernard's descriptions of reform or deterioration are filled with metaphors of uncovering, unclothing, or adding.[72] Although he occasionally uses the image of metamorphosis, Bernard does not think we simply become beasts. Rather, we add beastliness, covering and obscuring our humanity.[73] Indeed, nothing can even really be added, at least not intrinsically; Bernard often speaks as if roles and sins, despair and death, are only overclothing.[74]

Ironically, then, for all his sense of a radically disjunctive self, for all his references to "becoming like," Bernard's anthropology, his theory of the human person, has no real sense of what we would call "change." *Mutatio*, for Bernard, is not the replacement of one thing by another, whether instantaneously or incrementally. When he opens his advice to Eugene III by saying, "I am confident that this change [*hanc mutationem*] has been done to you rather than is of you [*in te … non de te*], that this promotion has not taken the place of your former role but rather is added to it [*nec priori statui successisse promotionem, sed accessisse*]," he sketches what is his normal understanding of change: something added to or subtracted from a perduring essence or substance.[75] In discussing the dissimilitude of sin in his eighty-second sermon on the Song of Songs, he says explicitly:

> When Scripture speaks of [the soul's] dissimilarity to God, it does not assert that the old similitude is deleted but that a new dissimilitude is added on [*superducta*]. Soul has not stripped herself of her original form but only clothed herself over with a foreign one [*non … exuit formam, sed superinduit peregrinam*]. It is that the latter is added on, not that the former is lost, and what is added on [*supervenit*] is able to obscure the natural one but does not exterminate it.[76]

Even though evil is intrinsic to the devil's temptation of humanity, Bernard speaks of the serpent as clothing himself (*induere*) with duplicity.[77] And for all his conviction that we are created *capax similitudinis*, his image of sin is also of something that cannot be replaced. In a masterful analogy that tells us about twelfth-century writing practice as well as about theology, Bernard writes that purifying memory means not wiping out sin but rather coming to remember it in a different, and distanced, way, as we might the sins of others. Just as an ink blot cannot be obliterated without destroying the parchment on which it is written, so the sin cannot be obliterated without replacing (and hence destroying) the memory itself. The passage is remarkable for suggesting an almost Lutheran sense of *simul justus et peccator*; it is the stance (God's and ours) toward the sin that makes the justifying difference, not its presence or absence. The image is also remarkable for epitomizing Bernard's perhaps not even fully conscious assumption that change means not that things are replaced by other things but that something (a quality or perspective) is added to or laid over something else.[78]

Bernard is aware, of course, that change can mean replacement. Such an understanding of change crops up quite incidentally in one of his discussions of miracles: the first sermon on Saint Victor. Bernard here returns to the theme of *imitatio/admiratio* and, once again, exhorts his monastic audience to drink the wine but put back the goblet, to follow strictness of life, not the allure of miracles: "I will not stretch out my hand to the glory of miracles, lest I lose even what I seem to have by grasping for what is not assigned to me."[79] He then implies a definition of miracle that is explicitly developed only in the thirteenth century: a miracle is not only that at which we wonder because it is unusual, even to us inexplicable; a miracle is something that violates the rules by which nature operates.[80] "I see new wine made from water.... I will not touch it. It is not destined for me.... I have not the power of changing the elements and transforming the nature of things." The point to notice here is that Bernard refers to a specific understanding of the rule not to be violated: it is the unchangeability of the elements, the set boundaries of the natures and species of things. Bernard assumes the atomism of his day.[81]

In the complex eighty-first sermon on the Song of Songs, Bernard actually defines change (*mutatio*) as replacement: *de uno ad aliud transit*. Hence in an argument that goes back at least to Plato, change is the replacement of something by nothing, that is, by the not-thing of what was there before. (A new thing can come only into the place of the not-thing; it cannot *be* the previous thing.) Death, then, is the ultimate change. Or is it? To understand what Bernard is saying, it is necessary to follow his argument in detail.

Sermon 80 begins by asking about the union of the soul with the Word. How can these two join together (*conjungere*), even though we know they have much in common (*cognatio*)? The answer is that, created *ad imaginem*, the soul is God-capable; she has suitability (*conventio*) for God. (Again we are struck by the *con*-words.)[82] Sermon 81 is then an exploration of this *convenientia*, which Bernard describes as an embrace, an affinity (*affinitas*) or closeness (*propinquitas*), between the soul and the Word. Yet embrace implies equality. And how can there be equality between majesty and poverty? Bernard's rhetoric here, in moves that are by now familiar to us, asserts — then denies — closeness. We are like (*similis*) the Word; we are different (*dispars*). What Bernard does not do is suggest a mean or midpoint between the extremes, a mediation. The argument then suddenly becomes a scientific one concerning the differences among types of souls. The souls of animals and plants are not by definition living, says Bernard. Animals and plants exist before as elements; when they die, they do not really cease to be; they dissolve (*dissoluere*), break apart, return (*redigere*) not to nothing (*in nihilum*) but to the bits (*partes, reliqua*) they were before: air to air, fire to fire, and so on. Bernard here denies replacement-change in the case of natural bodies, espousing a sort of atomism that goes back at least to Empedocles: nothing ceases; all returns to the elements. Plants and animals are not entities but a bundle of different constituents, composite in their natures: *ex pluribus constans*. We, then, Bernard argues, are alive by our very nature; we are like God because we live by our own essence, unlike because created (that is, our life is given by another). But if we live by definition, we cannot die. Nor can we change. For

> true and complete immortality excludes change as well as death [*non recipit mutationem*], since all change is the image of death. Indeed everything that undergoes change, while it passes from one thing to another, must necessarily die as what it is, so that it may begin to be what it is not [*Omne quod mutator, de uno ad aliud transit, moriatur quod est, ut esse incipiat quod non est*]. But how can you have immortality there where you have as many deaths as changes [*tot mortes quot mutationes*]?

The soul thus has immortality, true if imperfect, because she is the principle of life to herself. She can, says Bernard, as little fall from living as she can fall from being herself — that is, cease to be what she is and become something else (*cadat a se*).

Bernard has, however, now demonstrated too much. For if change is destruction of being, how can the soul change (*mutare*)? Yet change it must. Dissimilitude must become similitude. What Bernard is really struggling with in this subtle discussion is finding a model for spiritual change. For if change is really replacement, if all change is death, how can we grow psychologically or spiritually; if we cannot, how can "we" really move toward God?[83]

What I emphasize here about Bernard's discussion is that, having defined change as replacement, he finds that he must jettison the concept. The spiritual change that matters to him cannot be the replacement-change he has defined. Moreover, he is aided, in a sense, by the atomic tradition he somewhat distantly reflects. The natural philosophy available to him also denied ultimate coming to be and passing away, substituting instead dissolution into particles. Hence, for all the radical two-ness of his spirituality, Bernard does not conceive of something replacing something else

Mixture
② *replacement*

anymore than he conceives of a *mixtio* as a new entity arising from the fusion of opposites. We are not therefore surprised that his favorite images for *mutatio* are images of reclothing, adding onto or taking away from a perduring thing.

Having no way of employing the idea of mixture or the concept of what I have called "replacement-change" in his understanding of spiritual growth, Bernard thus tends to use various understandings of "with" (*con-*) that go very far toward union or unity. Here again we find that his language itself alternates between asserting radical oneness and asserting radical doubleness. In the *De diligendo Deo*, for example, he begins by speaking of growth or change (*mutatio*): through sin, we change our glory into the likeness of beasts and must therefore await renewing, remaking, by God.[84] Moreover, as is well known, Bernard's treatise, like the similar argument in the opening pages of the *De gradibus humilitatis*, explains for the beginning monk the stages of love by which the self moves toward God: from love of one's own enfleshed and unhappy self, to love of the similar, suffering other that is neighbor, to love of the enfleshed and suffering Christ, to love of God.[85] But Bernard's beautiful little treatise is not really an exploration of replacement-change. For, in a sense, if we are already similar to God, we do not really become; we are only cleansed or stripped. And if we are two, we are not one with — we are not even similar to — God. Yet Bernard asserts both: radically *similis*, radically *dispars*. As he does in the *De conversione*, he pulls soul and body radically together, yet forces them radically apart. Our bodies are specks of dust, distant from us; by them, we are joined to the likeness of beasts. As a sort of hybrid *homo-pecus*, we love God only for our own sakes; but if we love him for his, we must become *homo-deus*; we are never, as Javelet puts it, *homo-homo*.[86] Even the glorified body of the resurrection is only a garment added on. We are radically dual. Yet we not only love our

136

own flesh; we are so much at one with it that it becomes the vehicle for oneness with our neighbor's suffering flesh and hence with the suffering flesh of Christ. Moreover, we are also one with God. Daringly, Bernard asserts that a time will come when we will be "almost" annihilated in God (*paene annullari*). "To love this way is to be deified [*deificari est*]."[87]

Bernard here uses images of tasting and eating, of dissolving into, that seem at first glance to be images of replacement-change.[88] Eating God and being eaten by him, dissolving into him — such language seems to suggest that "we" cease to be ourselves and become God, as bread becomes flesh and blood in the stomach or a drop of water disappears in a barrel of wine. Bernard even suggests that our joining with God might be a pureness beyond *mixtio*. Rejecting "mixture" as a description of the good will, he uses the image of a fusion beyond *mixtio* to talk about mystical union: the deified self is dissolved from itself and poured into God.

But if we read this famous passage carefully, we see how the language pulls back from, even as it asserts, union:

[We ask for] chaste love … pure and sinless intention of the will … the more pure and sinless in that there is no admixture of self-will in it [*purior, quo in ea de proprio nil iam admixtum relinquitur*]. … To love this way is to be deified. As a drop of water seems to disappear completely in a quantity of wine [*deficere a se tota videtur*], taking on [*induit*] the wine's flavor and color; as a red-hot iron becomes very, very like [*simillimum fit*] the glow of fire and lays aside its own original form; as air suffused with the light of the sun is transformed [*transformatur*] into the brightness of the light, so that it seems [*videatur*] like light itself rather than only illuminated; so it is necessary that those who are holy, in an ineffable way, are liquified [*a semetipsa liquescere*] and inwardly poured away from themselves and into the will of God [*in Dei penitus transfundi voluntatem*]. How will God be all in all (I Cor. 15.26) if anything of man remains [*supererit*] in man? The substance remains, but in another form, another glory, another power [*Manebit quidem substantia, sed in alia forma, alia gloria aliaque potentia*].[89]

Hence Bernard asserts that the substance of the self perdures while taking on another form; and he asserts this as if he assumes it is what deification means. His language stresses that transformation is not the replacement of something by something else but rather the achievement of "very, very likeness;" the union is "seeming," not "becoming."[90] Yet how can "we" remain if God is to be all in all?

What Bernard really wants to explain in this early treatise is a process of "becoming one" that takes place, paradoxically, in a reality forever hybrid or dual. Although he does, as many scholars have pointed out, use notions of similitude and dissimilitude to express this, the relationship between likeness and unlikeness is (as many of the passages analyzed above suggest) a problematic one. A self that adds or subtracts bits of likeness never quite gets either to the dissimilitude of sin or to the exemplar to which it seeks assimilation. And how exactly does body, that crucial component of the self, fit in? God may be closer to the soul than the soul is to itself, certainly closer than soul is to body; but the human is a soul-body duo.[91] In early works such as the *De diligendo Deo*, Bernard seems to deal with this by asserting a radical union he then proceeds to deny. In later works, such as the sermons on the Song of Songs and the *De consideratione*, he moves to using *unitas* as a technical concept.[92] Deploying the kind of logical grammar typical of late eleventh-century thinkers,[93] Bernard struggles not just with the question of change but also with the implications of change for the problem of the nature of entities — that is, he asks not just how does something change, but also when and how is something what it is? A close analysis of sermon 71 on the Song of Songs and of book 5 of the *De consideratione* will make my point clearer.

Sermon 71 begins with the oppositions of which Bernard is so fond. The "lilies" he must gloss lead into a discussion of virtues as white, vices black, simplicity as whiteness, duplicity or doubleness as blackness.[94] Then, as so often, oppositions lead Bernard, through a series of biblical associations, to images of oneness and incorporation. Christ, who feeds among the lilies, "feeds by feeding." (The association is, on one level, from one "whiteness" to another; on a deeper level, however, the movement is from doubleness to unity.) Christ thus replenishes our souls with the food of his gladness. Yet we ourselves are *his* food. In a startling opposition that suggests our utter distance from God and yet affirms union, Bernard asserts: "I am ashes and eaten by him." Then in radically organic, biological language that is of course also eucharistic, he describes a union with God so perfect that we are lifted by it into equality with what we join:

I am masticated when I am reproved; I am swallowed when I am instructed; I undergo decomposition in the stomach when I change my life [*immutor*]; I am digested when I am transformed [*transformor*]; I am assimilated when I am conformed [*conformor*]. Wonder not at this! He feeds us and is fed by us in order to unite us more closely to himself. In no other way can we be perfectly united [*unimur*] with him ... in perfect union [*perfecta unitio*] ... [each feeding on the other] that there may be firm union and full combination, since I am in him and he will be totally in me [*firma connexio et complexio integra, cum ego in eo, et in me nihilominus ille erit*].[95]

Yet Bernard is troubled by his own language. He tries somehow to draw a distinction between the *confusio* we are not and the

139

[handwritten annotation: "∅ confused but conjoined"]

mastication (*manducatio*) or conjoining (*conjunctio*) we are. (The use of *conjunctio* in apposition to *manducatio* suggests that "eating" may not to Bernard imply quite the assimilation we might assume it to mean.)[96] We cannot claim we are one with God, he continues; we are ashes. Yet "we," dust and ashes, can adhere to God (*adhaerere*), one in spirit with him. But our oneness is less than the oneness of God the Father and God the Son. For Father and Son need not feed upon each other; their *unitas* is other than ours. They are *unum*. We, by mutual mastication, assimilate each other yet remain two; we become not *unum* but *unus spiritus*:

> Do you not see the difference [between our being one in spirit with God] and the consubstantial union of Father and Son? If you have paid attention, I have pointed out how we see this difference of unions in the distinction between *unum* [a substantive] and *unus* [adjective modifying a substantive], for the Father and Son are not called *unus* nor is it appropriate to speak of human and God as *unum*. Father and Son cannot be called *unus*, because one is Father and one is Son [that is, there are two persons]; but they can be called *unum* because there is one substance. It is quite other with God and human, for they are not one in substance or nature and cannot be called *unum*. But they can be called one spirit with certain and absolute truth if they inhere in each other with the glue of love [*glutino amoris*]. . . . Hence you see, I think, not only the diversity but also the disparity of these unities [*non modo diversitas sed et disparitas unitatum*].

There follows a great deal of discussion like this, in which the union of human with God is, alternatively, asserted and denied. What can be more different, asks Bernard, than the unity of one and the unity of many, *unum* and *unus*? *Quid tam distans a se, quam unitas plurimum et unius?* God simply is; *unum* means not merely

140

being one but being one entity. Hence the lesser oneness we are is a lesser oneness not just in the sense that our union with God has elements of two-ness but also in the sense that what joins with God (the body-soul duo that is "us") is less "one" as well. Bernard concludes with the startling paradox that our very mastication by God, our incorporation into his viscera (*inviscerati*), is a mark of the distance at which we lie from the *unitas* of God in himself. One-ing itself is a mark of two-ness. Bernard is introducing degrees into an idea of oneness where "one" means not only "not two" but also "being an entity."[97]

It is easier to see what Bernard is doing, perhaps, if we look at book 5 of the *De consideratione*. Many scholars have recently argued for the central role in this treatise of contradiction or paradox or enigma, while asserting the importance of Bernard's thesis that "consideration" is a mean between ethical extremes.[98] And it is certainly true that Bernard advises the monk-pope Eugene III to avoid being monster or *mixtio* by holding to the middle or mean (*medius, mediocritas*, or *modus*) between administrative frenzy and monastic withdrawal. What has not, however, been sufficiently stressed is the extent to which the entire treatise is a meditation on degrees of *unitas*.[99]

To be sure, Bernard sees every rung in the ladder of being as, in a sense, a mixture or mediation. All, except at the pinnacle, are in some sense multiple. Except for peak and nadir, all are, because they are in a hierarchy, between other points. Indeed Bernard establishes a scale of unities (or, in a sense, entities): from "stones in a pile," through "soul and body in one man," on through the "unity of desire" (that is, our clinging to God), to "soul and flesh in Christ without *confusio*," and finally to God himself (from the unity of Christ, to the unity of the Trinity, to the unity of the one God). But Bernard's point is not that every third term between two others in the hierarchy is a joining or midpoint — a new or a

Argue against middle concept

141

third thing. Rather, he tries to show how every level is simultaneously an entity (a *unitas*) and a two-ness.

Eugene, having added to himself the role of pope, must, to
be sure, find a way of living with the two-ness he has become. But
for all the ethical moderation he may achieve, he has not really become a new thing. He remains a hybrid. As we are hybrids. Bernard stresses that our union with God is closer than our unity
with ourselves. The point is once again made grammatically. We
can, says Bernard, "predicate man of God and God of man" but
"not soul of body or body of soul." In other words, we can say
"man (or humankind) is God" but not "body is soul." This is,
Bernard suggests, because the unity that is soul-body dissolves at
death; the components separate. But the union of God and human
transcends death; there can be no dissolving. "We" are a unity, an
entity, more of a something than a heap of stones is a thing called
a pile. But we (soul and body) are less of a unity than the union of
soul with God.[100]

Higher yet on the ladder of unities is the bread of Christ,
mixed and fermented in the Virgin's womb, a wonderful *commixtio* (the *mira mixtura* of the Christmas sermons). And this *commixtio* is, of course, a mediation. But what Bernard stresses is not its
middle-ness so much as its mysteriousness: it is a paradox, a *unitas*
that remains even when dissolved. Christ is Christ even in separation. For Christ is one, and one with both his body and his soul,
even during the three days between crucifixion and resurrection.
He is one, that is, in time as well as in place. There must be nothing new about the flesh that is in Christ, either at conception or
at death and resurrection. The union of soul and body that is the
human Christ and the union of human and God that is the God-
man must be an entity that is still what it was before.[101] For if
this *commixtio* really became a new (third) thing that replaced
what was there before, our flesh would not be incarnated in it or

142

saved when he rose from the tomb. We are reminded that Bernard rejected the doctrine of the Immaculate Conception (as it was available in the twelfth century), exactly because he insisted on the oneness of the flesh conceived in the Virgin with flesh of humankind from which she descended. If Mary's flesh was not the (sinful) flesh of humankind, at least for a moment, then the flesh into which Christ comes is not ours and we are not saved. The flesh of Mary and the flesh of Christ must be one with that of all humankind. The Christ incarnated in Mary's womb must be radically multiple (flesh and soul as human; human and God) as well as radically one.[102] *Unitas, unus, unum* become for Bernard technical terms to explore the natures of things and the boundaries between them. The medium that interests Bernard is not so much a midpoint as a unity between other unities. And such unity is also always a hybrid.

The ultimate ancestry of a notion of degrees of unity is, of course, Platonic; and the notion is deployed through the tool of logical grammar that Marcia Colish and R.W. Southern, among others, have seen to be so important in the years around 1100.[103] In a sense, then, Bernard's use of *unitas* is nothing new. But why does Bernard, with his radical sense of the doubleness of reality, turn to *unitas* as his way of categorizing entities? Personally as well as ontologically, he needed to be able to conceive of change in which one entity replaced another, in which a new entity came to life from elements of an old, in which mixing, grafting, or hybridization produced a new thing. He needed a concept of an absolute entity, not a hybrid or composite located on a scale of entities none of which were really unitary things. To put it more concretely, he needed the concept of a mixed life as one life or role — that is, a new entity or *ordo* formed from the opposites of action and contemplation. And he needed a concept of the unitary person, forever soul and body. Why then adopt *unitas* to categorize beings? Why not use a concept such as *mixtio*? The answer may be, in part, that terms such as *mutatio, mixtio*, and *manducatio* could not really serve, given the scientific and philosophical thought of Bernard's day, as metaphors for the unity or oneness he had to assert in the midst of duplicity.

Natural Philosophy as the Context of Bernard's Understanding

Bernard's works are sprinkled with ideas and images from the science of his day. As Karl Morrison has persuasively argued, his medical metaphors are sometimes Galenic. And it is worth noting that the Galenic person is, in a sense, an entity of multiples — that is, the person is a balance of opposing forces or factors more than a new, third thing.[104] Bernard's theological anthropology reflects natural philosophy in other ways as well. As sermon 80 on the Song of Songs suggests, his exegesis frequently assumes an atomism according to which nothing really disappears. Things merely aggregate or dissolve, returning to the elements, the ultimate parts or bits. Hence, in a sense, there cannot be change; a thing is merely more or less of what it is. Nor is a thing really itself; no matter how tightly held together, it is a composite, liable to dissolution. If there is replacement-change, it is negation: a thing ceases to be itself; something else replaces it; it is no more. Although Bernard uses atomism in sermon 80 to argue for the immortality of the soul as utterly immaterial (because it has no "bits," it cannot dissolve or be replaced), his sense of the human person is nonetheless driven by an acute awareness that not only the particles of flesh but also the two parts, body and soul, must be reaggregated at the end of time.[105]

What we might call "atomic" assumptions about entities and change are at work behind the notions of mixture and nutrition available in the 1130s and 1140s, when Bernard was writing. And

144

such assumptions meant that neither nutrition and digestion (*manducatio*) nor mixing (*mixtura*) were really processes that resulted in the production of something new. As I have argued elsewhere, Scholastic theologians in Bernard's day found growth and nutrition a hugely troubling conceptual problem, which they solved by asserting that food did not really become flesh or blood in the stomach. (To argue that it did seemed to raise technical, theological problems for understanding not only the consumption of the Eucharist but also the survival — in technical terms the "identity" — of the human body.)[106] Operating with a model in which the replacement of one thing by another was the death of an entity, theologians thus used Matthew 15.17 ("Whatsoever entereth into the mouth, goeth into the belly and is cast out into the privy") to posit the continuation of a core of human nature through the process of eating, digesting, and eliminating. As Peter Lombard remarked, our bodies grow "with help from foods but foods are not converted into human substance."[107] No replacement-change; no assimilation. To be sure, notions of growth and digestion were to change over the course of the next hundred years;[108] the standard position in the mid-thirteenth century asserted exactly the real *mutatio* (replacement-change) of food into flesh that the Lombard denies. But in view of the Lombard's position, echoed by other Scholastics for at least another quarter of a century, it seems likely that when Bernard used *manducatio* for our union with God,[109] he meant exactly what the Latin words in apposition to *manducatio* suggest he meant: not "turning into," but "conjoining," "conforming to," "being with."

It seems likely that notions of "mixture" were fraught with the same ambivalence in the 1130s and 1140s as notions of nutrition and growth. As we have seen, Bernard's use of the term consistently implies not the production of a new entity (what would today be called a chemical compound) but the coexisting of elements, or particles, that can be separated again. In this connection, it is interesting to compare Bernard's concept of *mixtio* (and indeed of change generally) with that of Marius, author of a little treatise, *De elementis*, probably written within twenty-five years of Bernard's death.[110]

Marius, who was in touch with the Salernitan and Aristotelian traditions although he did not know Aristotle directly,[111] displays the same resistance to and fear of species-crossing that we find lurking behind Bernard's metaphors. Like Bernard, he insists on species preservation. Soul cannot become non-soul; qualities or accidents can be added to or subtracted from substances, but if substance itself changes, we have simply the replacement of something by something else. And such a model would be terrifying if applied to the human person. Like Bernard's, Marius's model of spiritual change is that sin or dissimilitude is added onto soul. Soul cannot become non-soul, no matter how deformed it may be through the overlay of filth. Moreover, Marius's notion of the hybrid is that implicit in Bernard's metaphors. There can technically be hybridization where species are very close together, just as there can be grafting of closely related plants; but such addings of entity to entity are violations of nature, sterile and distasteful; moreover, hybrids are a "both ... and," not a new thing.[112]

In contrast to Bernard, however, Marius has begun to move in certain ways toward a new understanding of change. Not only does he hold digestion and assimilation to be real conversion — that is, incorporation of food into body — he attempts as well to explain how such change occurs. Marius has a notion of a kind of prime matter, an underlay, in which something really becomes something else. Differing from Peter Lombard and other theologians, he asserts that eating really changes the thing eaten into the eater. ("Likeness" still operates as a category; what is eaten turns into the nature of the eater — that is, is like him — and not into

something arbitrary. The bread I eat, for example, becomes human flesh, not dog flesh.) Even more important, Marius arrives
(without Aristotle) at an Aristotelian conception of mixture as
the production of a new, third thing. Going beyond Galenic contraries, he argues that in a genuine *mixtio* contraries attack each
other and each is altered; a *mixtio* is not just a hybrid or a mean; a
new, a third, thing emerges.[113]

Hence Bernard's *mixtio* is not Marius's; his understanding of
natural conversion is of the close adhering of particles, not of
true assimilation or replacement. But had Marius's understanding
been available to him, would Bernard have used it for the double
onenesses that were so central to his spirituality? If *mixtio* had,
to Bernard, really meant a new, third thing, would he have employed it to characterize entities other than the monstrous or the
marvelous?

Of course we can never know. Counterfactuals are dangerous
tools of analysis. But I do not want to suggest that Bernard's theological concepts were, in any ultimate sense, driven by assumptions drawn from natural philosophy, even though it is always
necessary to point out that people can think with only the concepts and assumptions they have. Nonetheless it seems to me that
Bernard's obsession with the two-ness of entities that must also
be one — his use, for example, of "both ... and" rather than a new
name to denominate new roles or things, his inability to conceive
of something really becoming something else — reflected not only
the conceptual apparatus available to him but also the deep psychological and spiritual divide in his life: the experience that led
him to call himself a chimera.

Twelfth-Century Religious Life as Context

I argued twenty years ago both that twelfth-century religious discourse generally was characterized by an intense interest in roles,

stimulated in part by new possibilities for making life choices, and that the Cistercians in particular felt ambivalence about the active life (service in the world), to which they were simultaneously drawn. In the case of Bernard and several other Cistercians of his generation, I pointed out that acute interest in roles and responsibilities, and ambivalence about them, was expressed in the use of complex and paradoxical gender imagery.[114] I do not need to repeat these ideas. Many others have made similar arguments, some laying more emphasis on the rhetorical reconciliations Bernard effected between lives or activities (offering different combinations and emphases to different statuses), others stressing his own internal contradictions.[115] The point I wish to make here is not only that the twelfth century created a stunning array of new religious roles, many of them hybrid (the military orders, the quasi-religious status only a little later called "beguines," and so on), but also that many of the "reforms" of older roles and statuses were a kind of hybridizing as well. Carthusians were a sort of cenobitic hermit; Premonstratensians a kind of cenobitic-eremitic cleric; Cistercians such as Bernard and Eugene III were drawn by new ideas of evangelism (whether through politicking, preaching, or writing) and radical notions of disengagement as well. Chroniclers and polemicists were aware of the new diversity, and some, such as Gerhoh of Reichersberg or the anonymous author of the *Libellus de diversis ordinibus*, struggled to devise ways of cataloging the proliferating groups. Abbots and novice masters in these new orders (Bernard, Aelred of Rievaulx, and Guerric of Igny are obvious examples) felt especially torn between conflicting ideals both because they had responsibility for other souls in addition to their own and because such responsibility offered special temptations to violation of the withdrawal that was one of the poles of their desire.[116] Thrust into prominence by requests from contemporaries and by his own perception of the dangers of his times,

Bernard could find models for others: the monk-pope Eugene should be a "mean" of consideration, his own monks "wells" of prayer, the Templars "twins" of prowess and self-abnegation. But he feared he himself was only a chimera, a "monster."[117]

We see Bernard's ambivalence, his deep sense of his own two-ness, if we look closely at his language. For Bernard is drawn not only to complex gender images to express his dual role but also repeatedly to images of animals and monsters. By this observation I mean not just that Bernard discusses his own sense of being torn between roles or lives, although this is obviously so. To cite only two passages: Bernard comments, in the *De diligendo Deo*, "prayer is my profession even if I do not live as though it were," and mourns, in sermon 30 on the Song of Songs, that he has under-taken care of others when not fit to care for himself.[118] But I also mean that the topic of roles leads Bernard into self-reflection. In sermon 51, for example, his discussion of Mary and Martha (the two lives) as "closely related to each other and liv[ing] under the same roof" slips into "let me tell you my own experience." Some-thing about the idea of alternating or combining roles tends to lead Bernard into self-justification: "I cannot grieve over the loss of contemplation . . . if I see the fruits and flowers of piety. I patiently allow myself to be withdrawn from the barren embrace of Rachel if I can obtain the abundant fruit of your advance-ment."[119] Moreover, something about images of monsters seems to trigger in Bernard a discussion of roles, and something about the topic of roles or lives leads him to slip into images of animals and hybrids.

We have already seen how the *Apologia* and the letter to Suger relate "monsters" to "marvelous variety" and then move to a con-sideration of responsibilities and statuses.[120] The sermon for Saint Benedict provides yet another example. In this sermon, a quite astonishing array of tropes groups around the story of Benedict casting unclean spirits into swine. We find here the injunction to be comforted by but not emulate miracles; not being saints, Bernard's brothers have (he argues) no power to effect apparent changes of outward form. We find as well a complex discussion of the pig as an unclean animal that "true Jews" — that is, Christians — do not eat. Swine flesh, when eaten, becomes "one flesh" with ours. (Bernard refers, quite astonishingly, to marriage [Matthew 19.6].) Hence those who lapse into gluttony violate God's precepts and "become one with" the devil. It is clear that the image of gluttony as digesting pig flesh or being digested by the devil is one in which digestion means "adhering" or being added to, not true metamorphosis; the oneness is that of marriage, in which the one remains also forever two. What is most interesting for my purposes, however, is the fact that Bernard goes from a discussion of men becoming beast-men — a discussion that he has already associated with marriage, a role that interested him a good deal — to a discussion of the abbot's role. And the discussion is one in which his ambivalence is clear. For what Bernard lauds here is not Benedict as wise father and counselor but a Benedict who shuns the temptations of leadership. Benedict was "the Lord's beast of burden" (note the animal image again), who avoided bringing forth fruit or shearing the flock too soon. Not only does change of men into swine remind Bernard of the duality of leadership, but leadership also reminds him of its temptations, which are here almost equated with the active life.[121]

Literature and Art as Context

Bernard's sense of his own two-ness seems rooted in a role confusion for which the only solution he can find is alternation between, or simultaneous and paradoxical assertion of, incompatible lives — a *unitas* that is forever two. Moreover, he is not alone among twelfth-century figures in imagining himself (and his enemies) as hybrids or monsters. Much of the literature of entertainment that ushered in the mania for marvels was produced by men who were, like Bernard, self-consciously hybrid. French-educated clerics such as Gerald of Wales, Walter Map, or Gervais of Tilbury, who returned to their English homes to find no university jobs waiting, described the new bureaucratic roles they filled at court as mix-tures or flux. Obsessed with monsters and revenants, these clerics seem to have expressed, in their stories of composites and bound-ary crossings, a sense of both the possibility and the horror of role combination. Walter Map, for example, insisted that the court he served was a hydra, a giant with many hands, a hell populated by monsters, and even used the entire discussion to question what it means for a group of individuals to be a unity, to have identity through change.[122]

It is hardly surprising that hydras, giants, and wer-animals occurred to authors such as Bernard or Walter as images for the self. Bernard after all described historiated capitals and gargoyles he actually saw; Gerald of Wales and William of Newburgh, to take only two examples, interviewed people who told of encoun-ters with vampires, werewolves, and ox-men.[123] Anxious about their responsibilities, thoughtful about their place in the world, in some cases disappointed in their aspirations, such men not only found images of bizarre combinations close at hand; they were also exposed to many discussions, whether scientific treatises such as Marius's, moralizing accounts such as the bestiaries, or grammatical exercises such as early Ovid commentary, in which natural oddities were used to explore theological or philosophical topics.[124]

Literary scholars and art historians have recently been inter-ested in the proliferation of hybrids and monsters in the literature and visual arts of the twelfth century. They have sometimes, in my judgment, exaggerated its presence or over-interpreted its significance.[125] Nonetheless the appearance of increasing numbers of monstrous figures in image and text is not to be dismissed as a context for writing such as Bernard's, Gerald's, or Walter's. And it is worth emphasizing that, in the twelfth century, such creatures are, for the most part, genuine composites, not the shape-shifters of European folklore. As is well known, hybrids began to appear with greater and greater frequency in historiated capitals and marginalia (see Figures 11–15); and scholars emphasize the extent to which these creatures were original and fantastic creations (by no means simply misunderstood animals, or classical tropes).[126] Giants, fairies, mer-people, and wer-animals proliferated in romances as the century drew to a close. One recent study has perceptively underlined the fact that twelfth-century tales feature genuine hybrids, which tend to disappear in the early thirteenth century and reemerge in the fourteenth not as composites but as shape-shifters, sites of metamorphosis.[127] Moreover, bestiaries never recount transformation. The bipartite creatures they describe have immutable natures; the processes by which composites emerge are never discussed.[128] Although it is always possible to ask whether a gargoyle or historiated capital represents a transformation frozen at a single moment of time, the fact that bestiary text, which might well explain metamorphic process, does not do so suggests that such monsters are not moments in a story but types or natures, intrinsically double. The miracle and marvel collections so popular in the years between 1150 and 1230 often featured hybrids, such as sirens or mermen, or tales of species-crossings (for example, the stories of the fairy Melusine), in which the point seems to be not genetic or developmental explanation but rather wonder at the multiple natures that inhabit a wondrous world.[129] As I have suggested elsewhere, mid-twelfth-century discussions of species boundaries — of grafting, for example, or alchemical manipulation — stress combination or resistance to

152

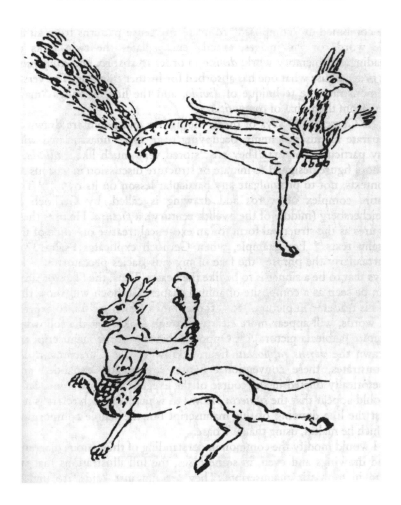

Figure 11. Two monstrous figures composed of *versus rapportati*, from fol. 255v of the twelfth-century *Hortus deliciarum*. Such figures, fashioned from animal and human parts, accompanied and represented Latin verses; both figures and verses were used as memory aids. They could be "read" only by a process of deconstructing and recomposing that trained the memory and carried its contents.

PA
VLTD

OS

DĀPN

turi
e sua
dia
cerui
ebat
ene g̃
udebt
s; Con
ibi sa
ge st.
· q̃e
rcem
te ex
il pn
sapi
umili
lisca
ptū ē
mentes;
ens
inc
eius
rem
omó
; za
mundi

REBVM·? POST FVNERA ROIE
post uulnera corporis·? post
ba male suadentis uxoris·?
contumeliosa dicta consol
tium·? post suscepta forti
cula tot dolor·. de tanta
tute constantie laudandi
audice beat' iob fuerat· 1
si ix depsenti scto eet euoca
dus; At post quā hic adh
duplicia recepturus ē· post
quā saluti pristine restitu

Figure 12. A traditional hybrid from the cloister of Cuxa in the Pyrenees, ca. 1130–1145: a siren, that is, a female head and torso with a serpent's tail. Now in the Cloisters Museum, New York.

Figure 13 (opposite). A series of hybrids from a Cistercian manuscript of the early twelfth century shows the power of the art to which Bernard of Clairvaux reacted. *Moralia in Job.* Dijon, Bib. pub. 173, fol. 103v (ca. 1111).

155

Figure 14. A monster from the cloister of Cuxa, still in situ. These large, distorted heads with human limbs may be hybrids, or they may represent monsters devouring humans. Whichever they evoke, the combination of human and animal here threatens species boundaries.

Figure 15. A classical monster with a novel addition: a griffin with a tail hand. From the collegiate church of St. Pierre in Chauvigny, second half of the twelfth century.

combination, not transformation.[130] Although shape-shifting, meta-morphosis, even metempsychosis were mentioned in the years around 1200 and feared as ontological possibilities, what engaged Bernard and many of his mid-twelfth-century contemporaries was not so much metamorphosis as hybrid.

Bernard's sense of himself as double echoes the fascination with composites, monsters, and marvels that enlivened the imaginative literature and art of his day. Such doubleness frightened him and tempted him to pride. Indeed, horror at doubleness goes very deep in Bernard's spirituality; witness the sensual disgust with which he reacts to the "beautiful deformity" of Romanesque art. But we must not forget that Bernard also sees the hybrid as a *mysterium* beyond *miraculum*. The God-man who saves and the virgin mother who mediates are the *mira mixta* of God. So is the unclean human heart in which such paradoxes nestle as belief.

Conclusion: Hybridity in the Spirituality of Bernard of Clairvaux

Hence the doubleness in *unitas* that permeates Bernard's work is rooted in more than the philosophical and scientific terminology available to him, more than the ambivalent situation in which he found himself as a twelfth-century Cistercian abbot, more than the fascination with oddity he undoubtedly shared with his contemporaries. A doubleness that must, paradoxically, be a unity is at the heart of Bernard's ontology, his understanding of what is.

To Bernard, humanity is hybrid. Although soul is created *imago* or *ad imaginem* (and much of Bernard's spirituality is devoted to the progress of this soul toward likeness), the self to Bernard is not soul. Soul may be closer to God than to body, but the self is body as well as soul, slime as well as spirit. Without the physical body, reassembled from all its bits at the end of time, we are not saved. [131] The body one misses during the period between death

158

and resurrection is not only a "retardation" of desire, a distraction we feel because we are dragged back earthward by our concern for it; it is also our access to experience and sensation, our means of sorrowing penitence while on earth, our access to ultimate joy when in heaven.[132] Yet the beloved body for which the soul longs is also a spider's filthy web, a disease.[133] And the soul itself is the site not only of glory but also of greed and despair, "like" animal as well as angel. Soul and body each are two. Together they are utterly incompatible yet joined for all eternity. Each, both, and neither is self. The *unitas* of person is ever in danger of fragmenting into parts, particles, *varietas*.

The radical contradiction, the incompatibility, the threat to boundary and entity, is crucial to both Bernard's conception and his method of presentation. In paragraph after paragraph, his powerful prose first pulls the person into dichotomies and then declares the parts to be each other. Again and again it proclaims us to be one with God yet totally other from him. Never linear, Bernard's rhetoric soars and dips, asserting and denying and asserting again. "Oh lowliness! Oh sublimity! ... in contradiction each to the other, cooperate for the good...."[134]

Thus for all Bernard's sense of the otherness of God, his spirituality is radically Christocentric. But his Christ is less mediation than contradiction, a hybrid of hybrids. For the human with which the divine-human Christ joins is itself double (soul-body). Divinity is revealed in a metamorphosis (the transformation of bread and wine into body and blood) that is, paradoxically enough, itself a hybrid.[135] Eucharistic change does not (like other metamorphoses) reveal its story by carrying signs of its becoming or transition, but rather its appearance contradicts its reality; it is thus the ultimate dialogic *unitas*, putting the material world we see in conversation with the otherness of Christ. Indeed, hybridity lingers at the highest levels of *unitas* Bernard can conceive or express. Although closer to our souls than we are to our own bodies, the God we approach through likeness is always "other," not only because unknown and unknowable but also because ontologically we are only "like." Likeness is a relative concept, a matter of degrees toward; one can never be one with the *unitas* of God through the addition of degrees of oneness, for degrees are multiple. Even at the heart of the experience of deification, Bernard is a *mixtura*, a substance *in alia forma*; digested, assimilated, and absorbed, he remains not the eater but the that-which-is-eaten.[136] His emphasis is less on the process, the linkage, the mediation, the transition than on the simultaneity of opposites, the coincidence of the *unitas* of self or world with the *unitas* that God is. It is as if the impossibility of our being a *unitas* is redeemed by the impossibility of the God-man. Redemption is not merely the growth of like toward like, shedding bits of accrued unlikeness; redemption is the elevation of our hybridity into God.[137]

"Hybridity" is, of course, not Bernard's term. Indeed, as I argued above, Bernard has no technical term except *unitas* for what we might call the entity-ness of the roles, positions, and beings that fill his world. Nonetheless at the distant poles of the universe — in his own confusion as chimera, and in Christ, the marvel that redeems — Bernard sees *mixtura*. Between the poles, where he finds *similitudo* and *transformatio*, the searching self remains dichotomous and contradictory, at once *sublimitas* and *vilitas*.

Hybridity is, as I have argued elsewhere, dialogic, because inherently two.[138] Its contraries are simultaneous and in conversation with each other. As Bernard himself saw, we understand the nature of white and black each more clearly if both are present. Slime and glory are in dialogue with each other not only in humankind but also in Christ. Moreover, hybrids both destabilize and reveal the world. For example, the bird-insect-ness of Arnold of Brescia reveals him to Bernard as hypocrite and heretic, having two tongues and two truths.[139] But Arnold's doubleness confounds expectations as well. Poor and humble in life, yet arrogant and false in doctrine, Arnold shakes our assumptions about the relationship between inner and outer, virtue and belief. In every hybrid, *sublimitas* and *vilitas* are in conversation — contradicting, undermining, complementing each other. Bernard's world is one in which every *unitas* is *diversitas*, unstable, multiple, itself and its opposite, speaking of what it is not as well as of what it is.

Hence "hybridity" seems to me an appropriate term for Bernard's rhetorical and ontological stance, for his characteristic patterns of speaking and thinking, for what he fundamentally assumes. An abbot and preacher, struggling to educate others and achieve some spiritual progress himself, Bernard nonetheless speaks less of radical transformation than of dichotomy, contradiction, opposition. The basic concept with which he thinks is not change, the series of little deaths that threaten being, but hybridity, the two-in-one-ness of an entity.

Great scholars such as Robert Javelet have sometimes spoken of Bernard's as a spirituality of metamorphosis. Yet close examination of such interpretations reveals that what they mean by metamorphosis is dynamism or process or return.[140] Bernard's is not a view of the world or of the self in which one entity turns into another. No matter how basic to Bernard is the concept of like returning to like, he fears replacement-change. It is surely, then, hybrid, not metamorphosis, that expresses Bernard of Clairvaux's basic assumptions. Paradox, not process, is at the heart of his understanding of religious roles, his definition of the human person, his belief in the God-man who saves, his hope for absorption into God. For Bernard's sense of the world is visual and dialogic, not narrative or historical.[141] His prose deploys contradiction, not linear development. His exegesis moves from terms to their opposites. His elaborations are seldom set in histories, whether of individuals, communities, or peoples. His fundamental category is a *unitas* forever encompassing two.

This characteristic way of thinking means that there are some things it is hard for Bernard to say and some things he says supremely well. His understanding of entities is the paradoxical notion that one plus one equals one. Nothing really holds the entity together except the assertion of unity. Two things do not to Bernard really come together to make a third thing. One thing does not become another. There is no real change; beings are only more or less themselves. But the radical two-ness of the world is preserved; at the heart of beings is not only a simultaneity of opposites but also a conversation between them. And the contrast makes each more vividly itself. Hence it should be no surprise that the Bernard who called himself a chimera could see the human person as vile slime united to glory and God himself as *mira mixtura*.

It seems clear that every rhetorical strategy and set of ontological assumptions presents advantages and disadvantages for grappling with what we persist in calling "reality." Conceptions of radical metamorphosis, because essentially narrative, grapple with history and personal development in a way Bernard, for all his dynamism, does not. Moreover they keep the focus on the question of identity. What I have called Bernard's hybridity, by which I mean both his ontology and his rhetoric, expresses something else. Bernard's language describes not how something changes, what constitutes an entity, how identity perdures; it simply affirms at every ontological level a simultaneity of opposites in which what *is* exists as A and not-A, one plus one, in conversation with — and being — itself. If metamorphosis leaves us finally with a question — for indeed how *can* something change and be the same thing? — the hybrid, at least in the hands of a master, bodies forth not question but paradox: the fact that the world is, and is contradictory.

CHAPTER FOUR

Shape and Story[1]

these scars bear witness
but whether to repair
or to destruction
I no longer know

> "Meditations for a Savage Child"
> Adrienne Rich[2]

The Problem of Personal Identity

For the past ten years, I have been fascinated by the question of personal identity in all three senses in which the word is used by present-day philosophers, sociologists, and literary theorists. Identity can mean individuality or personality. In this sense, identity is that which makes me particularly, distinctively, even uniquely me. But identity is also used in current debates to mean something almost the opposite; it can mean identity position. In this sense, my identity is that which signals group affiliation — often race or biological sex but sometimes also statuses generally understood as more socially shaped, such as class, language group, or religion. Finally, identity can mean spatiotemporal continuity. In this sense, identity refers to the fact that I am the same person I was a moment ago. This third understanding of identity carries the connotation of oneness or integrity. The same set of crumbs is not the identical piece of cake if it is divided into two portions.[3]

All three senses of identity can seem to slip away from one's intellectual grasp when examined closely. Moreover, they slip into each other. If we consider identity as individuality, what are its elements and limits? Does the emergence of depression or schizophrenia, for example, remove identity, however much it may alter personality? If outer behavior and inner intentionality seem fundamentally out of synchrony, as in the case of Tourette's syndrome, where does identity lie?[4]

Identity understood as identity position also raises questions — social, political, and philosophical. Feminists, queer theorists, specialists in ethnic studies, and politicians have recently asked, for example, who owns or bestows identifying labels, such as "black" or "queer." The difference between claiming identity for one's own group and naming an "other" is often the difference between self-assertion, on the one hand, and denigrating stereotype, on the other hand; and even this formulation is too simple. It is not quite true today, for example, that Poles can tell Polish jokes, whereas others may not. For even within identity groups the appropriateness of labels may be hotly contested. And terms such as "feminist" have, among people who describe themselves as such, varied, even contradictory, meanings. Moreover, theorists from almost every walk of life — biologists, sociologists, literary critics, lawyers and judges, political activists — query whether such "identities" as gay, female, Hispanic, elderly, are biologically determined or culturally constructed. Is there something basic to particular races or sexes either encoded in genes and carried by physiology or found so universally in world cultures as to be ineradicable even if elaborated by society from mere biological hints in musculature, pigment, or hormones?

The third understanding of identity — identity as spatiotemporal continuity — is today the least discussed outside of philosophical circles. Yet this sense of identity is often implicated in the other two. Moreover, it offers the deepest and rawest threat to our grounding as a self. For considering identity in this sense raises doubts about whether anything perdures — my personality, my cat, my briefcase if I take my eye off it for even a moment. If I have amnesia, does my body guarantee that I am "me" over time? What if *it* then undergoes a sex-change operation and complete cosmetic surgery? Is there any sense in saying that such an altered entity is "the same individual," whereas a donor mouse and its clone are two separate individuals?

Discussion of identity issues in all three senses of identity is everywhere today: in campus politics and debates over whose literary "canon" should be taught; in the pop culture of movies, television, and tabloids where consciousness is split or transplanted, bodies "beamed up"; in ethicists' agonized ruminations over cloning, organ donation, or recovered memory. Whether we read the *New York Review of Books*, *Newsweek*, or the *National Enquirer*, we are bombarded by the question: Are we genes, bodies, brains, minds, experiences, memories, or souls? How many of these can or must change before we lose our identity and become someone or something else? On what identity do we insist, if we claim rights for our identity position? What allows or entitles someone else to represent or empathize with that identity? How do we retain simultaneously a hope for freedom and a forgiving recognition of the limitations always imposed by body and history? The answers to these questions are not at all clear. But recent discussion has tended to fall into dichotomous terminology: mind (or consciousness or memory) versus brain or body; biology versus social or cultural construction; self versus other; freedom or agency versus essence. Such simple binaries seem to reduce individuals — both past and present — to a mere fraction of the complexity we, in our wiser and more intuitive moments, think we are. Hence we surely need a more labile and problematic understanding of identity, one that will not force us to choose between mind and body, socialization and biology, genes and desire, one not figured primarily in terms of transplants, splits, and dichotomies. Yet we seem at the present moment to lack images, metaphors, and stories that imagine a self possessing both individuality and identity position, a self that really changes while really remaining the same thing.

Some Stories About Werewolves: Ovid's Lycaon

Having now grounded the question in our current perplexities and, I hope, thereby thoroughly perplexed you, I want to remove myself a great way off and tell you three stories or sets of stories — stories that (I shall later contend) give us a new way of imagining identity. They are stories about werewolves — one from the first century of the common era, one from the late twelfth century, and a group from our own period. I hasten to underline that they are *stories* — not trial records, or medical accounts, or reportage. Although the Middle Ages is often associated in the popular press with the benighted, the monstrous, and the marvelous, the centuries between 500 and 1400 were not in fact the period of Western history most characterized by hunger for and terror of the bizarre. Indeed, the early Middle Ages prohibited and punished werewolf belief (although mildly — with a penance of bread and water); philosophical and theological experts of the high Middle Ages employed technical distinctions at least as complex as those of modern identity theorists to explain that, whatever people claimed they saw, human-animal metamorphosis did not occur.[5] It was the Renaissance of the sixteenth century, not the Middle Ages, that saw the flourishing of astrology, alchemy, and magic, the burning of witches and werewolves.[6] Such things are not, however, my topic. My topic is stories. Marvelous stories. Stories of metamorphosis and species transformation.

166

One more word of warning. These stories are not allegories, although literary critics in the first and twelfth centuries were perfectly capable of understanding werewolf stories as "about" the eruption of the beast within us; indeed, they developed the techniques for allegorical reading of such stories still sometimes used to interpret texts as different as Greek myths and the Bible.[7] The stories I speak of are, however, carefully constructed tales belonging to the literary genre Tzvetan Todorov has called "the marvelous" (that is, stories in which the characters accept the supernatural) as opposed to "the uncanny" (tales in which the supernatural is rationalized) or "the fantastic" (in which characters and readers vacillate between natural explanation and acceptance of the supernatural).[8] Realistic in their assessment of character and motivation, they hover in a world whose rules about boundary crossing — about identity — are internally consistent but different from ours; hence, in part, their power.

And so, with this as introduction, I tell you three tales. (I shall come to a fourth set of literary transformations at the end of the lecture, when I consider Dante.) The first is from Ovid's *Metamorphoses*, one of the great poems in the Western tradition, source of many of the stories familiar to us from legend, opera, and art. Ovid sings of a universe of change — "*in nova . . . mutatas . . . formas . . . corpora*," of bodies changed into new forms. One of the earliest stories he tells, in fifteen books of metamorphoses, is the story of Lycaon, whose savagery led Jove to destroy all but two members of the human race with a mighty flood. Explaining his anger to the other gods, Jove speaks:

> An infamous report of the age had reached my ears. Eager to prove this false, I descended from high Olympus, and as a god disguised in human form traveled up and down the land. . . . I approached the seat and inhospitable abode of the Arcadian king [Lycaon], just as the late

evening shades were ushering in the night. I gave a sign that a god had come, and the common folk began to worship me. Lycaon at first mocked at their pious prayers; and then he said: "I will soon find out, and that by a plain test, whether this fellow be god or mortal...." He planned that night while I was heavy with sleep to kill me.... And not content with that, he took a hostage who had been sent by the Molossian race, cut his throat, and some parts of him still warm with life, he boiled, and others he roasted over the fire. But no sooner had he placed these before me on the table than I, with my avenging bolt, brought the house down upon its household gods, gods worthy of such a master. The king himself flies in terror ...

We note that the poet suddenly, without a break in the narrative or a syntactic signal that he will change voice, shifts to the present tense. And we hear now not the majestic tones of the king of the gods recounting a story but the almost staccato beat of events unfolding before our eyes. The verbs rush the drama forward, until the last line, when Jove returns as narrator to pronounce judgment:

The king himself flies in terror and, gaining the silent fields, howls aloud, attempting in vain to speak. His mouth of itself gathers foam, and with his accustomed greed for blood he turns against the sheep, delighting still in slaughter. His garments change to shaggy hair, his arms to legs. He turns into a wolf, and yet retains some traces of his former shape [*veteris servat vestigia formae*]. There is the same grey hair, the same fierce face, the same gleaming eyes, the same picture of beastly savagery. One house has fallen but [it is] not one house alone [that] has deserved to perish.[9]

Ovid's great poem contains many kinds of metamorphosis — change of body for punishment, escape, or apotheosis, for seduc-

tion or betrayal, for discovery or revelation.[10] About the metamorphosis of Lycaon I make here only three points. First, the
Arcadian king (who is associated in a complex earlier image with
disloyalty to the emperor for whom Ovid writes) is not only an
impious tyrant, turning his people against Jove, ruler of the gods;
he is also a cannibal, committer of that ultimate metamorphosis
(human eating human — that is, human turning another person
not just into food but into himself). And the two vices are both
boundary crossings, mirroring each other and mirrored in the
tyrant's subsequent transformation. Lycaon violates both the divi-
sion between human and god, by preparing to kill Jove, and the
boundary between human and human, by killing a hostage for
cannibalism; hence his own species boundaries are violated by the
metamorphosis into wolf.

Second, Lycaon really changes; as the poetry pulses forward,
he becomes a wolf (*fit lupus*); his speech twists into howls, echo-
ing against silent fields. Clothes, the mark of civilization, become
hair; arms, signs of the creature who walks erect, become merely
two more legs.

And yet — my third point — Lycaon is what he was before:
"with his accustomed greed [*solitaeque cupidine*] for blood he
turns against the sheep, delighting still [*nunc quoque*] in slaughter."
The greed he carries into wolfhood was his already by custom and
practice. Thirst for blood and delight in killing have always been
there; only the object (sheep) is new. When the poet tells us that
Lycaon's joy in slaughter is "now also" or "still" present, the simple adverb emphasizes not new bloodthirstiness but continuing
bestiality. The poem not only states explicitly that *vestigia* (traces)
remain but also hammers away "same, same, same": " . . . the same
grey hair, the same fierce face [the word is not muzzle or snout
but *vultus*, a term for human face or expression], the same gleaming eyes, the same picture [*imago*] of beastly savagery." Lycaon's

169

visage is an *imago*, a representation or similitude, of savagery;
the term suggests both that the *vultus* portrays or bodies forth
the inner self and that this wolf-person as *imago* is *imago* not
of humanity's proper exemplar, the gods, but of a corruption, a
bestiality, that is what Lycaon is. Lycaon the wolf is "same . . . same
. . . same. . . ."

Some Stories About Werewolves:
Marie de France's Bisclavret

The medieval werewolf story I have chosen to tell is very different
— indeed almost opposite — from Ovid's. Equally artful and, like
Ovid's, in many ways typical of other stories of its day, the *lai* of
Bisclavret by Marie de France is a tale of the regaining (not the
loss) of civilization and nobility, a tale in which the metamorphosis, unlike Lycaon's, is reversed. Marie's poem begins:

> In the old days, people used to say —
> and it often actually happened —
> that some men turned into werewolves
> and lived in the woods.
> A werewolf [*garvalf*] is a savage beast [*beste salvage*];
> while his fury is on him
> he eats men, does much harm,
> goes deep in the forest to live.
> But that's enough of this for now:
> I want to tell you about the *bisclavret* [the Breton word for
>   werewolf].[11]

These few lines (clearly set off by "that's enough of this") are all
we hear about savagery and anthropophagy (that is, eating humans). Marie, with characteristic self-confidence, suggests her
divergence from folk tradition and establishes her authorial voice;

she is not repeating an old tale of shape-shifting or magic but creating a new story. She also distinguishes her *bisclavret* (known throughout the poem not by a name but only by this generic label) from the savage *garvalf* of tradition, a distinction that becomes crucial to the events that follow.

The story then unfolds. A fine and noble knight with an estimable wife has a habit of disappearing for three days a week. Nagged by his wife to reveal where he goes, he finally answers: "My dear, I become a werewolf." And when she inquires whether he keeps his clothes on, he replies, "Wife, I go stark naked," and reveals that he hides the garments carefully because he cannot return to his human shape without them. The wife, now understandably afraid and "never wanting to sleep with him again," contrives with the help of a lover to steal his clothes.

A year passes. Then the king, hunting in the forest, finds the werewolf, who runs and kisses his foot in its stirrup, begging for mercy. "My lords," calls the king to his courtiers, "Look at this marvel — this beast is humbling itself to me. It has the mind of a man [*sen d'hume*]. . . ."[12] So the king returns home with the werewolf, who "was so noble and well behaved that he never wished to do anything wrong." After some time, the wife of the bisclavret comes with rich presents for the king, and the werewolf, flying at her in rage, tears the nose off her face. The king, convinced there is a reason for the beast's hatred, tortures the woman until she confesses and restores the stolen clothes. The bisclavret is then allowed to retire into the king's chamber with the clothes, and when the king returns there, he finds the knight asleep in the royal bed. The wife is banished with her lover and "[has] several children who were widely known for their appearance: several women of the family were actually born without noses."

Marie's story raises complex questions about civilization, trust, and gender that I cannot explore thoroughly here.[13] But I call your

171

attention to four points relevant to the theme of identity. First, Marie's story, unlike Ovid's, is about transformation and return. The bisclavret is not left to howl forever in silent meadows. Having performed like a well-behaved dog at court, he becomes a well-beloved knight to a just and wise king.

Second, Bisclavret, unlike Lycaon, is presented throughout as still human. Marie insists several times (in the king's words): "This beast...has understanding and judgment [*Ceste beste ad entente e sen*]."[14] Not only is Marie's werewolf an innocent victim, both of the pattern of periodic bestiality with which he begins and of the wifely trick that freezes him in his wolf shape (yes, this tale by a woman may have misogynistic elements); he is also throughout rational — loyal to his king, vengeful only to those who betrayed him first, civilized enough to request privacy for the shocking act of metamorphosis and the nakedness that precedes it. Indeed, the wife's real crime (a natural enough reaction) is to confuse her bisclavret with the *garvalf* tradition, thus denying him the possibility of escaping from it. Her mistake (put in modern jargon) is stereotyping, identifying the bisclavret with what she takes to be his identity position.

Although the bisclavret is wolf-shaped and deprived of speech, we are dealing with a sharper soul-body or person-skin dualism than we met in Ovid's story. Whereas Ovid's wolf carries traces of a former self *on* his skin, there is in Marie a suggestion of over and under, inner and outer, of a person under the shaggy wolf. But the suggestion never becomes a claim that the skin is only covering or disguise; Bisclavret, although rational, is also a wolf. As Marie says, it is a "beast [*beste*]" that "has understanding and judgment [*entente e sen*]."

Third, Marie's werewolf seems, at least morally, to change *more* than Ovid's. Lycaon becomes a beast, but a beast he has always been. Bisclavret learns discretion and trust and teaches those around him. He is more reliable and courteous, wiser in judgment, as a werewolf than he was as a husband, wisest (and richest) of all as a retransformed knight. It is the wife, who does not undergo metamorphosis, who also does not learn.[15]

Finally, vestiges, or traces, are important in Marie's tale, as in Ovid's, but the traces important here are not on Bisclavret but on the wife. The werewolf's physical transformation both to wolf and to man goes undescribed. But his revenge marks the wife's body, and she passes this physical mark down to subsequent generations. It is her body finally that (however unfair we may feel it is) carries the story. Although very different from Ovid's sense that eyes, face, and foaming jaws carry Lycaon's identity, Marie's treatment of "the wife," individualized by name no more than her husband "the bisclavret," clearly draws on a deep-lying assumption that history, story, lasts only where it is borne by physical marks on body or in body's comportment. In some sense generic "king," "werewolf," and "wife," the characters in Marie's tale nonetheless have identity in the sense of individuality and in the sense of spatiotemporal continuity because of the vestiges of an earlier part of the story they bear in the bend of a knee or the scar of a face.

Stories About Werewolves and Metamorphosis: Angela Carter

The modern werewolf stories I have chosen to consider are from a collection by the British writer Angela Carter, who died in 1992. Metamorphosis was for Carter, as for Ovid, a complex theme, and there is no one meaning she gave to change, no single tone in which she sings of it, although Salman Rushdie seems correct when he says "It is Carter's genius...to make the [beast] fable a metaphor for all the myriad yearnings and dangers of sexual relations."[16] Carter's stories weave fairy-tale themes we all know—

especially "Little Red Riding Hood," "Beauty and the Beast," and "Bluebeard" — into standard European werewolf motifs, such as the notion that spilling a werewolf's blood will release him into his human form or that destroying his clothes will condemn him to lycanthropy forever, or the idea (sometimes called "repercussion" by folklorists) that any wound suffered on the werewolf's body will be found on the restored human form as well.[17] It is Carter's trademark to disrupt profoundly both our expectations of what should follow what in such tales and our customary moral and aesthetic response to them, whether the disrupted template is from classical myth or the Brothers Grimm.

For example, in the brief tale (it is only two pages in the collected stories) called "The Werewolf," the "good child" who sets out for grandmother's house manages to defend herself against the wolf in the forest by slashing off its right forepaw, only to find her grandmother with "a bloody stump where her right hand should have been." The longer story "The Company of Wolves" gives Red Riding Hood a more feminist reading.[18] Although the wolf eats grandma completely, the "wise child" does not flinch when she reaches grandmother's house. Rather she strips for the wolf. "The firelight shone through the edges of her skin," writes Carter; "now she was clothed only in her untouched integument of flesh." And when the wolf roars "All the better to eat you with,"

> The girl burst out laughing; she knew she was nobody's meat.
> ... She ripped off his shirt for him.

And so the reader waits for the denouement, which is surprisingly gentle for what has threatened to be a tale of rape and carnage:

> ... All silent, all silent.

Midnight; and the clock strikes. It is Christmas day, the werewolf's birthday. . . .

See! sweet and sound she sleeps in granny's bed, between the paws of the tender wolf.

In a parallel tale, "The Tiger's Bride," Beauty approaches her beast in terror (and he is a real beast, carnivorous and stinking with piss), only to hear him purring. Then, in one of the most beautiful descriptions I know of sexual arousal — and, yes, of love — the tiger licks his bride into his own species and the story ends:

> And each stroke of his tongue ripped off skin after successive skin, all the skins of a life in the world, and left behind a nascent patina of shiny hairs. My earrings turned back to water and trickled down my shoulders; I shrugged the drops off my beautiful fur.

Carter's werewolves and metamorphoses are clearly heirs both to Ovid's and to Marie's. Like Marie's, Carter's stories deal with sexual fulfillment and betrayal, although hers are more overtly erotic. Like Ovid's, her werewolves eat people, although anthropophagy in her tales is usually also the identity violation of rape whereas Lycaon's cannibalism is also impiety — the ontological violation of the boundary between human and god. (Is there a hint of this in Carter's suggestion that Christmas — the day of Christian metamorphosis of god to human — is the werewolf's birthday?[19]) Some of Carter's metamorphoses are unidirectional, like Lycaon's; others involve reversals, some of them salvific, like Bisclavret's. Most important for my purposes is Carter's clear sense — paralleling Marie's and Ovid's — that skin both *overclothes* and *is*. The "wise child" wears her own virgin skin, through which the firelight shines. Using the Latinate word "integument," which possessed in Marie de France's day the technical definition of "a story which covers and conveys meaning," Carter writes: "now she was clothed only in her untouched integument of flesh."[20] The "wise child" flaunts the nakedness of which the bisclavret was ashamed, but that naked skin *is* as well as *covers* self. Has she realized or lost a skin-self, been devoured, raped, or sexually fulfilled? What lies there when "she" (but it is, Carter insists, "she") sleeps in the arms of a wolf?

"The Tiger's Bride" makes identity fluid in similar ways. Like Lycaon, the bride becomes a beast. But vestiges, marks, remain. What is in one line a patina of hairs (still a human term) is in the next fur (an animal term); but an "I" still speaks, and even as the earrings drip away, the beauty of "my" skin-hair-fur perdures. Like the grandmother with her bloody stump, the bride carries something through species change. Enchanted, aroused, and decidedly uncomfortable, we readers wonder: Who, or what, is the tiger's bride?

Metamorphosis and Identity

And so we have three tales of metamorphosis, Ovid's, Marie's, and Carter's. But how, you may ask, do they help us think about identity? These stories seem to be about exactly the opposite — not identity but loss. Moreover, they seem, on the surface at least, preposterous, even offensive — the taste of other eras, which enjoyed the surely politically incorrect spectacle of women turned into trees or raped by wolves or carrying into future generations a facial deformity we would be inclined to blame on an unforgiving, even bestial husband. Even if Carter's Beauty is sometimes saved from the beast by her mother or Red Riding Hood stands up to the wolf, we may feel that these are hardly myths for our time.

I suggest that we think again. For these stories are not as preposterous as they first seem. We are surrounded, as even medieval commentators on Ovid knew, by metamorphosis. We do see change of species; we grapple with change of self. Caterpillars turn into butterflies; dead sticks flower in springtime; beloved children change into killers when schizophrenia erupts; healthy cells become cancer; people die.[21] Change is a staggering fact — one ancient philosophers struggled to explain. It is possible to argue that the great intellectual breakthrough of the centuries before Ovid was that of Aristotle, whose fundamental contribution to Western culture was to speak of what he called generation and corruption — coming to be and passing away — as not mere fluctuations of appearance, the adding and subtracting of qualities or "skins," but the replacement of one existing substance by another. Real change.[22] Without it there is no story; nothing happens. Aristotle the biologist knew that the chicken really replaces the egg; Aristotle the aesthetician knew that, in tragedy, the fortunes of the hero really reverse.[23] If change is not real, Lycaon's howls do not move us, nor is the bisclavret really trapped, speechless, in wolfhood by his wife's betrayal.

And yet there is no story if there is only change. If something does not continue, we have only discrete vignettes, a point the modern writer H.H. Munro (Saki) plays with in his story "The She-Wolf," where a group of bored society people are tricked into accepting metamorphosis by the rather crude substitution of a wolf for a woman in a conservatory. The story falls completely flat — which is perhaps, given the frisson of horror he evokes in other werewolf stories, exactly Saki's point.[24] If we see a tyrant in one frame, a shaggy wolf in the next, a running woman at one moment, and at the next a laurel tree, we are (unless we are environmentalists) unmoved and uninterested; there is no story. No matter how majestic or beautiful, a tree is only a tree. The horror and pain come because the wolf was (is?) Lycaon, the tree was (is?) Daphne. And I say "was (is?)" because there is no "was" for wolf or tree unless there is an "is." Unless the story is carried in some way in the present body or shape, we do not know what it was.[25] Hence the body carries the story. Lycaon's hair is still the same shaggy gray; the tiger's bride has her beautiful fur; even the bisclavret, although his appearance is completely undescribed, carries in his doglike comportment the knight's devotion to sovereign, as his wife carries in her face to future generations the story of betrayal.

As students of folklore and comparative religion tell us, there are profound differences between cultures in stories of metamorphosis or shape-shifting; nor are all such stories in the Western tradition the same.[26] Even Marie and Angela Carter, drawing on European werewolf traditions that go back in part to Ovid or Ovid's sources, do not tell the same story or take the same stance toward metamorphosis. Indeed, if we consider the two poles I just discussed — change and continuity — Marie, at least in an ontological sense, stresses continuity (a human seems to remain under the skin), whereas Angela Carter and Ovid push toward change.

Moreover, the contrast appears even starker if we embed the stories in their historical contexts. The whole range of metamorphoses in Ovid is situated in a Pythagoreanism that views all of nature as perpetual transformation and return: "nothing perishes in the whole universe; it does but vary and renew its form" (*Metamorphoses* 15. 254–55).[27] Orthodox Christian theologians in the Middle Ages rejected with horror the metempsychosis (or transmigration of souls from one body to another at death — certainly a form of shape-shifting) that Ovid used in book 15 of the *Metamorphoses* as a sort of frame and culmination for his sense of eternal change. In fact, theorists in Marie's day resisted metamorphosis so profoundly, even as an image, that they felt reading such stories was heretical.[28] Some twelfth-century people feared the ravages of actual werewolves; others were convinced that dissidents taught metempsychosis as a way of undermining the burial practices of ordinary pious folk; still others deplored the titillation or ontological scandal proffered by stories that suggested moral or metaphysical breaching of the boundary between animal and human.[29] The special-effects departments of Hollywood have no such qualms. Cinematographers compete to raise images of hybrids and metamorphosis to new heights of realism and horror, perhaps because today's viewers often react only to the technical skill or aesthetic impact, disregarding any implications for ontology.[30]

Nonetheless, despite the obvious contrast between ancient and modern embrace of the shape-shifting motif, on the one hand, and medieval resistance to it, on the other, stories in the European werewolf tradition are not fundamentally contradictory: all imagine a world characterized by both flux and permanence; all confront both the promise and the horror of change. Medieval thinkers struggled to explain, not erase, the metamorphoses of marvel, magic, and miracle: the change of chrysalis to butterfly in the world around them, of Lot's wife to salt in the stories of their holy scripture, of wine to blood in the central ritual of the Christian tradition. Indeed, Marie, surrounded by theorists suspicious of metamorphosis, makes in her oeuvre a more optimistic use of shape-shifting to express human potential and desire than either Ovid or Angela Carter.[31] Nor do Carter and Ovid see only change. The point made by Ovid's Pythagoras in book 15 of the *Metamorphoses* is not only that the energy of the universe perdures but also that it is a *self* that is reincarnated in many shapes. We must not forget that the historical Pythagoras is supposed to have remembered his former lives — surely a radical claim to continuity through metempsychosis. And Angela Carter's heroes and heroines often painfully resist change. In the last of her werewolf stories, "Peter and the Wolf," an intellectually gifted peasant boy who has grown up with wolf stories and has known a feral child, turns his back resolutely against metamorphosis, as he (the words are Carter's)

179

"tramps onwards into a different story." His last words upon leaving his peasant world forever behind are: "If I look back again . . . I shall turn into a pillar of salt." Metamorphosis here is trap.[32]

What, then, do we see in these stories of metamorphosis — stories that recur and recur in the Western tradition? Not a single meaning or message, not even a single definition of person or self. Stories don't give definitions. That is not how they work.[33] But I suggest we do find here a profound and powerful way of thinking about what we call "identity" in all its senses. I suggest that identity is what we find in these tales from Ovid, from Marie, from Angela Carter: the shape (or visible body) that carries story.

Shape and Story, Body and Narrative

Of course, both shape and story are complex notions — notions for which contemporary theory employs other, more freighted terms, in particular "body" and "narrative." It is in order to avoid the implications of structures, essences, ontologies often carried by these terms that I choose the simpler words "shape" and "story." But what I mean is not simple.[34]

By story I mean, as I said above, real change. In an Aristotelian sense, story involves *metabole*, the replacement of something by something else. Story spreads out through time the behaviors or bodies — the shapes — a self has been or will be, each replacing the one before. Hence story has before and after, gain and loss. It goes somewhere. Even if it is the story of repetition, or of salvation or destruction by a return whence it began, story has sequence.

Moreover, shape or body is crucial, not incidental, to story. It carries story; it makes story visible; in a sense, it is story. Shape (or visible body) is in space what story is in time. I thus prefer the ordinary word "shape," suggested by the theme of metamorphosis, rather than the now-popular concept "body" (whose ordinary associations seem to tie it too closely to the physiological and genetic) or the technical term "form" (whose medieval meaning makes it almost the opposite of body or matter).[35] The shape I speak of (Lycaon's wolf body, for example, or the bisclavret's dog-like comportment) encapsulates graphically and simultaneously the sequence, the before and after, of a self. But it can do this only paradoxically and partially, only in traces or vestiges, not fully. For what shape carries is story, and story is change; before must be (mostly) lost in order for there to be an after.

It should now be clear that the identity dealt with so complexly in the werewolf stories I have discussed is not an essence, an identity position, or even a personality. Indeed the shape of which Ovid, Marie, Saki, and Angela Carter speak is not either allegorical or mimetic. Although some later commentators read Ovid this way, he is not saying that Lycaon's essence is imitated or uncovered or revealed in his skin. None of these stories is, in modern jargon, essentialist.[36] None says we look like what we are. (*Bisclavret*, which comes the closest to speaking of under and over, inner and outer, does not speak of "looks like" at all.) None reduces us to an essence manifested (or hidden) in pigment or limbs, or allegorizes our bodies as signs of a characteristic or a character located within. Lycaon is not human greed symbolized by an animal; Carter's wild child is not a virgin soul or a virgin self or a virgin identity position manifested in translucent skin. As the literary critic Leonard Barkan says, shape matters; it matters too much to be only allegory or symbol.[37] Without it, there is no story, and hence no self. For my self is my story, known only in my shape, in the marks and visible behaviors I manifest — whether generic or personal. I am my skin and scars, my gender and pigment, my height and bearing, all forever changing — not just a performance, as some contemporary theory would have it, but a story.[38]

Hence identity is labile, problematic, threatening, and threatened. But metamorphosis is as much its guarantee as its loss. Like
Carter's peasant boy, we resist it, afraid we shall become a pillar
of salt, that our story will end in arbitrary change. But without
change, we have no story. All we can hope for is that the traces
of our story perdure in the body we are becoming. It is when
shape no longer carries story, when the traces or vestiges are completely erased, that identity is lost.[39] Narcissus is still in some
sense Narcissus as long as the flower bends to contemplate its
own image in the pond.[40] Lycaon is "still" Lycaon, even when his
"accustomed greed for blood" is turned toward sheep more than
men, as long as the "accustomed greed" and the fierce gray eyes
are "the same."

Metamorphosis in Dante

Perhaps I can better explain the complex way in which metamorphosis can carry identity if I turn, in closing, to a great work of the
Western canon, Dante's *Divine Comedy*.[41] I begin with one of the
most startling and dramatic — even brash — moments of self-consciousness and intertextuality in literature: the challenge to Ovid
in cantos 24 to 25 of the *Inferno*.[42]

In the eighth circle of hell, Dante the voyager meets five noble
thieves of Florence, some of whom first appear as reptiles, others
in human form. While Dante watches in horror, the human forms
merge with snakes and lizards, who have themselves before been
human. In the first of these metamorphoses (24.100–08), the
damned man, one Vanni Fucci, bitten at the neck by a great serpent, falls into a heap of ashes, which immediately resumes its
former shape. Dante audaciously compares this shape-shifting to
the phoenix (traditional Christian symbol of bodily resurrection),
which dies and is born again every five hundred years. Two more
thieves then merge with reptiles, who are themselves understood

by most commentators as metamorphosed thieves. The descriptions grow longer and more sexual, borrowing language from Ovid's story of the nymph Salmacis and the boy Hermaphroditus who fuse into a single bisexual being (*Metamorphoses* 4.356–88):

> If now, reader, you are slow to believe what I say, that will be no marvel, for I, who saw it, hardly allow it.
> As I was raising my brows toward them, a serpent with six feet threw itself on one of them and embraced him closely.
> Its middle feet it wrapped around his waist, with its forefeet it seized his arms; then it pierced both his cheeks with its fangs;
> its hind feet it spread along his thighs, and put its tail between them, extending it up along his loins:
> ivy never took root on a tree so tightly as the horrible beast grew vinelike around the other's limbs.
> After they had adhered to each other like hot wax and had mixed their colors, neither seemed what it had been
> . . . .
> Already the two heads had become one, so that two sets of features seemed mingled in one face, where two heads were lost.

Then Dante, in a well-established literary topos, flings down his challenge:

> About Cadmus and Arethusa let Ovid be silent, for if in his poetry he converts him into a serpent and her into a fountain, I do not envy him,
> for never two natures face to face did he transmute so that both forms were ready to exchange their matter.

What does Dante mean by this claim to have outdone Ovid at his own game of transmutation?

In one sense, of course, Dante is simply claiming to have described a more radical metamorphosis than Ovid — a change of one individual into another so total that the form-matter combination Dante understands as person is shattered in a way Ovid could not have imagined. But I think we can see here something else, without getting into the complexity (which is nonetheless surely relevant) of Dante's metaphysical categories.[43] For the metamorphosis of Dante's thieves, whether or not a literary advance on Ovid, is, in the terms I have been using, a complete loss of identity; shape does not carry story. It is story more than form that is erased. And story is erased not only because there are no traces left but also because the metamorphosis goes nowhere except to confusion. In an (to Dante) obscene parody of resurrection (hence the phoenix simile), the change from reptile to human goes on forever, but neither carries traces of the other. It is significant that later commentators must argue without decisive evidence (that is, without any identifying marks on the bodies) that the reptile in canto 25 line 50 is the same person (Cianfa) who disappears in line 43. This is thus a change in which identity does not endure. If the figure is Cianfa, "he" reemerges after a hiatus — something totally impossible to the natural world. Hence the metamorphosis is a parallel, although a corrupt, distorted, and unstable one, to the supra-natural return of resurrection.

So Dante's boast in *Inferno* 24–25 is that, in describing hell, he has produced a metamorphosis that outdoes Ovid's, one in which shape does not carry story. And if this were all Dante did with Ovid's poetry and his ideas, I might well have shown you merely that one of the most sophisticated passages in literature does *not* fit my theory of shape carrying story. That is, of course, not my point. Rather, I suggest that Dante employs metamorphosis where

no traces endure in a way that shows us the impossibility of identity perduring (in any logical sense) without the survival of vestiges of body or "shape."

Moreover, I use Dante to make a second point. For if we read
carefully, we must argue that Dante's true challenge, his best
claim, to rival his master Ovid rests not in the *Inferno* at all but
elsewhere. At the heart of both later segments of the poem — the
Purgatorio and the *Paradiso* — lies true Ovidian metamorphosis:
metamorphosis in which shape does carry self. That true Ovidian
metamorphosis is, of course, resurrection — as Dante's use of the
phoenix simile in the depths of hell broadly hinted.

In *Purgatorio* 24–25 (and it is no accident that these cantos
parallel exactly cantos 24–25 of the *Inferno*, where Dante challenges Ovid), the pilgrim asks why his physical fingers grasp only
air when he tries to embrace those he meets. In answer, the poet
Statius explains that souls generate aerial bodies in the afterlife as
embryos grow in the womb. Just as the account of the thieves in
Inferno 25 shows that loss of story, of sequence, is loss of self, so
Purgatorio 25 makes it clear that selfhood requires story-express-
ing shapes even in that period after death and before resurrection
when bodies are not necessitated by theological doctrine. Christians had, of course, been required since the second century to
adhere to the doctrine of the resurrection of the flesh, but that
tenet required the return of body only at the end of time. Dante's
poem sets himself to wander through the afterlife, as pilgrim,
before the Last Judgment. Hence the aerial bodies he gives his
shades are an innovation not required by theology, although they
are certainly suggested by the earlier European tradition of otherworld visions.[44] What Statius explains in canto 25 is not just how
and why all those technically disembodied souls Dante encoun-
ters appear as shades or aerial bodies but also the connection of
shape and recognizability — that is, the profound, yet also obvious,

connection of body and identity. The shades of heaven, hell, and purgatory unfold bodies out of their souls as the expression of their particularity, just as the evolving embryo expresses the soul that animates it.

Moreover, in cantos 22 and 30 of the *Paradiso*, where Dante asks to see souls as they truly are "with faces uncovered," the flower-souls he has encountered are suddenly transformed into the glorified and particular bodies of the resurrection. What souls unfold in the *Paradiso* are not just the aerial bodies of *Purgatorio* 25 — provisional shapes to carry story in that realm where no true shape can exist — but the real physical bodies that will return at Judgment. Yet there is true metamorphosis as well. After all, in the ethereal realm of pre-Last Judgment heaven, souls have been flowers and gems. It is only in the ultimate transmigration, resurrection, that soul regains its original shape — not in Ovid's eternal return but in a glorified state that is wonderfully new, although vestiges of the former self remain.

In one sense, then, just as he boasts, Dante outdoes Ovid in hell, by describing the eternal return of ashes to body to reptile to ashes, a metamorphosis with no perduring shape, no traces, no sequence, no story. But there where all boasts are forgotten — in paradise — Dante builds upon, yet also challenges, his great predecessor with the metamorphosis of resurrection: a metamorphosis in which the final shape, bearing traces of all that has unfolded before, is both radically changed *and* human. The balance of metamorphosis and continuity in Dante's *Paradiso* differs from that in Ovid's book 15, where there is also an apotheosis (that of Caesar to star). The differences are important; indeed they are in part Dante's point. But Dante clearly understood and used Ovid's metamorphosis. In defying Ovid and producing metamorphosis so total that identity is lost, he paradoxically underlines the Ovidian connection of shape and story as powerfully as he does in paradise, where glorified body expresses self. Thus the identities of Dante's *Commedia*, although understood in Scholastic terms of form and matter foreign to Ovid, are not so far from Ovid's, just as Angela Carter — for all her difference from Marie — is not so far from Marie's sense of skin and self as woven too closely together to be merely cover and core, disguise and essence.

Conclusion

It is now time to return where I began — with our modern woes and queries. And we are of course no closer than we were to answering the either-or questions of modern politics, or modern philosophy, or even modern television. I cannot tell you whether your race or gender is biologically given or culturally constructed, how far your sexual preference lies in your genes and hormones or in your education and your hopes. I cannot tell you whether you should erase some of your experience with cosmetic surgery or, like the bisclavret's wife, bear it no matter how unfair it may seem. Nor can I tell you whether you can or should be cloned and, if you are, whether your clone is you. But I can draw two conclusions.

First, these dichotomies of nature versus nurture, biology versus social construction, mind versus body, essence versus agency do not seem to me to give us the help we need to deal compassionately with ourselves or with others. In the complex decisions we must make as we gain and lose children, parents, lovers, friends, even the selves we thought we were, we need a sense of identity — identity as individuality, identity as group affiliation, identity as continuity — more labile and nuanced than these stark contrasts suggest. Who I am, who you are, is (as we all know at heart) seldom a matter of either-or.

Nor does the move to "both...and" help very much. For a hybrid, a "both...and," is often only a rather desperate — and

187

ultimately only rhetorical — effort to wiggle out of the trap of either-or we have fallen into. What we need to think with are not images of monsters and hybrids, creatures of two-ness or three-ness, stuck together from our own sense of the incompatibility of aspiration and situation, culture and genes, mind and body.[45] What we need are metaphors and stories that will help us imagine a world in which we really change yet really remain the same thing.

Second, the stories of the past, of the Western canon — great stories like those of Dante and Carter, Ovid and Marie de France — are worth studying, not least because they explore and comment on, elaborate and explode themselves. We cannot understand Dante and Marie unless we know Ovid, Ovid unless we understand Pythagoras; we will not grasp fully the intricate ways Carter or Saki disrupts our expectations at every twist of line and plot unless we know the entire European werewolf tradition and the Brothers Grimm. We read, however, not in order to understand the tradition (an academic enterprise) but in order to understand — through the tradition and its artful refigurings —ourselves. Behind these fantastic stories lie probing, parody, and evocation of that glorious, inexplicable, and (to postmodern eyes) totally improbable thing: identity.

For if my reading of these werewolf stories is persuasive, we have at hand images to think with that do not force us to choose between mind and body, inner and outer, biology and society, essence and agency. Rather, we are, as these odd old tales suggest, shapes with stories, always changing but also always carrying traces of what we were before. We are not Dante's thieves — a series of random shapes with no story. We are not the *garvalf* anticipated by Bisclavret's wife — a stereotypical pattern predicted by a generalized shape and tradition. But we are also not floating bundles of motives and memories without shape, separated souls without the aerial bodies Statius explains in the *Purgatorio*. Terrifying though it may be (but I hope I have shown that it is liberating as well), we are Bisclavret or the tiger's bride, really changing but bearing our story through the change and bearing it *out there in our bodies*, visible to others as well as to ourselves.

Indeed, I would suggest that we, as we reflect on the European tradition of metamorphosis, are like another of Ovid's transformations: Narcissus. For even if we gaze at our own reflection when we bow low over the pool of our literary past, that gazing is a mark of who we are, and who we are is, in part, what we have been.[46] The stories of our high tradition, like our folklore, are a significant component of what we think with. Hence our self-reflexivity, our tendency to study ourselves, is a mark of the self we carry with us as we bend over the pool. Our concern with how we can change yet be the same thing — our fascination with the question of identity in all its varieties — is inherited from our traditions. The identity we carry with us questions — and by questioning confirms — itself. In this sense, we are all Narcissus, as we are all also the werewolf, a constantly new thing that is nonetheless the same.

Afterword

In the fall of 1999, a friend of my daughter's began her first job in a high school in New Jersey. She teaches eighth-grade biology and physical science. Over supper with us a few weeks into the term, she described one of her first classes, which involved the simple experiment of heating baking soda in a test tube and observing the sudden appearance of water and something gas-like that displaces liquid in another tube. Excited by the students' reactions, she summarized their comments for us. "Ms. Baldwin, where did that come from? Did the baking soda just disappear, or did it, like, turn into something else? How did the water get there? Is that leftover white stuff baking soda? If not, where is the baking soda now?" This is the same question that, I would argue, excited many people in western Europe in the years around 1200 — a question not, of course, about baking soda but about the cosmos and the self.[1]

To say that our young friend's students worry about ontology — about change and the nature of things — is not to deny that they have other excitements, anxieties, and fears. They are thirteen. They worry about sex and gender roles, about families and friendship, about vocation and education, about God and evil; they undoubtedly fear insults and ostracism, acne and overeating, poor grades and lost homework assignments, more than change. And yet they manifest, through their excitement at the teacher's baking soda experiment, a fundamental curiosity about the world: Where does something go when it changes? Do things really change? Do we? The popularity of movies and TV shows about metamorphosis and monsters (for example, *Buffy the Vampire Slayer*, *Back to the Future*, *Star Trek*) attests to the same curiosity.

The argument of the essays collected here is that medieval discussions of werewolves and heretics, alchemy and cosmology express a similar concern. I argue not that medieval people worried about ontological problems in lieu of other anxieties but simply that they worried about ontological problems and that this worry has a history. Ways of conceptualizing change can themselves change.

Moreover, change, mutation, transformation are far more complicated notions than historians — even intellectual historians — have usually understood. Medieval discussions of *mutatio*, both explicit and implicit, are sophisticated, confusing, and enticing; they lure us below the surface of texts to deeper rhetorical strategies and philosophical assumptions. At the heart of such apparently disparate genres as epics and romances, hexaemeral commentaries, devotional literature, travelers' tales, theological discussions of demons, and treatises on minerals, fossils, and nutrition, the theme of *mutatio* throbs as the basic question about self and other.

The "change" I discuss in these essays elicited what I call in my first chapter a "significance-reaction" — a deep and burning sense that a particular event involves us in more than its specific details. To the historian William of Newburgh or the traveler Marco Polo, green children apparently born from the earth or the long-necked monster we call a giraffe pointed to something beyond themselves. That was what it meant to be a monster (*monstrum*): to point. To point to meaning, to ask for explanation. But explanation to a medieval writer could involve any of Aristotle's four causes, not merely efficient cause. In other words, an event or a being or an entity could be explained by what came before it sequentially and impelled it into action or being. But it could also be explained by what it was seen to be, its form or nature or definition (formal cause), or by the material that composed it (material cause), or by its *telos*, its purpose or destination (final cause). Any of these causes could be its significance or reason (*ratio*). Moreover, its significance could also be, in a more Platonic or Augustinian vein, its participation in the ultimate good or the way it signaled its origin as a vestige or footprint of God. The significance that instances of change seemed to demand was not simply a matter of finding regularity in the natural world, although regularity could be significant. But the *ratio* of an event or entity could also be moral, theological, or philosophical. Evolution, metamorphosis, or hybridity could point toward irrationality or transcendence as well as toward patterns of efficient causation.

To medieval writers, wonder was not merely a feeling of not understanding; it was a feeling of not understanding something significant, something that mattered. Hence the change, the wonder, triggered a search for *ratio*; and *ratio* always lurked just a little bit beyond the ordinary, the obvious explanation. Where does something go when it becomes something else? *Can* something become something else? Can *we*? How? What does it mean if we can? The powerful, funny, sophisticated, and awe-ful writings of Ovid, Bernard of Clairvaux, Marie de France, Gerald of Wales, and Dante indicate that the questions mattered enormously; they demanded answers.

I suggest that we still feel the same way.

Notes

INTRODUCTION: CHANGE IN THE MIDDLE AGES

1. On Gerald, see Robert Bartlett, *Gerald of Wales, 1146–1223* (Oxford: Clarendon Press, 1982). For the werewolf story, first recension, see the edition by John J. O'Meara in "Giraldus Cambrensis in Topographia Hibernie. Text of the First Recension," *Proceedings of the Royal Irish Academy* 52, sect. c.4 (1949), pp. 143–45. Later recensions are in Gerald of Wales, *Topographia Hibernica*, dist. 2, ch. 19, in J.S. Brewer, J.F. Dimock, and G.F. Warner (eds.), *Giraldi Cambrensis opera*, 8 vols., Rerum Britannicarum medii aevi scriptores 21 (London: Longman, 1861–1891; Kraus reprint, 1964–1966), vol. 5, pp. 101–107, quoted sections at pp. 104 and 106–107. The second recension was written before July 1189. See Chapter 2, nn.121–24 below.

2. The tendency to concentrate on the werewolf story rather than Gerald's later glosses has been stimulated in part by the fact that the readily available English translation of Gerald's *Topography* is of the first recension, not the later revised versions: Gerald of Wales, *The History and Topography of Ireland*, trans. John J. O'Meara (Harmondsworth, UK: Penguin Books, 1982).

3. See n.1 above. It may be that there are special precedents for this interest in types of change in the Irish culture Gerald encountered. Earlier texts in Irish survive that classify in quite technical ways and with imported Latin terminology the different denotations of *revolutio, metaformatio, suscitatio*, and such. See, for example, the seventh-century text *De mirabilibus sanctae scripturae*, known as

the Irish Augustine, cited by Marina Smith in "The Earliest Written Evidence for an Irish View of the World," in Doris Edel (ed.), *Cultural Identity and Cultural Integration: Ireland and Europe in the Early Middle Ages* (Portland, OR: Four Courts Press, 1995), p. 37, and the twelfth-century text "Tidings of the Resurrection," ch. 33, ed. Whitley Stokes, in *Revue celtique* 25 (1904), pp. 232–59, esp. pp. 250–51; see also the discussion of these texts in Chapter 2 nn.21 and 36 below. On "Tidings," see Benjamin Hudson, "Time Is Short: The Eschatology of the Early Gaelic Church," in Caroline Bynum and Paul Freedman (eds.), *Last Things: Death and the Apocalypse in the Middle Ages* (Philadelphia: University of Pennsylvania Press, 2000), pp. 101–23.

4. See Bartlett, *Gerald of Wales*; Joyce E. Salisbury, *The Beast Within: Animals in the Middle Ages* (New York and London: Routledge, 1994); and the works cited in Chapter 2, nn.75–77 and 125–28 below. Gerald discusses theories of eucharistic change in *Gemma ecclesiastica*, dist. 1, ch. 8, in Brewer et al. (eds.), *Opera*, vol. 2, pp. 25–28, but also without reaching a conclusion.

5. Peter of Poitiers (d. 1205) provides an example from the Schools: "There are however three kinds of change [*conversio*]. The first kind is when one substance [*substantia*] goes over [*transit*] into another so that the first, shaped by properties, is matter [*materia*] to the second. Thus an egg is said to be an animal in capacity [*potestate*] because it can be such through the operation of nature, and glass [Migne: *unitur*] from flint through the operation of artifice. And the second is when there is change [*mutatio*] of properties, as when the same substance has a variety of properties. Thus softness is put away and hardness taken up by decree, and stone [Migne: *panis*] is made, and thus the body of Lot's wife was changed into stone. And the third type of change is found here, when, that is, the substance of bread goes over into the substance of Christ, all the properties that were in the bread remaining." Peter goes on to consider whether the body of Christ is from (*ex*) bread as a statue is from bronze and decides against this. See *Sententiarum libri quinque*, bk. 5, ch. 12, in J.-P. Migne (ed.), *Patrologiae cursus completus: series latina*, 221 vols. (Paris: Migne, etc., 1841–1864) [hereafter PL], vol. 211, cols. 1246C–D and 1248D. For other examples of discussions of eucharistic change in the Schools that also consider theories of natural change,

see Hans Jorissen, *Die Entfaltung der Transsubstantiationslehre bis zum Beginn der Hochscholastik* (Münster: Aschendorf, 1965), esp. p. 37 n.105, p. 81 n.58, p. 107 n.154, pp. 136–37, p. 144 n.120.

6. In circa 200, Tertullian formulated the contrast similarly. To Aristotle, says Tertullian, "a thing that has changed ceases to be what it is and becomes something else"; but there is also a different conception of change, one in which "to be changed is to exist in a different form." Tertullian, *De resurrectione mortuorum*, ed. J.G.P. Borleffs, in *Tertulliani opera*, pt. 2: *Opera montanistica*, Corpus christianorum: Series latina (Turnhout: Brepols, 1954), ch. 55, pp. 1001–3, a work widely known in the twelfth and thirteenth centuries. Aristotle's conception of change, elaborated in *On Coming-to-Be and Passing-Away* (*On Generation and Corruption*) and the *Physics*, was directly known in the twelfth century only through the *Categories* (see n.7 below). Hence Aristotle was used more for classifying than for theorizing change until his understanding of substance was absorbed in the early thirteenth century. Although twelfth-century grammarians and theologians employed a number of different classifications of change (see Chapter 2, nn.55 and 88 below for examples), one frequent source was Guitmond of Aversa, *De corporis et sanguinis Christi veritate in eucharistia libri tres*, bk. 1, PL 149, cols. 1443C–44A. Guitmond gives four types of change; the third – of one substance into another – can be natural or miraculous, that is, either seed to grass or rod to serpent. (The examples are Guitmond's.) Another source for and stimulus to discussions of change was Peter Lombard, *Sententiae in IV libris distinctae*, 2 vols. (Grottaferrata: Collegium S. Bonaventurae ad Claras Aquas, 1981), bk. 4, dist. 11, ch. 1, vol. 2, p. 296.

7. This point was made for medieval thinkers by the axiom they often quoted as from Boethius: "omnis mutatio fit secundum aliquid commune." See Boethius, *Liber de persona et duabus naturis in Christo contra Eutychen et Nestorium*, ch. 6, PL 64, col. 1349D: "sola enim mutari transformarique in se possunt, quae habent unius materiae commune subjectum, neque haec omnia, sed ea quae in se et facere et pati possunt. Id vero probatur hoc modo: neque enim potest aes in lapidem permutari, nec vero idem aes in herbam...." The axiom expressed the Aristotelian idea that all change or motion is from contrary to contrary but

something must provide a connection. See Aristotle, *Categories*, ch. 14, trans. J.L. Ackrill in *Aristotle's Categories and De interpretatione* (Oxford: Clarendon Press, 1963), pp. 41–42; *On Coming-to-Be and Passing-Away (On Generation and Corruption)*, esp. bk. 1, chs. 3–4, trans. E.S. Foster, Loeb Classical Library 194 (Cambridge, MA: Harvard University Press, 1965), pp. 185–205; and *The Physics*, esp. bk 1, chs. 5, 8–9 and bk. 5, ch. 5, 2 vols., trans. Philip H. Wicksteed and Francis M. Cornford, Loeb Classical Library 228, 255 (Cambridge, MA: Harvard University Press, 1968–1970), vol. 1, pp. 50–58 and 82–96, vol. 2, pp. 60–68. To Aristotle, then, change presupposes both a process and an end or goal, a that-toward-which. See *Physics*, bk. 3, ch. 1, 201a, *ibid.*, vol. 1, pp. 194–98; and Sarah Waterlow, *Nature, Change, and Agency in Aristotle's Physics: A Philosophical Study* (Oxford: Clarendon Press, 1982), ch. 1.

8. Hugh of St. Victor, *De sacramentis*, bk. 1, pt. 6, ch. 37, in PL 176, cols. 285A–88A; see also *ibid.*, bk. 2, pt. 8, ch. 9, col. 468.

9. Otto of Freising, *Chronica sive historia de duabus civitatibus*, bk. 8, ch. 9, in Adolf Hofmeister (ed.), *Scriptores rerum Germanicarum in usum scholarum ex Monumentis Germaniae historicis separatim editi* (Hanover and Leipzig: Hahn, 1912), pp. 402–404. *Figura* here might also be translated as quality or appearance or even image.

10. See Chapter 2 nn.47–49 below.

11. On these themes, see Robert Javelet, *Image et ressemblance au douzième siècle de saint Anselme à Alain de Lille*, 2 vols. (Paris: Letouzey et Ané, 1967); Caroline Bynum, "Did the Twelfth Century Discover the Individual?" in *Jesus as Mother: Studies in the Spirituality of the High Middle Ages* (Berkeley: University of California Press, 1982), pp. 82–109; and the works cited in n.16 below. What I say here is not intended to deny the new and important stress on development in the twelfth-century romance.

12. Philip Lyndon Reynolds, *Food and the Body: Some Peculiar Questions in High Medieval Theology* (Leiden: Brill, 1999), passim and esp. pp. 1–66 and 407, and Joan Cadden, "The Medieval Philosophy and Biology of Growth: Albertus Magnus, Thomas Aquinas, Albert of Saxony, and Marsilius of Inghen on Book I, Chap. V of Aristotle's *De generatione et corruptione*, with Translated Texts of

Albertus Magnus and Thomas Aquinas" (Ph.D. diss., Indiana University, 1971). See also Chapter 2 at n.14 and Chapter 3 at nn.82, 83, 95, 96, 113.

13. See Chapter 2 nn.13, 52, 61–62, 100 below. Hugh of St. Victor, in the little treatise *De tribus diebus*, argued that the greatest marvel of all was the natural production of like by like; ch. 11, PL 176, col. 820. In the thirteenth century, Albert the Great used the principle of likeness to argue that, in miracles too, like produces like. When Christ healed the blind man, for example, he gave him an eye not an extra ear.

14. See Jorissen, *Die Entfaltung der Transsubstantiationslehre*, passim, and for the quotation from Magister Udo's Sentence Gloss, p. 28 n.70. See also David Burr, *Eucharistic Presence and Conversion in Late Thirteenth-Century Franciscan Thought*, Transactions of the American Philosophical Society 34.3 (Philadelphia: American Philosophical Society, 1984), pp. 1–15.

15. See n.7 above.

16. Karl F. Morrison, *Understanding Conversion* (Charlottesville: University Press of Virginia, 1992), pp. ix–xx. See also Denyse Delcourt, *L'Ethique du changement dans le roman français du XIIe siècle* (Geneva: Droz, 1990), pp. 29–30.

17. On alchemy and metamorphosis stories, see pp. 79–86, 92–98, and 105–109 above. On theories of growth, nutrition, and digestion, see Reynolds, *Food and the Body*; Cadden, "Medieval Philosophy and Biology of Growth"; and Michael Allyn Taylor, "Human Generation in the Thought of Thomas Aquinas: A Case Study on the Role of Biological Fact in Theological Science" (Ph.D. diss., Catholic University of America, 1982). On annihilation theory in eucharistic theology, see Jorissen, *Die Entfaltung der Transsubstantiationslehre*, pp. 24–50.

18. See n.6 above. The interpretation that sees the change between the twelfth and thirteenth centuries as the result of western Europe's acquiring of Aristotle is a standard one; see, for example, Fernand van Steenberghen, *Aristotle in the West: The Origins of Latin Aristotelianism*, trans. Leonard Johnston (Louvain: E. Nauwelaerts, 1955). Marie-Dominique Chenu, *La Théologie au douzième siècle* (Paris: J. Vrin, 1957), gives a different account, in which the discovery of

Aristotle is more result than cause, but the emphasis remains nonetheless on intellectual sources. Recent work places more emphasis on social, political, and psychological causes. See the works cited in n.21 below.

19. For two rather different statements of why this mattered philosophically, see Chapter 4 n.22 and Afterword n.1 below. Reynolds, *Food and the Body*, remarks (p. 407): "We, like most Christian thinkers before the thirteenth century, tend to regard substances as arrangements of atoms, and this perspective places the conservation of matter in the foreground (so much so, indeed, that we tend to reduce substantial change to accidental change). Aristotle, on the contrary, regards the terms of generation and corruption as the being and non-being of something. Something that did not exist comes into being, while something that existed passes away."

20. Texts can also, of course, be sought and used merely for reasons of prestige and with little understanding of their content; but the complicated engagement of a variety of early thirteenth-century discourses with Aristotle makes it clear that such was not the case here.

21. See, for example, R.I. Moore, *The Formation of a Persecuting Society: Power and Deviance in Western Europe, 950–1250* (Oxford: Basil Blackwell, 1987); Robert Bartlett, *The Making of Europe: Conquest, Colonization, and Cultural Change, 950–1350* (London: Allen Lane, 1993); and Dyan Elliott, *Fallen Bodies: Pollution, Sexuality, and Demonology in the Middle Ages* (Philadelphia: University of Pennsylvania Press, 1999). Brian Stock, *The Implications of Literacy: Written Language and Models of Interpretation in the Eleventh and Twelfth Centuries* (Princeton, NJ: Princeton University Press, 1983), pp. 472–99 and 522–27, sees the increasing role of texts and hence of hermeneutics as crucial in the awareness of change.

22. See pp. 147–58 above. The virulent polemic among religious orders I discussed in "Did the Twelfth Century Discover the Individual?" is surely evidence of self-consciousness (and defensiveness) about choosing, as is the concern in twelfth-century canon law with defining "vow," "clerical status," the requirements for *transitus* from one religious order to another, and so on.

23. An example of this sort of "thinking about" choice, identity, and bound-

aries through carefully deployed images of metamorphosis — inconceivable a hundred years earlier — is found in Marie de France's *Yonec*, in which a young knight becomes a bird to reach his unhappily married lover but a man to receive the Eucharist (itself, of course, a metamorphosis) with her.

24. We find such hesitation about replacement even in eucharistic theology, where the thirteenth-century resolutions of earlier questions were not just a matter, as is often said, of acquiring a real understanding of Aristotelian substance. Annihilation theory was rejected not only because it was a misunderstanding of "substance" (see Thomas Aquinas, *In Quattuor libros senteniarum*, bk. 4, dist. 11, q. 1, art. 2, in Robert Busa [ed.], *S. Thomae Aquinatis opera omnia*, 7 vols. [Stuttgart and Bad Cannstatt: Friedrich Frommann, 1980], vol. 1, pp. 475–76) but also because theologians wanted a tight connection — in Boethius's words "something common" — between the corporeality of bread and of Christ. See Innocent III's treatise (from about 1198) *Mysteriorum evangelicae legis et sacramenti eucharistiae libri sex*, bk. 4, ch. 20, PL 217, col. 870D, which insists that the change in question is not "secundum unionem" but "secundum transitionem" — a real change, not an adding on. The bread does not, however, "go into nothing or cease to be." For an overview of later positions, see Burr, *Eucharistic Presence and Conversion*, esp. pp. 1–7 and 99–107.

25. See nn.5 and 6 above and Chapter 2 n.14 below.

26. For references to recent scholarship on marvels as alterity, see Caroline Walker Bynum, "Miracles and Marvels: The Limits of Alterity," in *Vita Religiosa im Mittelalter: Festschrift für Kaspar Elm zum 70. Geburtstag* (Berlin: Duncker and Humblot, 1999), pp. 800–17, and Chapter 1 nn.5–6 and 8–9 below.

27. See Chapters 3 and 4, esp. Chapter 3 n.83.

28. M.M. Bakhtin, *The Dialogic Imagination: Four Essays*, ed. Michael Holquist, trans. Caryl Emerson and Michael Holquist (Austin: University of Texas Press, 1981), pp. 70–82 and 111–18.

29. For an explanation of this point in Ovid's *Metamorphoses*, see Charles Segal, "Ovid's Metamorphic Bodies: Art, Gender, and Violence in the *Metamorphoses*," *Arion* 5 (1997), pp. 9–41.

30. Chapter 3.

31. Chapter 4. And see Warren Ginsberg, "Ovid and the Problem of Gender," in Marilynn R. Desmond (ed.), *Mediaevalia: A Journal of Medieval Studies* 13 (1989, for 1987): *Ovid in Medieval Culture: A Special Issue*, pp. 9–28; and Leonard Barkan, *The Gods Made Flesh: Metamorphosis and the Pursuit of Paganism* (New Haven, CT: Yale University Press, 1986). For an interpretation of modernist metamorphosis that sees it as chaos — and yet nonthreatening because unreal — see the provocative essay by James Trilling, "The Flight from Enchantment: Ornament as a Threat to Reason and Reality," *Yale Review* 86.2 (1998), pp. 81–103.

32. For the contrast, see Wendy Doniger O'Flaherty, introduction to *Hindu Myths: A Sourcebook*, ed. and trans. Wendy Doniger O'Flaherty (Harmondsworth, UK: Penguin, 1975); *eadem, Women, Androgynes, and Other Mythical Beasts* (Chicago: University of Chicago Press, 1980); and James P. Carse, "Shape-Shifting," in Mircea Eliade (ed.), *Encyclopedia of Religion* (New York: Macmillan, 1987), vol. 13, pp. 225–29. Indian myths of ever-shifting figures, consuming and being consumed, make it clear that hybrids and shape-shifters, when considered in cross-cultural perspective, are usually *not* images of perduring identity. Moreover, the strict caste system that is the Indian context for such images of self-transformation and transgression suggests that there is no simple mirroring of social structure in image. A great deal of anthropological interpretation has made it a truism that images of chaos and lability often proliferate in strongly hierarchical cultures and express resistance to them. For an example of shape-shifters in Western folk material, see the ghost stories collected by the monk of Byland about 1400, in M.R. James, "Twelve Medieval Ghost Stories," *English Historical Review* 37 (1922), pp. 413–22. It is too simple, however, to see folk culture as resisting, high culture as supporting, an individualized self; see Chapter 2 n.67 below.

33. Doniger points out that in India, for example, there is no (Western) sense of the self as "like an artichoke with a core"; rather, the self peels away, like an onion, and nothing is left. Indians have, she argues, "come to terms with their impermanence." See Wendy Doniger O'Flaherty, *Other People's Myths: The Cave of Echoes* (New York: Macmillan, 1988), pp. 72–73. Her reading of Hindu meta-

morphosis stories is nonetheless not very different from my interpretation of metamorphosis in Chapter 4. See *ibid.*, pp. 77–79.

34. There is, for instance, a recent, lengthy study of beards; see Giles Constable, introduction to *Apologiae duae: Gozechini epistola ad Walcherum: Burchardi, ut videtur, Abbatis Bellevallis Apologia de barbis*, ed. R.B.C. Huygens, Corpus christianorum: continuatio mediaevalis 62 (Turnhout: Brepols, 1985), pp. 47–150. For some remarks on relating current issues to the medieval past, see my "Why All the Fuss About the Body? A Medievalist's Perspective," *Critical Inquiry* 22 (Autumn 1995), pp. 27–31.

35. See Chapter 2, at nn.121–26, and Chapter 3, at nn.114–17 and 122 above.

36. Since I wrote these essays, I have done more detailed work on theories of *mutatio* in the eucharistic debates of the eleventh to thirteenth centuries as well as on the parallel debates over the relics of Christ. Some of this work will appear as "Das Blut und die Körper Christi im Mittelalter: Eine Asymmetrie" in *Vorträge aus dem Warburg-Haus* (Hamburg: Akademie Verlag).

Chapter One: Wonder

1. This chapter was delivered as my presidential address for the American Historical Association on January 3, 1997, in New York City. I would like to thank Arnold Davidson, John Martin, and Pamela Smith for stimulating conversations that suggested the topic. I would also like to thank Lorraine Daston, Jeffrey Hamburger, Katharine Park, Edward Peters, and Stephen D. White for generously sharing their unpublished work, Joel Kaye, Dorothea von Mücke, and Guenther Roth for thoughtful readings, Kathy Eden for advice about Renaissance literary theory, and Philippe Buc and Jennifer Howard for help with the photographs. Marino is quoted in James V. Mirollo, "The Aesthetics of the Marvelous: The Wondrous Work of Art in a Wondrous World," in Joy Kenseth (ed.), *The Age of the Marvelous* (Hanover, NH: Hood Museum of Art, Dartmouth College, 1991), p. 61. Marino was speaking of poets.

2. Stephen Spender, *The Year of the Young Rebels* (New York: Vintage Books, 1969), p. 42.

3. Patricia Nelson Limerick, "Turnerians All: The Dream of a Helpful

History in an Intelligible World," *American Historical Review* 100 (June 1995), pp. 697–716, esp. pp. 704–12. For the same point made by an anthropologist, see Sherry B. Ortner, "Resistance and the Problem of Ethnographic Refusal," *Comparative Studies in Society and History* 37 (1995), pp. 173–93; her phrase for the danger is "thinning culture."

    4. John E. Toews, "Intellectual History After the Linguistic Turn," *American Historical Review* 92 (October 1987), pp. 879–907, esp. p. 906.

    5. For example, Stephen Greenblatt, *Marvelous Possessions: The Wonder of the New World* (Chicago: University of Chicago Press, 1991); Lorraine Daston and Katharine Park, *Wonders and the Order of Nature, 1150–1750* (New York: Zone Books, 1998); and Kenseth, *Age of the Marvelous*. In what follows, I have been greatly assisted and instructed by Daston and Park's magisterial study; I differ from them above all in including miracles and portents in my discussion of wonder.

    6. According to Todorov, "the marvelous" is a genre in which characters accept the supernatural; in the "strange" or "uncanny," it is rationalized; in the "grotesque" or "fantastic," characters vacillate between natural explanation and acceptance of the supernatural as supernatural. See Tzvetan Todorov, *Introduction à la littérature fantastique* (Paris: Editions du Seuil, 1970), esp. pp. 28–62. Medievalists have disagreed about whether Todorov's categories should be applied to medieval works of the imagination. See, for example, Jacques Le Goff, "The Marvelous in the Medieval West," in *The Medieval Imagination*, trans. Arthur Goldhammer (Chicago: University of Chicago Press, 1988), pp. 27–44, esp. p. 34; Lucienne Carasso-Bulow, *The Merveilleux in Chrétien de Troyes' Romances* (Geneva: Librairie Droz, 1976), pp. 11–17; Francis Dubost, *Aspects fantastiques de la littérature narrative médiévale (XIIe–XIIIe siècles): L'Autre, l'ailleurs, l'autrefois* (Geneva: Slatkine, 1991), esp. pp. 3–29. I have more sympathy with those such as Francis Dubost who argue that we can use modern critical notions of response and framing to identify a medieval "fantastic" than with those who would rule such analysis inappropriate. When Paul Freedman suggests that work in medieval cultural history divides between presentism and a taste for the grotesque, he has in mind the ordinary language

usage of "grotesque," not the one under discussion in literary theory; "The Return of the Grotesque in Medieval Historiography," in Carlos Barros (ed.), *Historia a Debate: Medieval* (Santiago de Compostela: Historia a Debate, 1995), pp. 9–19.

7. Wallace K. Ferguson, in *The Renaissance in Historical Thought: Five Centuries of Interpretation* (Boston: Houghton Mifflin, 1948), called the efforts of medievalists to recapture the idea of renaissance for various medieval cultural revivals "the revolt of the medievalists"; see pp. 329–85.

8. See, for example, Ronald C. Finucane, *Appearances of the Dead: A Cultural History of Ghosts* (London: Junction Books, 1982); Claude Kappler, *Monstres, demons et merveilles à la fin du moyen âge* (Paris: Payot, 1980); Claude Lecouteux, *Les Monstres dans la pensée médiévale européenne: Essai de présentation* (Paris: Presses de l'Université de Paris-Sorbonne, 1993); Michel Meslin (ed.), *Le Merveilleux: L'Imaginaire et les croyances en Occident* (n.p.: Bordas, 1984); Daniel Poirion, *Le Merveilleux dans la littérature française du moyen âge* (Paris: Presses Universitaires de France, 1982), esp. p. 82; Paul Rousset, "Le Sens du merveilleux à l'époque féodale," *Le moyen âge*, 4th ser., 62.11 (1956), pp. 25–37; Jean-Claude Schmitt, *Les Revenants: Les Vivants et les morts dans la société médiévale* (Paris: Gallimard, 1994); Pierre-André Sigal, *L'Homme et le miracle dans la France médiévale (XIe–XIIe siècle)* (Paris: Editions du Cerf, 1985); R.W. Southern, "The Place of England in the Twelfth-Century Renaissance," reprinted in *Medieval Humanism* (New York: Harper Torchbook, 1970), pp. 158–80, see esp. pp. 171–74; Benedicta Ward, *Miracles and the Medieval Mind: Theory, Record, and Event, 1000–1215* (Aldershot, UK: Scolar, 1982). Philippe Ménard, in "Le Monde médiéval: Les Curiosités profanes," in Meslin (ed.), *Le Merveilleux*, comments: "Le merveilleux a connu son âge d'or au XIIIe siècle" (p. 32).

9. Historians have tended to depict medieval enthusiasm for the marvelous either as extreme emotionality and credulity or as a site of resistance to clerical culture. Marc Bloch and Johan Huizinga, for example, characterized the Middle Ages as more "emotional" than modern times: Bloch, *Feudal Society*, trans. L.A. Manyon (Chicago: University of Chicago Press, 1961), p. 73; and Huizinga, *The Autumn of the Middle Ages*, trans. Rodney J. Payton and Ulrich Mammitzsch

(Chicago: University of Chicago Press, 1996), pp. 1–9. On this point, see Jean-Claude Schmitt, "'Façons de sentir et de penser': Un tableau de la civilisation ou un histoire-problème," in Hartmut Atsma and André Burguière (eds.), *Marc Bloch aujourd'hui: Histoire comparée et sciences sociales* (Paris: Editions de l'Ecole des Hautes Etudes en Sciences Sociales, 1990), 409–19; and Stephen D. White, "The Politics of Anger," in Barbara Rosenwein (ed.), *Anger's Past: The Social Uses of an Emotion in the Middle Ages* (Ithaca, NY: Cornell University Press, 1998), pp. 127–52, esp. p. 128. For magic, marvel, and folktale as resistance to elite culture, see Le Goff, "Marvelous," pp. 27–44; and Laurence Harf-Lancner, "La Métamorphose illusoire: Des théories chrétiennes de la métamorphose aux images médiévales du loup-garou," *Annales: Economies, sociétés, civilisations* 40.1 (1985), pp. 208–26. I am uncomfortable with the assumption that we can clearly distinguish popular and clerical cultures in the surviving documents. The phrase "le moyen âge qui baigne dans le merveilleux" is from Roger Caillois, *Images, images: Essais sur le rôle et les pouvoirs de l'imagination* (Paris: José Corti, 1966), p. 28.

10. I am using here something like the distinction suggested by Carol Z. Stearns and Peter N. Stearns between "emotionology" (formal psychological theories plus widely held and explicit values) and "emotions" (behavior and reactions), although I find the terminology awkward; see Stearns and Stearns (eds.), *Emotion and Social Change: Toward a New Psychohistory* (New York: Holmes and Meier, 1988), esp. p. 7. For recent work in the history of emotions, see n.58 below.

11. I have explained my own position on the complicated issue of presentism and the difference between responsible and irresponsible use of analogies from the past in "Why All the Fuss About the Body? A Medievalist's Perspective," *Critical Inquiry* 22 (Autumn 1995), pp. 27–31.

12. Paula Findlen, *Possessing Nature: Museums, Collecting, and Scientific Culture in Early Modern Italy* (Berkeley: University of California Press, 1994); Greenblatt, *Marvelous Possessions*; and Edward Peters, "The Desire to Know the Secrets of the World" (forthcoming). See also J.H. Elliott, *The Old World and the New, 1492–1650* (Cambridge, UK: Cambridge University Press, 1970); and Oliver Impey and Arthur MacGregor (eds.), *The Origins of Museums: The Cabinet*

of Curiosities in Sixteenth- and Seventeenth-Century Europe (Oxford: Clarendon Press, 1985).

13. The phrase from Columbus, which gave Edward Peters the title for his wonderful essay cited above, is found in Cesare de Lollis (ed.), *Scritti di Cristoforo Colombo*, 2 vols. (Genoa: L. Ferrari, 1892–1894), vol. 2, pt.1, p. 79. José de Acosta's statement comes from his *Historia natural y moral de las Indias*, 2nd ed., ed. Edmundo O'Gorman (Mexico City: Fondo de Cultura Económica, 1962), p. 112, quoted in Elliott, *Old World and New*, pp. 30–31.

14. See, for example, Daston and Park, *Wonders and the Order of Nature*; and Ward, *Miracles and the Medieval Mind*, pp. 6–8.

15. Thomas Aquinas, *On the Power of God*, 3 vols., trans. the English Dominican Fathers (London: Burns Oates and Washbourne, 1933), q. 6, art. 2, vol. 2, pp. 162–64; *De potentia Dei*, in Robert Busa (ed.), *S. Thomae Aquinatis opera omnia*, 7 vols. (Stuttgart and Bad Cannstatt: Friedrich Frommann, 1980), vol. 3: *Quaestiones disputatae*, p. 232.

16. Hence Francis Bacon, writing in 1605, would call wonder the "seed of knowledge"; see Bacon, *The Advancement of Learning and Novum Organum*, intro. J.E. Creighton (New York: Colonial Press, 1899), p. 4. Bacon also said (p. 5): "the contemplation of God's works produces knowledge . . . with regard to him; not perfect knowledge but wonder, which is broken knowledge." For major medieval figures in this tradition, see at n.33. Some scholars would date the tendency to rationalize the marvelous as far back as Adelard of Bath in the early twelfth century.

17. René Descartes, *The Passions of the Soul*, trans. S. Voss (Indianapolis, IN: Hackett, 1989), pt. 2, arts. 70 and 53, quotations at pp. 56–57 and 52, respectively.

18. *Ibid.*, art. 71, pp. 57–58. Compare the treatment in Albert the Great's commentary on Aristotle's *Metaphysics*; Albertus Magnus, *Metaphysica libri quinque priores*, ed. Bernard Geyer, bk. 1, tract. 2, ch. 6, in Albertus Magnus, *Opera omnia*, 37 vols., ed. Institutum Alberti Magni Coloniense (Münster: Aschendorff, 1951–), vol. 16, pt. 1, p. 23, which gives a physiological description of *admiratio*. J.V. Cunningham, *Woe or Wonder: The Emotional Effect of Shakespearean Tragedy*

(Denver, CO: University of Denver Press, 1951), pp. 79–80, and Greenblatt, *Marvelous Possessions*, pp. 81 and 176–77, have recently made much of this passage, but it is also important to note, as Daston and Park point out, that *admiratio* here is a kind of fear. See also Thomas Aquinas, *Summa theologica*, 3 vols., trans. the English Dominican Fathers (New York: Benziger, 1947), pt. 1 of pt. 2, q. 41, art. 4, vol. 1, pp. 766–67, and pt. 2 of pt. 2, q. 180, art. 3, vol. 2, pp. 1932–33.

19. See, for example, Rom Harré, "An Outline of the Social Constructionist Viewpoint," and Claire Armon-Jones, "The Thesis of Constructionism," in Rom Harré (ed.), *The Social Construction of Emotions* (Oxford: Blackwell, 1986), esp. pp. 2–3, 34, 40. For a neo-Darwinian and unabashedly reductionist interpretation, see John Onians, " 'I Wonder...': A Short History of Amazement," in John Onians (ed.), *Sight and Insight: Essays on Art and Culture in Honour of E.H. Gombrich at 85* (London: Phaidon, 1994), pp. i1–34.

20. Stephen Greenblatt, in his moving essay "Resonance and Wonder," in I. Karp and S.D. Lavine (eds.), *Exhibiting Cultures: The Poetics and Politics of Museum Display* (Washington, DC: Smithsonian Press, 1991), pp. 42–56, contrasts "wonder," or the power to stop viewers in their tracks, with "resonance," the evoking of cultural context. Although I am in sympathy with Greenblatt's valuing of both the particular and its context, I would suggest that his formulation of wonder is early modern, even Darwinian, and that a medieval understanding would include what he calls "resonance" in wonder.

21. Aristotle's *Poetics*, which might have stimulated such discussion, was virtually unknown until the fifteenth century. His *Rhetoric*, available in Latin after the mid-thirteenth century, was generally understood as a book of moral philosophy, not a guide to composition or preaching. It associated wonder with pleasure and desire, also with the unfamiliar and foreign (see bk. 1, ch. 11, and bk. 3, ch. 2); see James J. Murphy, *Medieval Rhetoric: A Select Bibliography* (Toronto: University of Toronto Press, 1971), p. 35; *idem*, introduction to *Three Medieval Rhetorical Arts*, ed. James J. Murphy (Berkeley: University of California Press, 1971), p. xv; and John O. Ward, "From Antiquity to Renaissance: Glosses and Commentaries on Cicero's *Rhetorica*," in James J. Murphy (ed.), *Medieval Eloquence: Studies in the Theory and Practice of Medieval Rhetoric* (Berkeley: Uni-

versity of California Press, 1978), p. 55. Giles of Rome's thirteenth-century commentary on the *Rhetoric* — one of the few to treat the entire work — pays only scant attention to the two crucial passages on wonder but does, in its brief treatment, stress the element of delight; see Aegidius Romanus [Giles of Rome], *Commentaria in Rhetoricam Aristotelis* (Venice, 1515; facs. reprint, Frankfurt: Minerva G.M.B.H., 1968), fols. 38v–39v and 92v.

22. Discourses can be distinguished by subject matter, by genre, by the institutional location of authors, and so on. I am using a combination of these factors. I have excluded the romance from consideration because the genre itself dictates a certain matter-of-factness of response, the analysis of which is a complex matter of literary interpretation; see the works cited in n.6 above, and Morton Bloomfield, "Episodic Motivation and Marvels in Epic and Romance," in *Essays and Explorations: Studies in Ideas, Language, and Literature* (Cambridge, MA: Harvard University Press, 1970), pp. 96–128.

23. Walter Map, *De nugis curialium: Courtier's Trifles*, ed. and trans. M.R. James, revised by C.N.L. Brooke and R.A.B. Mynors (Oxford: Clarendon Press, 1983).

24. In the medieval Germanic tongues (Anglo-Saxon, Old Frisian, Middle High German), the word is *wunder*, from the Indo-European *uen* (desire); in medieval Latin, the term is *admiratio*, whose root in Latin *mir* implies "seeing" (and goes back to an Indo-European word for "smile") and whose legacy in the Romance tongues gave French by the twelfth century the term *merveille* and Middle English a little later *marveyle*. See Le Goff, "Marvelous," pp. 27–29; Claude Lecouteux, "Introduction à l'étude du merveilleux médiéval," *Etudes germaniques* 36 (1981), pp. 273–90; Dubost, *Aspects fantastiques*, pp. 31–88; and James P. Biester, "Strange and Admirable: Style and Wonder in the Seventeenth Century" (Ph.D. diss., Columbia University, 1990), pp. 7–9.

25. Writing in the early thirteenth century, Caesarius of Heisterbach gave the classic definition of "miracle" in his *Dialogus miraculorum*, 2 vols., ed. J. Strange (Cologne: Heberle, 1851), dist. 10, ch. 1, vol. 2, p. 217: "What is a miracle? . . . We call a miracle whatever is done contrary to the usual course of nature [*contra solitum cursum naturae*], hence we wonder."

209

26. Aristotle, *Metaphysics*, trans. Hippocrates G. Apostle (Bloomington, IN: Indiana University Press, 1966), bk. A 983a, ll. 13-21, p. 16.

27. Augustine of Hippo, *De civitate Dei*, 2 vols., ed. B. Dombart and A. Kalb, Corpus christianorum: series latina 47, 48 (Turnhout: Brepols, 1955), bk. 21, chs. 8 and 4, vol. 2, pp. 771 and 761-63, respectively. (The example of lime had a long history already when Augustine used it.) For a later citation, see Gervais of Tilbury, *Otia imperialia*, in G.W. Leibniz (ed.), *Scriptores rerum Brunvicensium*, 3 vols. (Hanover: N. Foerster, 1701-1711), decisio 3, ch. 2, vol. 1, p. 961.

28. Augustine, *De utilitate credendi*, ch. 16, in *Augustini opera omnia*, in J.-P. Migne (ed.), *Patrologiae cursus completus: series latina*, 221 vols. (Paris: Migne, etc., 1841-1864) [hereafter PL], vol. 42, col. 90.

29. Anselm of Canterbury, *De conceptu virginali et originali peccato*, ch. 11, in Francis S. Schmitt (ed.), *Opera omnia*, 6 vols. (1940-1961; reprint, Stuttgart: Friedrich Frommann, 1984), vol. 2, pp. 153-54. Both this passage and Augustine's definition from *De utilitate credendi* are used by Aquinas, in *On the Power of God*, q. 6, art. 2, vol 2, pp. 162-64. The contrast went back to Plato; see Marie-Dominique Chenu, *La Théologie au douzième siècle* (Paris: J. Vrin, 1957), pp. 44-50.

30. See Aquinas, *On the Power of God*, q. 6, art. 2, vol. 2, p. 164; and *idem*, *De potentia*, in Busa (ed.), *Opera*, vol. 3, p. 232. And see n.25 above for Caesarius of Heisterbach.

31. B. Ward, *Miracles and the Medieval Mind*, pp. 3-32; John Hardon, "The Concept of Miracle from St. Augustine to Modern Apologetics," *Theological Studies* 15 (1954), pp. 229-57; and Bernhard Bron, *Das Wunder: Das theologische Wunderverständnis im Horizont des neuzeitlichen Natur- und Geschichtsbegriffs* (Göttingen: Vandenhoeck und Ruprecht, 1975), pp. 14-16. See also Eberhard Demm, "Zur Rolle des Wunders in der Heiligkeitskonzeption des Mittelalters," *Archiv für Kulturgeschichte* 57 (1975), pp. 300-44. By about 1200, a clear termi-nological distinction was emerging in Latin between *mirabilia* (wonders or mar-vels), *miracula* (miracles), and *phantasmata* (phantasms or fantasies), although the reaction *admiratio* was not limited to any single category of event. Somewhat later, the vernaculars came to sort out the terms also. For example, in the *Show-*

ings of the fifteenth-century mystic Julian of Norwich, there is a clear and consistent terminological distinction (although no consistency in the spelling of
terms) between miracle (*meracle*), which is done by God directly or through the
saints outside the ordinary course of nature, marvels (*marvelye, merveyle*), which
are mysteries or natural things of great significance, and phantasms or hallucina-
tions (*raving*), which are evil and false appearances owing to demons.

32. Natural causes may, however, be manipulated by demons or magicians
with God's permission; see Aquinas, *Summa theologica*, pt. 2 of pt. 2, q. 178, art.
2, vol 2, pp. 1925-26. This position allowed for a comfortable distinguishing of
magic and miracle while admitting — as theologians felt compelled to do on the
basis of scriptural evidence — that magic happened.

33. Nicole Oresme, *De causis*, ch. 1, in Bert Hansen (ed.), *Nicole Oresme and
the Marvels of Nature: A Study of His* De causis mirabilium (Toronto: The Pontifical Institute of Mediaeval Studies, 1985), pp. 160-63; for the quotations from
William of Auvergne's *De universo* and the pseudo-Albert's *Liber de mirabilibus
mundi*, see p. 51 n.3 and p. 61 n.36.

34. See, for example, Oresme, *De causis*, ch. 3, pp. 206-207, 210-13,
216-19, 222-23. In ch. 4, pp. 278-79, Oresme observes, "Who but God alone
knows in how many ways two sticks can be unequal?" And in his *Recapitulatio*,
pp. 360-61, he summarizes his argument thus: "[I]t is not necessary to have
recourse because of the diversity and marvelousness of effects [*diversitatem effec-
tuum et mirabilitatem*] to the heavens and unknown influence, or to demons, or
to our glorious God ... since it has been sufficiently demonstrated in the above
chapters that effects just as marvelous (or nearly so) are found here below."

35. On Roger Bacon's arguments concerning those who live without eating,
see my *Holy Feast and Holy Fast: The Religious Significance of Food to Medieval
Women* (Berkeley: University of California Press, 1987), p. 88; on the resurrection, see *The Opus Majus of Roger Bacon*, 2 vols., trans. R.B. Burke (Philadelphia:
University of Pennsylvania Press, 1928), pt. 6, vol. 2, pp. 617-25; on charms and
amulets, see pt. 3, ch. 14, and pt. 4, vol. 1, pp. 112-15, 409-11. On the Eucharist,
the magnet, the bent twigs, and the housefly, see pt. 7, vol. 2, pp. 820-22; pt. 6,
ch. 12, vol. 2, pp. 630-31; and pt. 1, ch. 10, vol. 1, p. 24, respectively. And see

Fratris Rogeri Bacon opus majus, ed. S. Jebb (London: William Bowyer, 1733), p. 474.

36. For Albert, see n.18 above. For Oresme on the physiology of pleasure and fear, see *De causis*, ch. 4, pp. 346–49.

37. Aquinas, *Summa theologica*, pt. 1 of pt. 2, q. 32, art. 8, vol. 1, p. 732; pt. 1 of pt. 2, q. 3, art. 8, vol. 1, pp. 601–602; pt. 3, q. 30, art. 4, reply to obj. 1, vol. 2, p. 2182; and pt. 3, q. 15, art. 8, vol. 2, p. 2111, respectively. Concerning Christ's wonder, he said: "Hence, if we speak of Christ with respect to His Divine Knowledge, and His beatific and even His infused knowledge, there was no wonder in Christ. But if we speak of Him with respect to empiric knowledge, wonder could be in Him; and He assumed this affection for our instruction, i.e. in order to teach us to wonder at what He Himself wondered at" (pt. 3, q. 15, art. 8, vol. 2, p. 2111).

38. On the claim of certain Scholastic authors to "de-wonder" remarkable phenomena by providing natural explanations, see Katharine Park, "The Topography of Wonder: *Admiratio* in Medieval and Renaissance Europe," Lecture for the University of Bielefeld, June 1993. She cites the phrase from the mid-sixteenth-century treatise *On the Variety of Things* by Girolamo Cardano. For a famous interpretation of twelfth-century wonder that sees it as focused exactly on the regularity of nature, see Chenu, *La Théologie au douzième siècle*, pp. 21–44.

39. André Vauchez, in his influential *Les Laïcs au moyen âge: Pratiques et expériences religieuses* (Paris: Editions du Cerf, 1987), esp. pp. 49–92, argued that medieval saints' lives shifted around 1150 from an emphasis on miracles and charismatic gifts (which were to be marveled at) to an emphasis on the virtues (which were to be imitated). He has since then (rightly, in my judgment) modified his argument to claim that both threads are present generally in medieval hagiography. See Vauchez, "Saints admirables et saints imitables: Les Fonctions de l'hagiographie ont-elles changé aux derniers siècles du moyen âge?" in *Les Fonctions des saints dans le monde occidental (IIIe–XIIIe siècle)* (Rome: Ecole Française de Rome, 1991), pp. 161–72. Particularly good on the wonder response to hagiographic accounts are Brigitte Cazelles, *Le Corps de sainteté d'après Jehan Bouche d'Or, Jehan Paulus, et quelques vies des XIIe et XIIIe siècles*

(Geneva: Droz, 1982); and Michel de Certeau, "Hagiographie," *Encyclopaedia universalis*, 20 vols. (Paris: Encyclopaedia Universalis France, 1968–1975), vol. 8, pp. 207–209. On miracles and saints generally, see Jaroslav Pelikan, *The Christian Tradition: A History of the Development of Doctrine*, vol. 3: *The Growth of Medieval Theology (600–1300)* (Chicago: University of Chicago Press, 1978), pp. 174–84.

40. For examples of the topos in medieval hagiography, see Richard Kieckhefer, *Unquiet Souls: Fourteenth-Century Saints and Their Religious Milieu* (Chicago: University of Chicago Press, 1984), pp. 13–14; and Bynum, *Holy Feast and Holy Fast*, pp. 85 and 336 n.82. On the topos of "fleeing the bad and imitating the good," see Gertrud Simon, "Untersuchungen zur Topik der Widmungsbriefe mittelalterlicher Geschichtsschreiber bis zum Ende des 12. Jahrhunderts," *Archiv für Diplomatik* 5–6 (1959–1960), pp. 94–112. In Renaissance aesthetic theory, the *imitatio/admiratio* contrast became a contrast between the verisimilar and the marvelous. See Biester, "Strange and Admirable"; Douglas Biow, *Mirabile Dictu: Representations of the Marvelous in Medieval and Renaissance Epic* (Ann Arbor: University of Michigan Press, 1996); Cunningham, *Woe or Wonder*; Baxter Hathaway, *Marvels and Commonplaces: Renaissance Literary Criticism* (New York: Random House, 1968); and Bernard Weinberg, *A History of Literary Criticism in the Italian Renaissance*, 2 vols. (Chicago: University of Chicago Press, 1961).

41. Augustine, sermon 280 on Saints Perpetua and Felicity, PL 38, col. 1281.

42. Kieckhefer, *Unquiet Souls*, pp. 13–14; and Bynum, *Holy Feast and Holy Fast*, pp. 85 and 336 n.82.

43. See, for example, Caesarius, *Dialogus miraculorum*, dist. 2, ch. 3, and dist. 6, ch. 6, vol. 1, pp. 63, 356.

44. See Bernard of Clairvaux, *De gradibus humilitatis et superbiae*, chs. 28–30, in Jean Leclercq, C.H. Talbot, and H.M. Rochais (eds.), *Sancti Bernardi opera*, 8 vols. (Rome: Editiones Cistercienses, 1957–1977), vol. 3, pp. 38–40; and Bernard, *Apologia*, ch. 29, in Conrad Rudolph, *The "Things of Greater Importance": Bernard of Clairvaux's Apologia and the Medieval Attitude Toward Art* (Philadelphia: University of Pennsylvania Press, 1990), app. 2, p. 282.

45. In addition to the sermons cited in nn.48 and 49 below, see Bernard of Clairvaux, *Vita sancti Malachiae episcopi*, in *Opera*, vol. 3, pp. 306–78; *De*

consideratione, bk. 5, sect. 13, chs. 27–32, in *Opera*, vol. 3, pp. 489–93; Fourth Sermon for the Vigil of the Nativity, vol. 4, pp. 220–28; Second Sermon for Christmas Day, vol. 4, pp. 251–56; Sermons for St. Benedict and St. Martin, vol. 5, pp. 1–12, 399–412; and the Sermon for St. Andrew, vol. 6, pp. 144–49.

46. Hugh of St. Victor, *De institutione novitiorum*, ch. 7, PL 176, cols. 932–33. On Suso, see Jeffrey Hamburger, "Medieval Self-Fashioning: Authorship, Authority, and Autobiography in Suso's *Exemplar*," in *The Visual and the Visionary: Art and Female Spirituality in Late Medieval Germany* (New York: Zone Books, 1998), pp. 233–78. On *imitatio* generally, see Robert Javelet, *Image et ressemblance au douzième siècle de saint Anselme à Alain de Lille*, 2 vols. (Paris: Letouzey et Ané, 1967); and Giles Constable, "The Ideal of the Imitation of Christ," in *Three Studies in Medieval Religious and Social Thought: The Interpretation of Mary and Martha, The Ideal of the Imitation of Christ, The Orders of Society* (Cambridge, UK: Cambridge University Press, 1995), pp. 143–248.

47. The best place to see this assumption is in Bernard of Clairvaux's *De gradibus*, chs. 1–9, in *Opera*, vol. 3, pp. 16–37, and Bernard, *De diligendo Deo*, in *Opera*, vol. 3, pp. 119–54. For a stimulating interpretation of the medieval sense of alterity that differs from my own, see Karl F. Morrison, *"I Am You": The Hermeneutics of Empathy in Western Literature, Theology, and Art* (Princeton, NJ: Princeton University Press, 1988).

48. Bernard of Clairvaux, First Sermon for St. Victor, in *Opera*, 6, pp. 30–31.

49. See Bernard of Clairvaux, Third Sermon for the Vigil of the Nativity, in *Opera*, vol. 4, pp. 211–19, esp. pp. 216–17.

50. Map, *De nugis,* dist. 1, ch. 24, p. 80.

51. As, for example, in Map, *De nugis*, dist. 1, ch. 31, pp. 126–28.

52. William of Newburgh, *Historia rerum Anglicarum*, 2 vols., ed. Richard Howlett, Rerum Britannicarum medii aevi scriptores 82, pts. 1–2 (1884–1885; reprint, Wiesbaden: Kraus reprint, 1964), bk. 1, ch. 27; bk. 2, ch. 19; bk. 4, ch. 6; and bk. 5, ch. 33, vol. 1, pp. 82–84, 147–48, 307–308, and vol. 2, pp. 497–99. See also Nancy Partner, *Serious Entertainments: The Writing of History in Twelfth-Century England* (Chicago: University of Chicago Press, 1977), ch. 2.

53. Gervais, *Otia imperialia*, decisio 3, preface and chs. 42 and 92, pp. 960–61, 974–75, 991. There is discussion of Gervais and a French translation of book 3 of the *Otia imperialia* in Gervais of Tilbury, *Le Livre des merveilles: Divertissement pour un empereur (Troisième partie)*, trans. Annie Duchesne, preface by Jacques Le Goff (Paris: Les Belles Lettres, 1992).

54. Gervais, *Otia imperialia*, decisio 3, ch. 10, p. 963.

55. John of Salisbury, *Policraticus*, ed. K.S.B. Keats-Rohan, Corpus christianorum: continuatio mediaevalis 118 (Turnhout: Brepols, 1993), ch. 22, p. 131: "cum admirationem ratio tollit et exemplorum inductio singularitatem excludat." For the transformation of water to wine as a speedup of natural processes, see ch. 12, pp. 91–92. (The argument went back to Augustine; see Chapter 2, n.61 below.) Although the explanation naturalizes the miraculous, John also speaks here of venerating and wondering at the richness of the wisdom of God.

56. James of Vitry, *Historia orientalis* (Douai, 1597; reprint, Farnborough, UK: Gregg International, 1971), pp. 215–16 (cited by Daston and Park, *Wonders and the Order of Nature*, p. 35); and *The Travels of Sir John Mandeville with Three Narratives in Illustration of It* (London, 1900; reprint, New York: Dover Press, 1964), ch. 22, p. 138. On the problems surrounding Mandeville's text, see Mary B. Campbell, *The Witness and the Other World: Exotic European Travel Writing, 400–1600* (Ithaca, NY: Cornell University Press, 1988), ch. 4. For Gosswin, see Lecouteux, *Les Monstres*, p. 11.

57. See "The Journey of William Rubruck," in Christopher Dawson (ed.), *Mission to Asia* (1955; reprint, Toronto: Medieval Academy of America, 1980), ch. 28, p. 150. And see Kappler, *Monstres*, p. 219. It is significant that William's account did not become very popular, probably because of its sober tone.

58. There has recently been debate in the fields of anthropology and history between the social constructivists and those who see emotional reactions as essentially psychobiological processes, with the victory going generally to the constructivists. Related to this is a debate over whether there is a universal core reaction to which we would refer with an emotion-word (for example, "anger"), whether or not a particular culture has a word translatable by our

"anger." See, for example, J.R. Averill, "A Constructivist View of Emotion," in Robert Plutchik and Henry Kellerman (eds.), *Theories of Emotion* (New York: Academic Press, 1980), pp. 305–40; Roy G. d'Andrade and Claudia Strauss (eds.), *Human Motives and Cultural Models* (Cambridge, UK: Cambridge University Press, 1992); Harré, "Outline of the Social Constructionist Viewpoint," pp. 2–14; Armon-Jones, "Thesis of Constructionism," pp. 32–56; Catherine A. Lutz and Lila Abu-Lughod (eds.), *Language and the Politics of Emotion* (Cambridge, UK: Cambridge University Press, 1990); and Shula Sommers, "Understanding Emotions: Some Interdisciplinary Considerations," in Stearns and Stearns (eds.), *Emotion and Social Change*, pp. 23–38. Although historians will, by training, tend to reject psychobiological reductionism, they do well to avoid complete constructionism as well, for it tends to leave them unable to make comparisons across cultures and language groups or even across time. The position called "chastened particularism" by my fellow medievalist William I. Miller seems to me the most satisfactory. Miller argues that "even in the absence of a specifically dedicated vocabulary," emotions that are "not completely congruent with ours" will nonetheless "bear sufficient points in common so that comparison, recognition, and rough mutual understanding are achievable." This seems to me a sensible assumption with which to conduct research. See William I. Miller, *Humiliation and Other Essays on Honor, Social Discomfort, and Violence* (Ithaca, NY: Cornell University Press, 1993), pp. 12–13.

59. Bernard, *Vita sancti Malachiae*, in *Opera*, vol. 3, p. 307; and see Sermon on St. Martin, in *Opera*, vol. 5, pp. 399–412, which, although it stresses that miracles are to be admired and virtues imitated, nonetheless treats miracles as sources of delight that move us toward imitation. For another example of miracles as a source of delight, see Reginald of Durham, *Life of Oswald*, bk. 1, ch. 44, in Thomas Arnold (ed.), *Symeonis monachi opera omnia*, 2 vols., Rerum Britannicarum medii aevi scriptores 75 (London: Longman, 1882–1885), vol. 1, pp. 369–70.

60. Luca Robertini (ed.), *Liber miraculorum sancte fidis* (Spoleto: Centro Italiano di Studi sull'Alto Medioevo, 1994). The stories really are quite funny; see, for example, bk. 4, chs. 21 and 28, pp. 255–56 and 263–66. And see Amy

G. Remensnyder, "Un Problème de cultures ou de culture? La Statue-reliquaire et les *joca* de sainte Foy de Conques dans le *Liber miraculorum* de Bernard d'Angers," *Cahiers de civilisation médiévale* 33 (1990), pp. 351–79.

61. Gerald of Wales, *Topographia Hibernica*, in J.S. Brewer, J.F. Dimock, and G.F. Warner (eds.), *Giraldi Cambrensis opera*, 8 vols., Rerum Britannicarum medii aevi scriptores 21 (London: Longman, 1861–1891; Kraus reprint, 1964–1966), dist. 1, ch. 16, vol. 5, p. 49: "naturae ludentis opera contulit admiranda." And see the second preface (for Henry II), vol. 5, p. 20: "et occultis natura ludit excessibus." On the bearded woman, see dist. 2, ch. 20, vol. 5, p. 107; on kingfishers, grasshoppers, and storks, see dist. 1, chs. 14–21, vol. 5, pp. 51–54.

62. Robert of Basevorn, *Forma praedicandi*, trans. L. Krul in Murphy (ed.), *Three Medieval Rhetorical Arts*, pp. 146–47. A number of scholars have pointed out that "wonder" in Tudor-Stuart England tended to include dread: see Cunningham, *Woe or Wonder*; and Biester, "Strange and Admirable."

63. Gerald, *Topographia Hibernica*, dist. 2, chs. 19–21, vol. 5, pp. 101–109. And see Harf-Lancner, "La Métamorphose illusoire," pp. 208–26. Isidore of Seville names the "wonderful" as one of five kinds of rhetorical cases and says that (as opposed to "honest cases," to which we agree immediately, and "humble matters," which we tend to ignore) the wonderful (*admirabile*) is that by which the spirit (*animus*) of the hearer is alienated (*alienatus*) or shocked; Isidore of Seville, *Etimologías: Edición bilingüe*, 2 vols., ed. J. Oroz Reta and M.-A. Marcos Casquero (Madrid: Biblioteca de Autores Cristianos, 1982), bk. 2, ch. 8, nos. 1–2, vol. 1, p. 370.

64. On mechanical devices, see Richard Kieckhefer, *Magic in the Middle Ages* (New York: Cambridge University Press, 1989); William Eamon, "Technology as Magic in the Late Middle Ages and the Renaissance," *Janus: Revue internationale de l'histoire des sciences, de la médecine, de la pharmacie, et de la technique* 70 (1983), pp. 171–212; and Merriam Sherwood, "Magic and Mechanics in Medieval Fiction," *Studies in Philology* 44 (1947), pp. 567–92. On food, see Bynum, *Holy Feast and Holy Fast*, pp. 60–61. The thirteenth-century theologian William of Auvergne described a "trick" that would make a house appear full of snakes; see Kieckhefer, *Magic*, 92.

65. C.N.L. Brooke, "Religious Sentiment and Church Design in the Later Middle Ages," *Bulletin of the John Rylands Library* 50 (1967), pp. 13–33; Peter Browe, *Die Verehrung der Eucharistie im Mittelalter* (Munich: Hueber, 1933); F. Baix and C. Lambot, *La Dévotion à l'eucharistie et le VIIe centenaire de la Fête-Dieu* (Gembloux: Duculot, 1964); Miri Rubin, *Corpus Christi: The Eucharist in Late Medieval Culture* (Cambridge, UK: Cambridge University Press, 1991).

66. See Joseph Braun, *Die Reliquiare des christlichen Kultes und ihre Entwicklung* (Freiburg: Herder, 1940), plates 73–81; and the works on museums cited in n.12 above.

67. *Abbot Suger on the Abbey Church of St.-Denis and Its Art Treasures*, 2nd ed., ed. and trans. Erwin Panofsky (Princeton, NJ: Princeton University Press, 1976), pp. 116–19. For another example of wondering at the beauty and richness of both the materials and the craftsmanship of art, see Theophilus, *The Divers Arts: The Foremost Medieval Treatise on Painting, Glassmaking, and Metalwork*, trans. J.G. Hawthorne and C.S. Smith (1963; reprint, New York: Dover, 1979), prologue to bk. 3, pp. 77–80. On wonder at craftsmanship, see Rudolph, "*Things of Greater Importance*," pp. 57–66. On attitudes toward relics, see Caroline Walker Bynum, *The Resurrection of the Body in Western Christianity, 200–1336* (New York: Columbia University Press, 1995), pp. 200–25, 318–29.

68. On mystical women, see Bynum, *Holy Feast and Holy Fast*; on beauty, see Carasso-Bulow, *Merveilleux in Chrétien*, pp. 16–17. Gerald of Wales marvels at animals — not all animals but those that behave in seemingly purposive ways; see nn.61 and 63 above and nn.70 and 81 below.

69. Aelfric, *The Homilies of the Anglo-Saxon Church: The Homilies of Aelfric*, 2 vols., ed. Benjamin Thorpe (1844–1846; reprint, New York: Johnson, 1971), vol. 1, pp. 184–86, 292, 304; and see Karen Louise Jolly, *Popular Religion in Late Saxon England: Elf Charms in Context* (Chapel Hill: University of North Carolina Press, 1996), pp. 82–85. See also Bernard, *De consideratione*, bk. 5, sect. 13, chs. 27–32, in *Opera*, vol. 3, pp. 489–93, and First Sermon for All Saints, in *Opera*, vol 5, p. 330.

70. Gerald, *Topographia Hibernica*, dist. 2, ch. 41, in *Opera*, vol. 5, p. 126.

71. Marco Polo, *Milione: Versione toscana del Trecento*, ed. Valeria Bertolucci

Pizzorusso (Milan: Adelphi, 1994), chs. 176 and 189, pp. 276-78 and 294. And see the discussion in Campbell, *Witness and the Other World*, pp. 92-112.

72. The classic study is Rudolf Wittkower, "Marvels of the East: A Study in the History of Monsters," *Journal of the Warburg and Courtauld Institutes* 5 (1942), pp. 159-97; see also Richard Bernheimer, *Wild Men in the Middle Ages: A Study in Art, Sentiment, and Demonology* (Cambridge, MA: Harvard University Press, 1952); Lecouteux, *Les Monstres*; Kappler, *Monstres*; and Katharine Park and Lorraine Daston, "Unnatural Conceptions: The Study of Monsters in Sixteenth- and Seventeenth-Century France and England," *Past and Present* 92 (1981), pp. 20-54. On the relative appeal of various travelers' accounts, see Campbell, *Witness and the Other World*; and Greenblatt, *Marvelous Possessions*.

73. Walter of Châtillon, *The Alexandreis*, trans. R. Telfryn Pritchard (Toronto: The Pontifical Institute of Mediaeval Studies, 1986), bk. 8, ll. 374-90, pp. 190-91.

74. Peter the Venerable, *De miraculis libri duo*, ed. Denise Bouthillier, Corpus christianorum: continuatio mediaevalis 73 (Turnhout: Brepols, 1988), bk. 2, ch. 25, pp. 142-46; for the first account, see bk. 1, ch. 23, pp. 68-72. See also Denise Bouthillier and Jean-Pierre Torrell, "'Miraculum': Une Catégorie fondamentale chez Pierre le Vénérable," *Revue thomiste: Revue doctrinale de théologie et de philosophie* 80 (1980), pp. 357-86. On Roger Bacon, see n.35 above; on Caesarius, see n.43 above.

75. Map, *De nugis*, dist. 2, ch. 4, p. 136. And compare the passage cited at n.50 above.

76. *A Book of Showings to the Anchoress Julian of Norwich*, 2 vols., eds. Edmund Colledge and James Walsh (Toronto: The Pontifical Institute of Mediaeval Studies, 1978), Long Text, chs. 49-52, pp. 505-53, esp. pp. 546-47 ("we haue in vs a mervelous medelur both of wele and of woo") and p. 548.

77. William of Newburgh, *Historia rerum Anglicarum*, bk. 1, ch. 28, pp. 84-87.

78. Isidore of Seville, *Etimologías*, bk. 11, ch. 3, nos. 1-4, vol. 2, p. 46: "Nam portenta dicta perhibent a portendendo.... Monstra vero a monitu dicta"; see also Oresme, *De causis*, ch. 3, p. 260 n.118.

79. To say this is not to argue that there was no conquest, appropriation, and exploitation in the Middle Ages, nor is it to forget that the "perspectivalism" of medieval travelers owes much to their limited ability to do anything other than gaze in wonder.

80. I have done a quick search through a large number of representations of key moments in Christian iconography that might be candidates for wonder: the Annunciation to Mary, Christ's Transfiguration, the Last Supper, Christ's Resurrection, the "Noli me tangere," the appearance to Thomas the Doubter, Christ's Ascension, Pentecost, the miracles of Christ and the saints, and Old Testament events such as the sacrifice of Isaac and the Burning Bush. Although some scholars have asserted that one can see a universal wonder-reaction in paintings such as Leonardo's *Last Supper*, the matter is exceedingly complicated, not only because a number of different gestures in art seem clearly to express roughly the same reaction to unusual events but also because the same unusual event seems to garner a wide range of different emotional responses according to the time and circumstance of depiction — from humble acceptance (even resignation) to terror (or even rage). It thus seems to me that the close parallels between sixteenth- and seventeenth-century painting and Le Brun's drawings of the emotions are more likely to reflect artists learning from psychological and anatomical theory than artists reproducing unmediated biological responses. In other words, the art suggests not physiological reductionism — as Darwin and his latter-day followers such as John Onians have argued — but rather cultural and extremely complex construction of emotional response. Merely to consult the array of depictions of the Annunciation, Transfiguration, and Ascension in a standard reference work such as Gertrud Schiller, *Ikonographie der christlichen Kunst*, 5 vols. (Gütersloh: Mohn, 1966–1980), shows what a wide range of hand gestures accompanies response to the unexpected — a response that is clearly not always what we would think of as wonder. It is also, however, significant that when the response does seem to be what we would think of as wonder, there is often some hand gesture (though not always the same one). See Figure 3.

81. Gerald of Wales and Vincent of Beauvais accepted the story that barna-

cle geese were born from trees in Ireland, although Albert the Great rejected it, saying that barnacle birds had been observed having sexual intercourse and laying eggs like other birds; see Lynn Thorndike, *A History of Magic and Experimental Science*, 8 vols. (New York: Macmillan, 1923–1958), vol. 2, pp. 464–65. The travelers' accounts of Sir John Mandeville and Friar Odoric of Pordenone used the marvel of the barnacle goose to justify the story of Eastern trees whose fruit contained lambs. See *Travels of Sir John Mandeville*, ch. 29, p. 174; and Kappler, *Monstres*, p. 62. See Figure 10.

CHAPTER TWO: METAMORPHOSIS, OR GERALD AND THE WEREWOLF

1. This chapter was originally delivered as my presidential address to the Medieval Academy of America on March 28, 1998, in Stanford, California. I would like to thank Peter Brown, Jeffrey Hamburger, Joel Kaye, Adam Kosto, Dorothea von Mücke, and Guenther Roth for their suggestions. Much of the research was done at the Wissenschaftskolleg zu Berlin; I am grateful both to the staff there and to the visiting scholars, especially Carolyn Abbate, Karine Chemla, Arnold Davidson, Jean-Claude Schmitt, and Pamela Smith, with whom I shared ideas.

2. Charles Homer Haskins, *The Renaissance of the Twelfth Century* (Cambridge, MA: Harvard University Press, 1927). Haskins, in his introduction, treats renaissance as a general "revival" or "cultural flowering" and makes it clear that he omits vernacular literature because he feels it has to date been more studied than the corpus of Latin literature. But the fact that he included the word "renaissance" in the title of his book and treated Latin material, especially in the context of its use of classical models, led many of his followers to take the content of his study as a definition of "renaissance."

3. See Robert L. Benson and Giles Constable with Carol D. Lanham (eds.), *Renaissance and Renewal in the Twelfth Century* (Cambridge, MA: Harvard University Press, 1982).

4. Gerhard B. Ladner, "Terms and Ideas of Renewal," in Benson and Constable (eds.), *Renaissance and Renewal*, pp. 1–33, and see Chapter 3 n.1 below.

5. R.I. Moore, *The Formation of a Persecuting Society: Power and Deviance in*

Western Europe, 950–1250 (Oxford: Basil Blackwell, 1987), and Caroline Walker Bynum, "Miracles and Marvels: The Limits of Alterity," in *Vita Religiosa im Mittelalter: Festschrift für Kaspar Elm zum 70. Geburtstag* (Berlin: Duncker and Humblot, 1999), pp. 800–17.

6. Gerhard Ladner, *The Idea of Reform: Its Impact on Christian Thought and Action in the Age of the Fathers* (Cambridge, MA: Harvard University Press, 1959), pp. 3–5; see also Giles Constable, "Renewal and Reform in Religious Life: Concepts and Realities," in Benson and Constable (eds.), *Renaissance and Renewal*, pp. 37–67.

7. Caroline Walker Bynum, *Holy Feast and Holy Fast: The Religious Significance of Food to Medieval Women* (Berkeley: University of California Press, 1987), *eadem*, *The Resurrection of the Body in Western Christianity, 200–1336* (New York: Columbia University Press, 1995), and *eadem*, "Miracles and Marvels." The reception of *Holy Feast and Holy Fast* by recent scholars has sometimes laid more emphasis on peculiarity than the account itself, or the medieval material presented, really warrants. Much more attention has been paid, for example, to the few instances I cited of pus drinking and mystical pregnancy than to the many pages of analysis of mystical metaphors and eucharistic devotion. Moreover, as Esther Cohen has recently observed, much work inspired by *Holy Feast and Holy Fast* seriously misrepresents both its argument and the argument of *Resurrection of The Body* by virtually equating body with person. The argument of my work over the past fifteen years has been that, in medieval anthropology, the person was a psychosomatic unity; see Esther Cohen, "The Animated Pain of the Body," *American Historical Review* 105 (Feb. 2000), p. 41.

8. See Chapter 1, nn.59–61 above.

9. Bynum, *Resurrection of the Body*, esp. pp. 117–225 and 318–43.

10. *Ibid.*, pp. 122–54 and 213–20.

11. *Ibid.*, p. 217 n.59. Heretics were charged both with teaching transmigration of souls and with reducing resurrection to spiritual rebirth in this life. For Caesarius of Heisterbach's condemnations of both antinomians and dualists, see n.116 below. For the reappearance of such themes in the fourteenth-century treatise *Schwester Katrei*, see Barbara Newman, *From Virile Woman to Wom-*

anChrist: Studies in Medieval Religion and Literature (Philadelphia: University of Pennsylvania Press, 1995), pp. 179–81.

12. I use "identity" in three senses: in the sense of spatiotemporal continuity (being the "same" thing over time — for example, the "same" Jane from cradle to grave); in the sense of particular nature or individuality (for example, curly-haired, vivacious, courageous Jane, which, if we don't encounter, we say she's "not herself"); and in the sense of classification (belonging to a group or species — for example, Jane as human being, as woman, as medievalist, and so on). The second sense is the least important in Scholastic discussion. See Chapter 4 above, pp. 163–66.

13. The topos "like from like" was classical; the idea is frequently borrowed by medieval theologians and philosophers from Augustine's *Literal Commentary on Genesis*, bk. 9, par. 17, ed. Joseph Zycha, Corpus scriptorum ecclesiasticorum latinorum 28, pt. 1 (Prague: F. Tempsky, 1894), pp. 290–92. The technical argument that generation produces only specifically but not numerically the same individual is often linked in high Scholasticism to Aristotle, *On Coming-to-Be and Passing-Away* (*On Generation and Corruption*) bk. 2, ch. 11, 338b, trans. E.S. Foster, Loeb Classical Library 194 (Cambridge, MA: Harvard University Press, 1965), p. 329.

14. Peter Lombard, *Sententiae in IV libris distinctae*, 2 vols., ed. Collegium S. Bonaventurae (Grottaferrata: Collegium S. Bonaventurae ad Claras Aquas, 1971–1981), bk. 2, dist. 30, ch. 15, vol. 1, pp. 504–505. And see Bynum, *Resurrection of the Body*, pp. 125–26. Even in Peter Lombard's day, Schoolmen were aware that the patristic tradition contained authorities that argued for real digestion and against a completely literal understanding of Matthew 15.17. Since I wrote this article, the Lombard's position and its *fortuna* in high Scholastic philosophy have been definitively studied by Philip Lyndon Reynolds, *Food and the Body: Some Peculiar Questions in High Medieval Theology* (Leiden: Brill, 1999); see esp. pp. 1–49, 172–214, 429–30, 439–40.

15. For additional texts, see Caroline Bynum, "Why All the Fuss About the Body? A Medievalist's Perspective," *Critical Inquiry* 22 (Autumn 1995), nn.52–59, and Brian Stock, *The Implications of Literacy: Written Language and*

Models of Interpretation in the Eleventh and Twelfth Centuries (Princeton, NJ: Princeton University Press, 1983), pp. 473–74.

16. Giles Constable, *The Reformation of the Twelfth Century* (Cambridge, UK: Cambridge University Press, 1996), p. 299; Bruno of Segni, *Homilia 143 in dedicatione ecclesiae*, in J.-P. Migne (ed.), *Patrologiae cursus completus: series latina*, 221 vols. (Paris, 1841–1846) [hereafter PL], vol. 165, col. 860C–D. Bruno writes: "[Christus], cum sit immutabilis secundum divinitatem, nostras mutationes in carne sua suscepit." Herman of Reun's rather gruesome Advent sermon makes the same point: "When we are born, we begin at once to sicken. The sickness ends only with death.... What therefore is...health, brother? Transitory, fragile, about to perish, vain." Cited in Bynum, *Resurrection of the Body*, p. 173.

17. Walter of Châtillon, moral-satirical poem 7a, published in Franco Munari, *Ovid im Mittelalter* (Zürich and Stuttgart: Artemis, 1960), pp. 52–58; my translation. Walter Map, one of the collectors of prodigies I discuss above, ends his *De nugis* with an invocation of flux that might sound quite positive (even Ovidian) except for the fact that he then defines hell as constant change and draws an analogy to his own situation at court (*in motu tamen immobiliter est*); Walter Map, *De nugis curialium: Courtier's Trifles*, ed. and trans. M.R. James, revised by C.N.L. Brooke and R.A.B. Mynors (Oxford: Clarendon Press, 1983), dist. 5, ch. 7, p. 500.

18. Peter Dronke, *Fabula: Explorations into the Uses of Myth in Medieval Platonism*, Mittellateinische Studien und Texte 19 (Leiden and Cologne: Brill, 1974), pp. 160–61; ed. and trans. on p. 90.

19. Barbara Obrist, "Die Alchemie in der mittelalterlichen Gesellschaft," in Christoph Meinel (ed.), *Die Alchemie in der europäischen Kultur- und Wissenschaftsgeschichte*, Wolfenbütteler Forschungen 32 (Wiesbaden: Harrassowitz, 1986), p. 44.

20. On the *Canon episcopi*, see Dennis M. Kratz, "Fictus Lupus: The Werewolf in Christian Thought," *Classical Folia: Studies in the Christian Perpetuation of the Classics* 30.1 (1976), p. 62. For patristic texts that assert metamorphosis to be impossible, see Joyce E. Salisbury, *The Beast Within: Animals in the Middle Ages* (New York and London: Routledge, 1994), p. 160. On the bodies of angels, see

Dyan Elliott, *Fallen Bodies: Pollution, Sexuality, and Demonology in the Middle Ages* (Philadelphia: University of Pennsylvania Press, 1999), esp. pp. 127–60.

21. From the seventh-century text *De mirabilibus sanctae scripturae*, known as the Irish Augustine, cited by Marina Smith in "The Earliest Written Evidence for an Irish View of the World," in Doris Edel (ed.), *Cultural Identity and Cultural Integration: Ireland and Europe in the Early Middle Ages* (Portland, OR: Four Courts Press, 1995), p. 37.

22. Marius, *On the Elements: A Critical Edition and Translation*, ed. Richard C. Dales (Berkeley: University of California Press, 1976), pp. 62–70. Marius knew little of Aristotle directly; see Dales, introduction to *ibid.*, pp. 18–30.

23. Marius, *On the Elements*, pp. 164–76. Even intermediates are not true hybrids but rather beings that belong to one category and possess elements of another; an oyster, for example, is a plant with the feeling of an animal.

24. Obrist, "Die Alchemie," pp. 43–45; *eadem*, introduction to *Constantine of Pisa: The Book of the Secrets of Alchemy: Introduction, Critical Edition, Translation, and Commentary* (Leiden: Brill, 1990), pp. 3–43; and William R. Newman, introduction to *The "Summa Perfectionis" of Pseudo-Geber: A Critical Edition, Translation, and Study* (Leiden: Brill, 1991), pp. 1–38. The complexity of the question of species inviolability can be seen in the fact that Roger Bacon changed his mind over the course of his career about species transformation. See n.103 below.

25. Albertus Magnus, *Book of Minerals*, bk. 1, chs. 6 and 8; bk. 3, tract. 1, ch. 9, tract. 2, ch. 6; trans. Dorothy Wyckoff (Oxford: Clarendon Press, 1967), pp. 24–25, 52–53, 177–78, 199–200. On hybrids, see Albertus Magnus, *De animalibus*, bk. 22, ch. 55 [105], in *Man and the Beasts: De animalibus (Books 22–26)*, trans. James J. Scanlan (Binghamton, NY: Center for Medieval and Early Renaissance Studies, 1987), pp. 148–49. Paul of Taranto, writing after 1250, simply uses the *De congelatione* to support species change but also affirms that alchemy is limited in the changes it can effect because it cannot infuse soul. See Newman, *"Summa Perfectionis"*, p. 29.

26. For more on this topic, see n.52 below.

27. Leonard Barkan, *The Gods Made Flesh: Metamorphosis and the Pursuit of*

Paganism (New Haven, CT: Yale University Press, 1986), p. 97; Denyse Delcourt, *L'Ethique du changement dans le roman français du XIIe siècle* (Geneva: Droz, 1990), p. 25; Kratz, "Fictus Lupus"; Salisbury, *Beast Within*, pp. 1-11.

28. Elliott, *Fallen Bodies*.

29. Bynum, *Resurrection of the Body*, pp. 32-33, 112-14. It seemed significant to me that eschatological language often equated grave and stomach and that fear of chain consumption (of bodies being eaten by animals, who might in turn be eaten by humans) often slipped into fear of cannibalism and metempsychosis. Whether animal eating human, human eating human, or human changed into animal (naturally or magically), the root fear seemed to me to be fear of loss of self through loss of body.

30. Marie-Dominique Chenu, *La Théologie au douzième siècle* (Paris: J. Vrin, 1957).

31. For example, in Thierry of Chartres's hexaemeral work, unity or stasis is contrasted with mutability (*mutabilitas*), diversity, and alterity (*alteritas*). See Brian Stock, *Myth and Science in the Twelfth Century: A Study of Bernard Sylvestris* (Princeton, NJ: Princeton University Press, 1972), pp. 240-47.

32. Laurence Harf-Lancner, introduction to *Métamorphose et bestiare fantastique au moyen âge*, ed. Harf-Lancner (Paris: Ecole Normale Supérieure, 1985), p. 3, citing H. Nais, says that it is only in the sixteenth century that the word "metamorphosis" becomes synonymous with transformation and even then it is employed mostly in poetic contexts for the metaphorical change of a lover or convert from one situation to another.

33. Thomas the Cistercian, *Commentarium in Cantica Canticorum*, bk. 4, PL 206, col. 249. The idea of metamorphosis as metaphorical change into animals derives from Boethius, *Consolation of Philosophy*, 4 prose 3; see Kratz, "Fictus Lupus," p. 58. Almost a hundred years later, Roger Bacon makes the same point; see Bacon, *The Opus Majus of Roger Bacon*, 2 vols., trans. R.B. Burke (Philadelphia: University of Pennsylvania Press, 1928), vol. 2, p. 672. For a Renaissance example, see Pomponazzi, cited in Charlotte Otten (ed.), *A Lycanthropy Reader: Werewolves in Western Culture* (Syracuse, NY: Syracuse University Press, 1986), p. 225. On metamorphosis as moral slippage or advance, see Barkan, *Gods Made*

Flesh, pp. 103-17.

34. William of Conches, *Glosae super Platonem: Texte critique avec introduc-tion, notes et tables*, ed. Edouard Jeauneau, Textes philosophiques du moyen âge 13 (Paris: Vrin, 1965), pars. 123 and 161-62, pp. 218-19 and 269-70. And see Paule Demats, *Fabula: Trois Etudes de mythographie antique et médiévale* (Geneva: Droz, 1973), pp. 147 and 154 n.209; and Barkan, *Gods Made Flesh*, pp. 122 and 128. On return to God as return to likeness, see Robert Javelet, *Image et ressem-blance au douzième siècle de saint Anselme à Alain de Lille*, 2 vols. (Paris: Letouzey et Ané, 1967).

35. Conrad of Hirsau, *Dialogus super auctores*, ed. R.B.C. Huygens, Collec-tion Latomus 17 (Berchem and Brussels: Latomus, 1955), p. 51; Conrad defines "metamorphosis" as "transformatio substantiarum." Conrad found Ovid par-ticularly objectionable because he apparently knew the "unknown God" of the Athenians (Acts 17.23) and therefore should have eschewed the theme of meta-morphosis. And see Demats, *Fabula*, pp. 133 and 145. The *Summa breves dies hominis sunt* (probably 1195-1210), quoted by Jorissen, argues that there are four types of change: accidental (as when a white thing becomes black), substantial with matter remaining (as in the miracle at Cana), material (as in the transub-stantiation of matter to matter in the Eucharist), and natural, which the philoso-phers teach (as when earth is dissolved into water). But, says the text, the Church does not accept what we read in the poets "de conversione rei inanimatae in rem animatam." Hans Jorissen, *Die Entfaltung der Transsubstantiationslehre bis zum Beginn der Hochscholastik* (Münster: Aschendorf, 1965), p. 109 n.163.

36. "Tidings of the Resurrection," ch. 33, ed. Whitley Stokes, in *Revue cel-tique* 25 (1904), pp. 232-59, esp. pp. 250-51. The interest in classifying types of change, which is echoed in Gerald of Wales's gloss on his own werewolf story, is itself worthy of note; see n.123 below and Introduction n.1 above.

37. Isidore of Seville, *Etimologías: Edición bilingüe*, 2 vols., ed. J. Oroz Reta and M.-A. Marcos Casquero (Madrid: Biblioteca de Autores Cristianos, 1982), bk. 11, ch. 4, vol. 2, p. 55; Vincent of Beauvais, *Speculum naturale* (1624; reprint, Graz: Akademische Druck- und Verlagsanstalt, 1964), bk. 31, ch. 122, col. 2390. The fact that the following sentence quotes Ovid makes it clear that Isidore

and Vincent have metamorphosis in mind. See Simone Viarre, *La Survie d'Ovide dans la littérature scientifique des XIIe et XIIIe siècles* (Poitiers: Centre d'Etudes Supérieures de Civilisation Médiévale, 1966), pp. 85 and 148–49. The passage from Vincent and that quoted in n.35 above from the *Summa breves dies hominis sunt* show that by the end of the twelfth century philosophers were struggling to explain the change of one substance into another in the natural realm, although (as the passage quoted in n.35 also suggests) the meaning of "substance" was complicated. See Jorissen, *Die Entfaltung der Transsubstantiationslehre*, pp. 110–14 and passim.

38. Gervais of Tilbury, *Otia imperialia*, in G.W. Leibniz (ed.), *Scriptores rerum Brunvicensium*, 3 vols. (Hanover: N. Foerster, 1701–1711), decisio 3, ch. 120, vol. 1, p. 1003: "Saepe apud doctos quaestio movetur, si Nabuchodonosor per injunctum tempus poenitentiae in bovem verum fit divina virtute mutatus...."

39. For the Ovid revival, see Marilynn R. Desmond (ed.), *Mediaevalia: A Journal of Medieval Studies* 13 (1989, for 1987): *Ovid in Medieval Culture: A Special Issue*, and Munari, *Ovid im Mittelalter*. I am not concerned here with the reception of the rest of Ovid, for which see Ralph Hexter, *Ovid and Medieval Schooling: Studies in Medieval School Commentaries on Ovid's Ars amatoria, Epistulae ex Ponto, and Epistulae Heroidum* (Munich: Arbeo, 1986).

40. Viarre, *Survie d'Ovide*. This is not to deny that Ovid was also taken to be a mythographer and used for his stories; see Demats, *Fabula*, p. 107.

41. I cite Ovid from *Metamorphoses*, 2 vols., 3rd ed., trans. F.J. Miller, revised by G.P. Goold, Loeb Classical Library 42–43 (Cambridge, MA: Harvard University Press, 1977).

42. On metamorphosis as return to Exemplar, see William of Conches and the texts cited in nn.33 and 34 above. See also Marie-Magdeleine Davy, "Notion de l'homme et de l'univers au XIIe siècle," *Les Etudes philosophiques*, n.s., 16.1 (1961), p. 38.

43. Arnulf, *Allegoriae* (ca. 1174), in Fausto Ghisalberti (ed.), *Arnolfo d'Orléans: Un Cultore di Ovidio nel secolo XII*, Memorie del Reale Istituto Lombardo di Scienze e Lettere, Classe di lettere, scienze morali e storiche 24 (Milan: Ulrico

Hoepli, 1917-1939), bk 1, no.7, p. 202; bk. 3, no.4, p. 208; and bk. 2, no.1, p. 204, respectively. It is also important to note that Arnulf singles out for attention the scientific tidbits one can find in Ovid, such as the discussion of coral (example of both hybridization and metamorphosis); *ibid.*, bk. 4, no.20, p. 212; cf. Ovid, *Metamorphoses*, 4.740-52, vol. 1, p. 230. About sixty years later, John of Garland gives similar interpretations; *Integumenta Ovidii, poemetto inedito del secolo XIII*, ed. Fausto Ghisalberti, Testi e Documenti inediti o rari 2 (Messina and Milan: Giuseppe Principato, 1933), vv. 87-90 and 115-16, pp. 42 and 44. John takes the fountain of Salmacis (*Metamorphoses* 4.285-87) as the cell of the womb within which hermaphrodites are conceived: vv. 193-94, p. 52. An anonymous early thirteenth-century commentary, found in MS Hauniensis Gl. kgl. S. 2008, rejects as untrue the "transformation of things into natures contrary to themselves" but isolates the cosmological parts of Ovid for special attention as an account that can be read naturally; see Demats, *Fabula*, pp. 151-56, esp. p. 155 n.212, and apps., pp. 187-88.

44. John J. Fitzgerald, "'Matter' in Nature and the Knowledge of the World: Aristotle and the Aristotelian Tradition," in Ernan McMullin (ed.), *The Concept of Matter in Greek and Medieval Philosophy* (Notre Dame, IN: University of Notre Dame Press, 1965), p. 59. See also Joseph Owen, "Matter and Predication in Aristotle," in *ibid.*, pp. 88-90.

45. *Profuit ignaris*, vv. 137-56. The poem is found in a manuscript from Tegernsee (Clm 19488) and has been edited by Peter Dronke in *Medieval Latin and the Rise of European Love-Lyric*, vol. 2: *Medieval Latin Love-Poetry* (Oxford: Clarendon Press, 1966), pp. 452-57 (trans. on pp. 457-61), and see pp. 232-38. See also Demats, *Fabula*, pp. 137-39; and Winthrop Wetherbee, *Platonism and Poetry: The Literary Influence of the School of Chartres* (Princeton, NJ: Princeton University Press, 1972), pp. 137-41.

46. *Profuit ignaris*, vv. 175-77, trans. Dronke, in *Medieval Latin*, p. 461.

47. See Stock, *Myth and Science*, pp. 14, 78-161, 187-92, 231-34; Winthrop Wetherbee, introduction to *The "Cosmographia" of Bernardus Silvestris: A Translation with Introduction and Notes* (New York: Columbia University Press, 1973); and Dronke, *Fabula*, pp. 93-94 and 121-25. The poem by Milo and the glosses

on Plato by William of Conches discussed above (nn.18 and 34) belong to the same intellectual tradition as the *Cosmographia*.

48. Bernard Sylvestris, *De mundi universitate, libri duo; sive, Megacosmus et microcosmus*, ed. C.S. Barach and J. Wrobel (reprint, Frankfurt am Main: Minerva, 1964), bk. 2, ch. 8, ll. 27–28, 37–46, pp. 51–52; trans. Wetherbee, "*Cosmographia*," pp. 109–10.

49. *De mundi universitate*, bk. 2, ch. 14, ll. 171–76, pp. 70–71; trans. Wetherbee, "*Cosmographia*," p. 126.

50. Hugh of St. Victor, *De sacramentis*, bk. 1, pt. 6, ch. 26; PL 176, cols. 278–80. Even in the mid-twelfth century, theologians knew that natural philosophers (*physici*) held digestion and growth to be processes in which real assimilation occurs. But we should note, first, that natural philosophical arguments became available only slowly and, second, that theologians generally preferred self-multiplication as an explanation for all growth until the thirteenth century. See Reynolds, *Food and the Body*, and Introduction, p. 22–26.

51. See Peter Lombard, *Sententiae*, bk. 2, dist. 30, ch. 15, par. 2, vol. 1, p. 505.

52. Thomas Aquinas, *De potentia Dei*, in Robert Busa (ed.), *S. Thomae Aquinatis opera omnia*, 7 vols. (Stuttgart and Bad Cannstatt: Friedrich Frommann, 1980), vol. 3: *Quaestiones disputatae*, q. 3, arts. 7–9, pp. 201–205, and q. 5, art. 9, pp. 228–29; *idem, Summa theologica*, pt. 1, q. 65; q. 73, art. 1, reply to obj. 3; and q. 110, art. 2, in *ibid.*, vol. 2, pp. 279–80, 287, 342. Albertus Magnus, *Summa theologiae*, in S.C.A. Borgnet (ed.), *Opera omnia*, vols. 31–33 (Paris: Vives, 1895), pt. 2, tract. 8, q. 31, membrum 2, art. 2, particula 2, vol. 32, pp. 343–46. And see nn.13 and 23 above. William of Auvergne thought human-animal hybrids were possible and gave a natural explanation. In *De universo*, pt. 3 of pt. 2, ch. 25, in *Opera omnia*, 2 vols. (Paris, 1674; reprint, Frankfurt am Main: Minerva, 1963), vol. 1, pp. 1071–72, he tells the story of a bear who stole a woman and had children with her; William then explains that bear semen is sufficiently similar to human semen to make this possible. Albert and Thomas wavered on the question of alchemical transformation, but Thomas seems to have thought change of bodies by art was not possible; see Obrist, "Die Alchemie," p. 48, and Newman,

"Summa Perfectionis", pp. 30–32.

53. Peter Lombard, *Sententiae*, bk. 2, dist. 7, chs. 5–10, vol. 1, pp. 361–65 (taken in part from Augustine, *On the Trinity*, bk. 3, chs. 7–9) and dist. 8, chs. 1–4, vol. 1, pp. 365–70 (taken in part from Augustine, *On the Trinity*, bk. 2, chs. 7–18 and bk. 3, chs. 10–11). Albertus Magnus, *Summa theologiae*, tract. 8, q. 30, membra 1–2, vol. 32, pp. 319–327. Thomas Aquinas, *De potentia Dei*, q. 6, arts. 5–8, pp. 234–38; *idem, Summa theologica*, pt. 1, q. 114, pp. 347–48; *idem, Summa contra Gentiles*, bk. 3, ch. 104, in Busa (ed.), *Opera*, vol. 2, p. 95. And see Elliott, *Fallen Bodies*, pp. 127–60.

54. Benedicta Ward, *Miracles and the Medieval Mind: Theory, Record, and Event, 1000–1215* (Aldershot, UK: Scolar, 1982), notes that the predominant miracle changes from vengeance to curing in the course of the twelfth century. It is also important to note that there was a strong anti-miracle vein in twelfth-century monastic writing; authors stress repeatedly that the highest glory is not miracle-working but virtue, that neither the Virgin Mary nor John the Baptist worked miracles. See Chapter 1, n.39 above. Peter the Venerable, author of an early miracle collection, echoes in places this anti-miracle theme.

55. For Scholastic authors and texts important in sorting out the distinction between *miracula* and *mirabilia*, see Ward, *Miracles*, pp. 4–10. Jacques Le Goff has argued that the distinction first clearly emerges in the introduction to Gervais of Tilbury, *Otia imperialia*; see Le Goff, preface to Gervais of Tilbury, *Le Livre des merveilles: Divertissement pour un empereur (Troisième partie)*, trans. Annie Duchesne (Paris: Les Belles Lettres, 1992), pp. ix–xvi. It also seems present in the organization of distinctio 2 of Gerald of Wales's *Topographia*; see n.68 below. It is important to note that William of Conches, commenting on the *Timaeus*, uses the same distinction, which he appears to draw from Chalcidius: *Glosae super Platonem*, ed. Jeauneau, par. 37, p. 104: "... omne opus vel est opus Creatoris, vel opus nature, vel artificis imitantis naturam." Commentators on Ovid use a similar distinction for types of change: natural, artificial or magical (that is, done by human craft), and spiritual; see Arnulf of Orleans cited at n.88. Later commentators on Dante use Arnulf's list and add "miraculous"; see Barkan, *Gods Made Flesh*, p. 166. Not merely the theologians but the grammarians and poets as

well were interested in categorizing types of change.

56. Pseudo-Albert, *Liber de mirabilibus mundi*; quoted in *Nicole Oresme and the Marvels of Nature: A Study of His* De causis mirabilium, ed. Bert Hansen (Toronto: The Pontifical Institute of Mediaeval Studies, 1985), p. 61 n.36. And see Chapter 1, n.33 above.

57. For a later example, see the fourteenth-century Schoolman Nicolas Oresme, *De causis*, ch. 1, in *Nicole Oresme and the Marvels*, ed. Hansen, pp. 160–63.

58. Peter Lombard, *Sententiae*, bk. 2, dist. 7, chs. 6–8, vol. 1, pp. 362–64; the Lombard quotes Augustine, *On the Trinity*, bk. 3, ch. 8.

59. John of Salisbury, *Policraticus*, ed. K.S.B. Keats-Rohan, Corpus christianorum: continuatio mediaevalis 118 (Turnhout: Brepols, 1993), bk. 1, ch. 10, p. 56. John also argued that "... nichil fit in terra sine causa.... Ex quo consequenter patet ad phisicam omnia pertinere"; *Policraticus*, bk. 2, ch. 1, p. 72. Elsewhere, however, he held to the old Augustinian idea that miracle is a matter of perspective; *ibid.*, chs. 11–12, pp. 89–91.

60. Thomas Aquinas, *Summa theologica*, pt. 1, q. 114, art. 4, p. 343; *ibid.*, pt. 2 of pt. 2, q. 178, arts. 1 and 2, pp. 741–42; *Summa contra Gentiles*, bk. 3, ch. 104, p. 95; *De potentia Dei*, q. 6, art. 5, reply to obj. 8, pp. 234–35. A century earlier, Peter the Venerable thought that the distinction was between Christian and counterfeit miracles. Counterfeit ones (such as those of Pharaoh's magicians) vanish quickly and take much education to perform; Christian ones are solid and real, firmly fixed in matter. See Peter, *Adversus Iudeorum inveteratam duritiem*, ch. 4, ed. Yvonne Friedman, Corpus christianorum: continuatio mediaevalis 58 (Turnhout: Brepols, 1985), pp. 106–18; *idem*, *Contra Petrobrusianos haereticos*, PL 189, cols. 802–03. And see Denise Bouthillier and Jean-Pierre Torrell, "'Miraculum': Une Catégorie fondamentale chez Pierre le Vénérable," *Revue thomiste: Revue doctrinale de théologie et de philosophie* 80 (1980), pp. 357–86, esp. pp. 363–65.

It is worth noting that the seventh-century Irish text cited at n.21 above seems to have gone so far as to deny that even Moses transformed his staff; see Marina Smith, "Earliest Written Evidence," p. 37.

61. John of Salisbury, *Policraticus*, bk. 2, ch. 12, pp. 91–92. Rupert of Deutz, *Commentaria in evangelium S. Joannis*, bk. 2, PL 169, cols. 276–77. The argument comes from Augustine, *In Iohannis evangelium tractatus CXXIV*, Corpus christianorum: series latina 36 (Turnhout: Brepols, 1990), bk. 8, ch. 1, pp. 81–82, and in Augustine's hands is an argument that everything is a miracle — that is, done by the power of God. What the clouds pour forth is changed each season into wine in grapes, and we take this as commonplace; but we marvel at the feast at Cana, because it is rare. There is such power, however, in every grain of seed.

62. Peter the Venerable, *Contra Petrobrusianos*, cols. 803–804. Peter argues (col. 804): "Fit igitur hoc modo omnibus notissimo de pane caro, de vino sanguis, et hoc non in uno homine, sed in omni homine: nec in uno tempore, sed in omni tempore. Quare ergo non creditur, quare dubitatur Deum hoc posse per virtutem, quod potest natura per digestionem?" The argument is found earlier in Guitmond of Aversa, *De corporis et sanguinis Christi veritate in eucharistia libri tres*, bk. 1, PL 149, cols. 1431A–D.

63. Albertus Magnus, *Summa theologiae*, tract. 8, q. 32, membrum 2, vol. 32, p. 360. Thomas Aquinas, *Summa theologica*, pt. 1, q. 114, art. 4, obj. 2, p. 347, says (quoting Augustine), "vera miracula per aliquam corporum immutationem fiunt." See also Alexander of Hales, *Summa theologica*, ed. Bonaventura Marrani and the Collegium S. Bonaventurae, vol. 2, pt. 1 of bk. 2 (Quarrachi: Collegium S. Bonaventurae, 1928), inquisitio 2, tract. 3, sect. 2, q. 3, tit. 3, q. 43, pp. 296–300: "Mutatio virgae Aaron in serpentem vere fuit facta, similiter et mutatio virgarum magorum in dracones vere facta est, et non phantastice tantum, sive collectione seminum sive aliter, secundum vult Augustinus" (col. 297).

David Burr explains nicely apropos the Eucharist how the miraculous could be an inducement to philosophical elaboration: "The primary responsibility placed upon theologians . . . was not to prove the unprovable or explain the unexplainable . . . but to talk sense, to use words responsibly. There was nothing wrong with affirming that eucharistic presence entailed one or more miracles. There was something very wrong in phrasing those miracles in sentences that violated the very meaning of the words used. The great scholastics did not shrink from the possibility that there was something supernatural about Christ's body being in several places at once, but they certainly wanted to counter the charge that it was flatly self-contradictory to say ... so. ..." Burr, *Eucharistic Presence and Conversion in Late Thirteenth-Century Franciscan Thought*, Transactions of the American Philosophical Society 34.3 (Philadelphia: American Philosophical Society, 1984), pp. 6–7.

64. There is general agreement among scholars that the late twelfth and early thirteenth centuries saw an increased interest in marvels. See R.W. Southern, "The Place of England in the Twelfth-Century Renaissance," reprinted in his *Medieval Humanism* (New York: Harper Torchbook, 1970), pp. 158–80; Robert Bartlett, *Gerald of Wales, 1146–1223* (Oxford: Clarendon Press, 1982), pp. 104–22; Jacques Le Goff, "The Marvelous in the Medieval West," in *The Medieval Imagination*, trans. Arthur Goldhammer (Chicago: University of Chicago Press, 1988), pp. 27–44; Lorraine Daston and Katharine Park, *Wonders and the Order of Nature, 1150–1750* (New York: Zone Books, 1998), and Chapter 1, n.8 above.

65. An example of cynicism about miracles is Walter Map; see Monika Otter, *Inventiones: Fiction and Referentiality in Twelfth-Century English Historical Writing* (Chapel Hill: University of North Carolina Press, 1996), pp. 93–128, esp. p. 124. Among English historians writing at roughly the same time, Richard of Devizes is also quite dismissive of miracles; William of Newburgh simply avoids them, using the conventional topos that lauds virtue as rarer and more wonderful than miracle. See n.113 below.

66. Le Goff, "Marvelous"; see also James V. Mirollo, "The Aesthetics of the Marvelous: The Wondrous Work of Art in a Wondrous World," in Joy Kenseth (ed.), *The Age of the Marvelous* (Hanover, NH: Hood Museum of Art, Dartmouth College, 1991), pp. 61–79.

67. For recent interest in the grotesque, see Paul Freedman, "The Return of the Grotesque in Medieval Historiography," in Carlos Barros (ed.), *Historia a debate: Medieval* (Santiago de Compostela: Historia a Debate, 1995), pp. 9–19, and Paul Freedman and Gabrielle Spiegel, "Medievalisms Old and New: The Rediscovery of Alterity in North American Medieval Studies," *American Historical Review* 103 (1998), pp. 677–704. On the transgressive, see David Williams,

Deformed Discourse: The Function of the Monster in Mediaeval Thought and Literature (Montreal: McGill-Queen's University Press, 1996), which, in my opinion, overestimates attention to the monstrous, and Salisbury, *Beast Within*, pp. 138–66. On the disgusting, see William I. Miller, *The Anatomy of Disgust* (Cambridge, MA: Harvard University Press, 1997). Some recent scholarship seems almost to suggest that resistance to metamorphosis is clerical, while metamorphosis is popular or folk; see Harf-Lancner (ed.), *Métamorphose et bestiare fantastique*, and *eadem*, "La Métamorphose illusoire: Des théories chrétiennes de la métamorphose aux images médiévales du loup-garou," *Annales: Économies, sociétés, civilisations* 40.1 (1985), pp. 208–26. Le Goff, "Marvelous," draws a broader contrast in which wonders are the resistance of a courtly class to clerical culture. Such dichotomies are not convincing, however. Peter Brown, among others, has taught us to reject a simple two-tiered model of analysis that reduces contrasts to clerical versus lay, educated versus illiterate, Christian versus Celtic or pagan or folk; Brown, *The Cult of the Saints: Its Rise and Function in Latin Christianity* (Chicago: University of Chicago Press, 1981), ch. 1. See also Daston and Park, *Wonders and the Order of Nature*, which criticizes Le Goff for grouping together under a modern notion of marvel all sorts of events and entities that medieval analysis would have distinguished. It should be clear from the material I have chosen to treat that stories of shape-shifting were used, problematized, and questioned in many genres and among many groups and statuses.

68. Writing just at the moment when a distinction between *miracula* and *mirabilia* was emerging, the authors tend to define the distinction and then not really use the categories they have developed. See Gerald of Wales, *Topographia Hibernica*, introduction to dist. 2, in J.S. Brewer, J.F. Dimock, and G.F. Warner (eds.), *Giraldi Cambrensis opera*, 8 vols., Rerum Britannicarum medii aevi scriptores 21 (London: Longman, 1861–1891; Kraus reprint, 1964–1966), vol. 5, pp. 74–76, and preface to *Expugnatio Hibernica*, in *ibid.*, pp. 209–11; and Gervais of Tilbury, *Otia imperialia*, ed. Leibniz, decisio 3, prologue, vol. 1, pp. 960–61. On Walter Map's categories, see Francis Dubost, *Aspects fantastiques de la littérature narrative médiévale (XII–XIII siècles): L'Autre, l'ailleurs, l'autrefois* (Geneva: Slatkine, 1991), pp. 36–45.

69. For example, early bestiaries have few hybrids; see Lesley Kordecki, "Making Animals Mean: Speciest Hermeneutics in the *Physiologus* of Theobaldus," in Nona C. Flores (ed.), *Animals in the Middle Ages: A Book of Essays* (New York: Garland, 1996), p. 98. Moreover, as Sylvie Lefevre has pointed out ("Polymorphisme et métamorphose: Les Mythes de la naissance dans les bestiaries," in Harf-Lancner [ed.], *Métamorphose et bestiare fantastique*, pp. 215–46), bestiaries never recount metamorphosis. See Chapter 3 at n.128.

70. Walter Map, *De nugis*, dist. 4, ch. 13, p. 368. Gervais of Tilbury, *Otia imperialia*, decisio 2, ch. 12, vol. 1, p. 921, reports the same story and calls the individual, one Nicolas Pappa, a man.

71. Walter Map, *De nugis*, dist. 2, chs. 12–13, and dist. 4, ch. 8, pp. 158–60 and 344.

72. William of Newburgh, *Historia rerum Anglicarum*, 2 vols., ed. Richard Howlett, Rerum Britannicarum medii aevi scriptores 82, pts. 1–2 (1884–1885; reprint, Wiesbaden: Kraus reprint, 1964), bk. 1, chs. 27–28, vol. 1, pp. 82–87, esp. pp. 86–87. William comments that magicians do, with God's permission, change rods into serpents, but he can find no reason why such green children would appear.

73. Gervais of Tilbury, *Otia imperialia*, decisio 3, chs. 85, 86 and 93, vol. 1, pp. 987–89, 991–92; for similar discussion, see Walter Map, *De nugis*, dist. 2, chs. 11–14, pp. 148–62, and dist. 4, chs. 6–11, pp. 322–62.

74. Gerald of Wales, *Topographia*, dist. 2, chs. 21–24, and dist. 3, chs. 10, 19, 25, vol. 5, pp. 108–11, 149–53, 164–65, 169; and *idem*, *Itinerarium*, bk. 1, ch. 2, vol. 6, pp. 27–28 and 32. It is worth noting that Gerald quotes Ovid's *Metamorphoses* both to make the point that seeds are necessary if frogs are to be born from mud (*Metamorphoses* 15.375) and, in the context of considering an animal-human hybrid, to underline the difference of man from other creatures (*Metamorphoses* 1.85); *Topographia*, dist. 1, ch. 32, vol. 5, p. 66, and dist. 2, ch. 21, p. 109, respectively. There are other quotations from Ovid in Gerald, but they have nothing to do with issues of change; see, for example, *Gemma ecclesiastica*, dist. 1, ch. 54, in *Opera*, vol. 2, p. 164, and *Itinerarium*, bk. 1, ch. 3, vol. 6, p. 43. It is typical of twelfth-century Ovid use that Gerald quotes from books 1 and 15 of the *Meta-*

morphoses and that the passages quoted are about generation and the nature of species, not metamorphosis.

75. Gerald of Wales, *Topographia*, dist. 2, ch. 19, pp. 101–107, and Gervais of Tilbury, *Otia imperialia*, decisio 3, ch. 120, p. 1003. And see the Latin poem of the thirteenth century "The Wonders of Ireland," edited from MS Cotton Titus D 24, fol. 74v, in Thomas Wright and J.O. Halliwell (ed.), *Reliquiae Antiquae: Scraps from Ancient Manuscripts...*, 2 vols. (London: Pickering, 1841–1843), vol. 2, p. 105, for a short description of werewolves. Philippe Ménard, "Les Histoires de loup-garou au moyen âge," *Symposium in honorem prof. M. de Riquer* (Barcelona: Universitat de Barcelona, 1984), p. 209, calls attention to the number of werewolf stories at just this moment; as do Salisbury, *Beast Within*, pp. 160–65, and Leslie Dunton-Downer, "Wolf Man," in J.J. Cohen and B. Wheeler (eds.), *Becoming Male in the Middle Ages* (New York: Garland, 1997), p. 211. Manfred Bambeck, "Das Werwolfmotiv in 'Bisclavret,'" *Zeitschrift für Romanische Philologie* 89 (1973), p. 146, goes so far as to speak of a "werwolf thematic" in late twelfth-century England.

76. For recent literature on the werewolf, see Otten (ed.), *Lycanthropy Reader*, and Gaël Milin, *Les Chiens de Dieu: La Représentation du loup-garou en Occident (XIe–XXe siècles)* (Brest: Centre de Recherches Bretonne et Celtique, 1993). The much-criticized work by Montague Summers, *The Werewolf* (1933; reprint, New Hyde Park, NY: University Books, 1966), is still useful, if one corrects for the obvious bias. And see the works cited in nn.77–80 below.

77. The author of *Mélion* stresses (v. 218) that the werewolf retains the "sens e memoire" of a man; see *Mélion* in Prudence M. O'Hara Tobin, *Les Lais anonymes des XIIe et XIIIe siècles* (Geneva: Librairie Droz, 1976), p. 303. There is similar language in *Bisclavret* (vv. 154, 157, 208; see *Les Lais de Marie de France*, ed. Jean Rychner [Paris: Honoré Champion, 1966], pp. 66–67); *Guillaume de Palerne* (v. 7345; see *Guillaume de Palerne: Roman du XIIIe siècle*, ed. Alexandre Micha [Geneva: Droz, 1990], p. 256); and *Biclarel* in *Le Roman de Renart le Contrefait*, ed. Gaston Raynaud and Henri Lemaître (Paris, 1914; reprint, Geneva: Slatkine, 1975), p. 235. Gerald of Wales's account also stresses the wolf's rationality; see at n.124.

NOTES TO PAGE 95

On the twelfth-century werewolf as "sympathetic" or "kindly", see Kirby F. Smith, "An Historical Study of the Werwolf in Literature," *Publications of the Modern Language Association of America* 9.1 (n.s., 2.1) (1894), pp. 1–42; Kate Watkins Tibbals, "Elements of Magic in the Romance of William of Palerne," *Modern Philology* 1 (1903–1904), pp. 355–71; Charles W. Dunn, *The Foundling and the Werwolf: A Literary-Historical Study of Guillaume de Palerne* (Toronto: University of Toronto Press, 1960), pp. 116–18; Kratz, "Fictus Lupus," pp. 69–71; Mihaela Bacou, "Des quelques loups-garous," in Harf-Lancner (ed.), *Métamorphose et bestiare fantastique*, pp. 29–50; Carolyn Oates, "Démonologues et lycanthropes: Les Théories de la métamorphose au XVIe siècle," in *ibid.*, p. 76; and Dunton-Downer, "Wolf Man," p. 205.

78. On the medieval werewolf as "faux loup-garou," see Ménard, "Histoires de loup-garou," p. 212; on the distinction between constitutional and involuntary werewolves, see K. Smith, "Historical Study." The constitutional werewolf is double by nature; the involuntary werewolf is changed by magic. On Marie's *Bisclavret*, see above, pp. 170–73.

79. See, for example, Harf-Lancner, "Métamorphose illusoire." Thus conceptualized, the werewolf becomes an example of what Ovid commentator Arnulf of Orleans sees as the second general category of change: magical change — that is, "change of body not of soul"; see Arnulf, Accessus or *Vita Ovidii,* in Ghisalberti (ed.), *Arnolfo d'Orléans*, p. 181.

80. See Norman Hinton, "The Werewolf as *Eiron*: Freedom and Comedy in William of Palerne," in Flores (ed.), *Animals in the Middle Ages*, pp. 133–46, and Matilda T. Bruckner, "Of Men and Beasts in *Bisclavret*," *Romanic Review* 81.3 (1991), pp. 251–69.

81. "Arthur and Gorlagon," ed. George L. Kittredge, in *Studies and Notes in Philology and Literature* 8 (1903), sect. 5, p. 154. *Arthur and Gorlagon* is a Latin translation of a probably Welsh tale from the thirteenth century or earlier.

82. It is worth noting that in Marie's *Yonec*, which seems to be closer to Breton sources, the change of man to bird occurs in full view of the participants and the reader without either comment or description. It is a bit of the magical world in which the story unfolds. But *Bisclavret*, realistic in its treatment of char-

acter and setting, moves the transformation into a private space and leaves it unseen by the reader.

83. See nn.27 and 66 above.

84. William of Auvergne, *De universo*, pt. 3 of pt. 2, ch. 13, *Opera omnia*, vol. 1, pp. 1040–44, esp. p. 1043. William of Malmesbury, *De gestis regum Anglorum*, 2 vols., ed. William Stubbs, Rerum Britannicarum medii aevi scriptores 90 (1889; reprint, Weisbaden: Kraus reprint, 1964), vol. 1, bk. 2, par. 171, pp. 201–202, writing about 1125, gives the traditional story of men who seem to be changed into beasts of burden. The pseudo-Augustinian *De spiritu et anima*, ch. 26, PL 40, col. 798 (probably from the late twelfth century), says some believe that men can be changed into wolves and pack animals but this is not so; neither mind nor body can be changed materially into an animal, but people can be tricked by phantasms: "... quoniam daemones naturas non creant, sed aliquid tale facere possunt, ut videant esse quod non sunt. Nulla enim arte vel potestate animus, nec corpus quidem aliqua ratione in membra et lineamenta bestialia veraciter converti potest. Sed phantasticum hominis..., sopitis aut oppressis corporeis hominis sensibus, ad aliorum sensuum figuras corporeas perduci potest...." (And see below, Chapter 3, n.58.) Vincent of Beauvais (*Speculum naturale*, bk. 2, chs. 104–06, cols. 146–47) gives a similar argument, and in ch. 109, col. 148, reports the same event.

85. K. Smith, "Historical Study," p. 26; Kittredge (ed.), "Arthur and Gorlagon," p. 170 n.3. And see n.94 below.

86. See Bynum, *Resurrection of the Body*, pp. 229–78 and 318–19, and Reynolds, *Food and the Body*, pp. 429–40.

87. See nn.18, 33, 34, 42, 48 above.

88. Arnulf's accessus, *tituli*, allegories, and a small sample of the glosses are edited in Ghisalberti (ed.), *Arnolfo d'Orléans*; the accessus is on p. 181. John of Garland's commentary (ca. 1234) is edited by Ghisalberti in *Integumenta Ovidii*. Paralleling Arnulf, John's opening verses catalog types of change and then discuss cosmology; see pp. 35–39. And see Ralph Hexter, "Medieval Articulations of Ovid's Metamorphoses: From Lactantian Segmentation to Arnulfian Allegory," in Desmond (ed.), *Mediaevalia,* pp. 63–82, and Fausto Ghisalberti, "Medieval

Biographies of Ovid," *Journal of the Warburg and Courtault Institutes* 9 (1946), pp. 1–110.

89. Arnulf, Accessus or *Vita Ovidii,* in Ghisalberti (ed.), *Arnolfo d'Orléans,* p. 181.

90. Arnulf, *Allegoriae,* ed. Ghisalberti, bk. 10, no.5, p. 223. See also bk. 9, no.8, p. 221: "Iphis from woman to man" is glossed simply "and this means nothing other than that he held himself first in the womanly position, then *viriliter.*" Scholars have in general failed to notice how often Arnulf, and John of Garland after him, employs that popular medieval tool etymology to isolate and underline significance; see, for example, Arnulf, *Allegoriae,* bk. 10, no.4, pp. 222–23. Etymological analysis – the unpacking of elements of a word (often down to single letters) in order to unpack the structure of things – is of course not a method conducive to stress on development or change. On etymology in this period, which should not be confused with modern philological research into the historical roots of words, see Roswitha Klinck, *Die lateinische Etymologie des Mittelalters* (Munich: Wilhelm Fink, 1970).

91. Arnulf, *Allegoriae,* ed. Ghisalberti, bk. 2, no.13, p. 207; and John of Garland, *Integumenta Ovidii,* ed. Ghisalberti, vv. 151–52, p. 47.

92. Material is organized so as to lengthen the list of instances of change; passing phrases in Ovid are expanded into full-blown episodes. See, for example, Arnulf, *Tituli* or *Mutationes,* in Ghisalberti (ed.), *Arnolfo d'Orléans,* bk. 4, nos.8–12, p. 209; cf. Ovid, *Metamorphoses* 4.277–84, vol. 1, p. 198.

93. Arnulf, *Tituli* or *Mutationes,* in Ghisalberti (ed.), *Arnolfo d'Orléans,* bk. 1, no.10, and bk. 10, no.1, pp. 201 and 221. See also bk. 2, nos.5–6, p. 204: "Parrasis…from modesty to immodesty, from immodesty to childbirth, from childbirth to a bear, from bear to star…."

94. John of Garland, *Integumenta Ovidii,* ed. Ghisalberti, vv. 85–86, p. 42: "Si lupus est arcas, lupus est feritate lupina / Nam lupus esse potes proprietate lupi." The Neoplatonic commentary found in MS Hauniensis Gl. Kgl. S. 2008, an excerpt from which is edited in Demats, *Fabula,* pp. 187–88, also resists metamorphosis, arguing: "Quod si ad fabulas referatur, planum est, sicut de Licaone qui versus fuit de homine in lupum; siquidem eius substantia non mutata

fuit sed forma."

95. Arnulf, *Allegoriae*, in Ghisalberti (ed.), *Arnolfo d'Orléans*, bk. 10, nos.10–11, p. 223. See nn.43 and 74 above.

96. Hexter, "Medieval Articulations of Ovid's Metamorphoses," and Demats, *Fabula*.

97. Modern interpretation sees Ovid's central subject as identity and the slippage of identity, not the flux or mutability emphasized in medieval readings. Among recent work, I have found especially helpful William S. Anderson, "Multiple Change in the *Metamorphoses*," *Transactions of the American Philological Association* 94 (1963), pp. 1–27; Leo C. Curran, "Transformation and Anti-Augustanism in Ovid's *Metamorphoses*," *Arethusa* 5.1 (1972), pp. 71–91; Barkan, *Gods Made Flesh*; Warren Ginsberg, "Ovid and the Problem of Gender," in Desmond (ed.), *Mediaevalia*, pp. 9–28; and Jasper Griffin, "Cosmic Leg-Pull," *New York Review of Books,* April 20, 1995, pp. 10–14.

98. See Frank Coulson, "The Vulgate Commentary on Ovid's *Metamorphoses*," in Desmond (ed.), *Mediaevalia*, pp. 29–61, for a mid-thirteenth-century commentary that interests itself both in scientific material and in questions of interpretation.

99. The early fourteenth-century commentator Giovanni del Virgilio condemned metempsychosis as heretical; see Demats, *Fabula*, pp. 158–75. For a twelfth-century monastic warning against reading about metempsychosis, see n.35 above.

100. Albertus Magnus, *Summa theologiae*, pt. 2, tract. 8, q. 31, membrum 1, art. 4, vol. 32, pp. 336–37. Cf. n.63 above.

101. Hugh of St. Victor, *De sacramentis*, bk. 1, pt. 1, ch. 15, PL 176, col. 199.

102. Thomas Aquinas, *Summa theologica*, pt. 3, q. 44, art. 4, reply obj. 4, p. 837. Note that the position differs from that of Hugh of St. Victor and Peter Lombard, which asserts that no new matter is added at all (cf. n.14 above, and see Reynolds, *Food and the Body*, pp. 1–2 and 35–37). Thomas allows for real growth but resists creation of new matter ex nihilo in the course of time. In *ibid.*, pt. 1, q. 65, art. 1, p. 279, Thomas says that matter perdures: "At least according to matter, all creatures continue forever, because what is created will never return

to nothing, although it be corruptible."

103. On resurrection, see Bacon, *Opus majus*, ed. Burke, pt. 1 of pt. 7, vol. 2, p. 651. Alchemy, which Bacon came to support after first having opposed it, also relied on reduction to first matter; see Obrist, "Die Alchemie," p. 44, and Newman, *"Summa Perfectionis"*, pp. 20–26. But to Bacon, alchemy was more a matter of achieving balance between humors and elements than a transformation; see Bynum, *Resurrection of the Body*, pp. 323–26.

104. Augustine, *De civitate Dei*, 2 vols., ed. B. Dombart and A. Kalb, Corpus christianorum: series latina 47, 48 (Turnhout: Brepols, 1955), bk. 18, ch. 18, vol. 2, pp. 608–10. Augustine did not, of course, oppose all metamorphosis; he accepted the change of rods into serpents in Exodus 7, for example. Scholarship on the question of metamorphosis has been flawed by a tendency to confuse an author's position on the human-animal transformation with his/her attitude toward any metamorphosis.

105. Augustine, however, accepted hybrids and saw the monstrous races as fact. See *ibid.*, bk. 21, ch. 8, vol. 2, pp. 770–74, where he argues that if God can create dog-men, he can certainly raise the bodies of the dead; and see n.124 below. Daston and Park, *Wonders and the Order of Nature*, make the important point that medieval authors felt horror and unease at individual hybrids or monsters, which occurred locally, and took them as omens; monstrous races, located on the margins of the world, were taken matter-of-factly as other beings. See also Mary B. Campbell, *The Witness and the Other World: Exotic European Travel Writing, 400–1600* (Ithaca, NY: Cornell University Press, 1988), pp. 75–86.

106. Kratz, "Fictus Lupus." Summers, *Werewolf*, is probably right in seeing thirteenth-century ideas as moving toward witch belief; on the sixteenth-century discussion, see Oates, "Démonologues et lycanthropes."

107. Peter Lombard, *Sententiae*, bk. 2, dist. 8, ch. 2, vol. 1, pp. 367–68.

108. Cf. Thomas Aquinas, *Summa theologica*, pt. 1, q. 114, art. 4, pp. 347–48, with *idem*, *De potentia Dei*, q. 6, arts. 7–8, pp. 236–38. See also Bonaventure, *Expositiones in librum I et II Sententiarum*, in *Opera*, vol. 4 (Lyons: Phil. Borde, L. Arnaud, and Petrus Borde, 1668), bk. 2, dist. 7, pt. 2, art. 2, q. 2 (on demons using the seeds in things to change their shapes), and dist. 8, pts. 1 and 2 (on how

angels and demons assume bodies), pp. 97–98 and 101–15; and Alexander of Hales, *Summa theologica*, inquisitio 2, tract. 3, sect. 2, q. 3, tit. 3, q. 43, vol. 2, pp. 296–304 (on the changes produced by demons), and inquisitio 2, tract. 3, sect. 2, q. 2, tit. 2, q. 183, vol. 2, pp. 238–47 (on demons and angels assuming aerial bodies).

109. Good angels do not, of course, do such things at all. Aquinas, *De potentia Dei*, q. 6, art. 8, reply obj. 5, p. 238; Bonaventure, *Expositiones in librum... II Sententiarum*, bk. 2, dist. 8, pt. 1, art. 3, q. 1, p. 107.

110. The theologians go to lengths to stress that angels are not composed of the corporeal. Bonaventure, for example, *Expositiones in librum... II Sententiarum*, bk. 2, dist. 3, pt 1, art. 1, q. 1, vol. 4, pp. 40–41, argues that angels, although composite because mutable, are composed of matter and form, not body and spirit.

111. On miracle collections, see Ward, *Miracles*, pp. 192–200, and Chapter 1 n.8 above; on demonic possession, see Barbara Newman, "Possessed by the Spirit: Devout Women, Demoniacs, and the Apostolic Life in the Thirteenth Century," *Speculum* 73.3 (1998), pp. 733–70. Early collections, such as Peter the Venerable's and Caesarius of Heisterbach's, are more collections of *exempla* (moral stories) than *miracula* in the later Scholastic sense and include many events we do not find particularly extraordinary. See Bouthillier and Torrell, "'Miraculum'... chez Pierre le Vénérable," pp. 357–86, and *eidem*, "De la légende à l'histoire: Le Traitement du 'miraculum' chez Pierre le Vénérable et chez son biographe Raoul de Sully," *Cahiers de civilisation médiévale: Xe– XIIe siècles* 25.2 (1982), pp. 81–99.

112. See, for example, Herbert of Clairvaux, *De miraculis*, PL 185, pt. 2, cols. 1271–384.

113. I cannot treat here the complex topic of miracles in hagiography. Scholars have disagreed about even so basic a question as whether the thirteenth century saw an increase or a decrease. See Chapter 1 n. 39 above. I have argued elsewhere that the thirteenth century saw a new emphasis on bodily miracles, often of a quite astonishing sort, especially in the lives of women saints; see Caroline Walker Bynum, "The Female Body and Religious Practice in the Later

Middle Ages," in *Fragmentation and Redemption: Essays on Gender and the Human Body in Medieval Religion* (New York: Zone Books, 1991), pp. 186–95.

It seems clear that miracle is sorted out from marvel in the writings of historians in the later twelfth century and virtually disappears. In early twelfth-century historians, such as Symeon of Durham, miracle and marvel flow naturally together; both induce delight. By the time of Robert of Torigny (ca. 1140), *mira* tends to refer to natural wonders, such as Stonehenge, or to portents; *miracula* is coming to be reserved for the extraordinary acts of the saints. By the late twelfth century, William of Newburgh, who worries a good deal about portents, gives no miracles of saints; Richard of Devizes, like such writers of entertainment literature as Walter Map and Gervais of Tilbury, becomes quite cynical about miracles. See Nancy Partner, *Serious Entertainments: The Writing of History in Twelfth-Century England* (Chicago: University of Chicago Press, 1977).

114. Caesarius of Heisterbach, *Dialogus miraculorum*, 2 vols., ed. J. Strange, (Cologne: Heberle, 1851), dist. 4, ch. 86, vol. 1, p. 252.

115. *Ibid.*, dist. 3, chs. 11–12, dist. 5, ch. 15, dist. 12, ch. 56, in vol. 1, pp. 123–25 and 293–94, vol. 2, pp. 359–60.

116. *Ibid.*, dist. 5, chs. 21–22, vol. 1, pp. 300–307.

117. Ward, *Miracles*, p. 16. On eucharistic miracles generally, see Peter Browe, *Die Eucharistischen Wunder des Mittelalters*, Breslauer Studien zur historischen Theologie, NF 4 (Breslau: Müller and Seiffert, 1938) and Miri Rubin, *Corpus Christi: The Eucharist in Late Medieval Culture* (Cambridge, UK: Cambridge University Press, 1991), pp. 108–29.

118. An especially graphic example of a counter-miracle is one recounted by Gerald of Wales in the *Gemma ecclesiastica* in which the Host is half bread and half flesh — in short, a hybrid, half of which reveals accidents and half substance. Gerald, *Gemma*, dist. 1, ch. 11, in *Opera*, vol. 2, p. 40, describing the miracle of Arras of 1176. For other witnesses to the miracle, see Browe, *Die Wunder*, p. 19.

119. Bacon, *Opus majus*, ed. Burke, pt. 7, vol. 2, pp. 820–22. On concern that partaking of the Eucharist might be cannibalism, see Gary Macy, *The Theologies of the Eucharist in the Early Scholastic Period: A Study of the Salvific Function of the Sacrament According to the Theologians, c. 1080–c. 1220* (Oxford: Clarendon

Press, 1984), pp. 28–51, 72, 108. The argument that the Eucharist should be veiled because of *horror cruoris* was traditional and went back to Ambrose; see Jaroslav Pelikan, *The Christian Tradition: A History of the Development of Doctrine*, vol. 3: *The Growth of Medieval Theology (600–1300)* (Chicago: University of Chicago Press, 1978), p. 199; Rubin, *Corpus Christi*, p. 91 n.56; Marsha Dutton, "Eat, Drink, and Be Merry: The Eucharistic Spirituality of the Cistercian Fathers," in John R. Sommerfeldt (ed.), *Erudition at God's Service*, Studies in Medieval Cistercian History 11 (Kalamazoo, MI: Cistercian Publications, 1987), pp. 9–10; and Klaus Berg, "Der Traktat des Gerhard von Köln über das kostbarste Blut Christi aus dem Jahre 1280," in Norbert Kruse and Hans Ulrich Rudolf (eds.), *900 Jahre Heilig-Blut-Verehrung in Weingarten 1094–1994: Festschrift zum Heilig-Blut-Jubiläum am 12. März 1994* (Sigmaringen: Thorbeke, 1994), pp. 442 and 449–50.

120. Gervais of Tilbury, prologue to *Otia imperialia*, decisio 3, vol. 1, p. 960, says we marvel especially at change (*mutatio*) in the natural course of things. In discussing Nebuchadnezzar, he questions whether the biblical account is literal or moral; about the chimera, he tells us that some say it is a fiction, others think it a mountain described metaphorically. See n.38 above.

121. Gerald of Wales, preface to *Expugnatio*, in *Opera*, vol. 5, p. 209.

122. Gerald of Wales, *The History and Topography of Ireland*, trans. John J. O'Meara (Harmondsworth, UK: Penguin Books, 1982), ch. 52 [dist. 2, ch. 19], pp. 69–71. The text of the first recension (written ca. 1187) is edited by O'Meara in "Giraldus Cambrensis in Topographia Hibernie. Text of the First Recension," *Proceedings of the Royal Irish Academy* 52, sect. c.4 (1949), pp. 143–45. The second recension was written before July 1189. I cite the later recensions from the Rolls Series ed., *Opera*, vol. 5, pp. 101–107. See also Introduction nn.1–4 above.

123. Toward the end of recensions two through four, Gerald suggests that they are outer change only, although earlier he inserts in the fourth recension the notion that two natures might co-inhere, as when Christ became man: "Nor should it be disputed . . . that the divine nature assumed human nature for the salvation of the world, since in this case by no less a miracle [*non minori mirac-*

ulo], human nature assumed that of a wolf, at God's bidding alone, in order to declare his power and vengeance." *Topographia*, dist. 2, ch. 19, in *Opera*, vol. 5, p. 104, which is not (according to Dimock's notes) in the earlier recensions.

124. In his emphasis on the wolf's rationality, Gerald refers explicitly to Augustine, *De civitate Dei*, bk. 16, ch. 8, vol. 2, pp. 508–10, and argues, as does Augustine, that any rational being descended from a human is human, regardless of its appearance. *Topographia*, dist. 2, ch. 19, in *Opera*, vol. 5, p. 105.

125. Jeanne-Marie Boivin, "Le Prêtre et les loups-garous: Un Episode de la *Topographia Hibernica* de Giraud de Barri," in Harf-Lancner (ed.), *Métamorphose et bestiare fantastique*, pp. 51–69, discusses the wolf's skin as a disguise.

126. On the clothing motif, see François Suard, "'Bisclavret' et les contes du loup-garou: Essai d'interprétation," *Marche Romane: Mediaevalia 80.* 30.3–4 (1980), pp. 267–76.

127. Tibbals, "Elements of Magic." Many of those who comment on the werewolf romances observe that the removing and donning of clothes represents rejecting and reacquiring civilization; see, for example, Ménard, "Histoires de loup-garou." Salisbury, *Beast Within*, uses the werewolf motif as evidence for the late medieval attenuation of barriers between animal and human. This may be to take the stories too literally; as Harf-Lancner, *Métamorphose et bestiare fantastique*, p. 10, observes, the opposition in metamorphosis stories is not between the human and animal realms but between true being and appearance.

128. Dubost, *Aspects fantastiques*, p. 565.

CHAPTER THREE: MONSTERS, MEDIANS, AND MARVELOUS MIXTURES

1. See Robert Javelet, *Image et ressemblance au douzième siècle de saint Anselme à Alain de Lille*, 2 vols. (Paris: Letouzey et Ané, 1967); Colin Morris, *The Discovery of the Individual: 1050–1200* (New York: Harper, 1972); Caroline Bynum, "Did the Twelfth Century Discover the Individual?" in *Jesus as Mother: Studies in the Spirituality of the High Middle Ages* (Berkeley: University of California Press, 1982), pp. 82–109; David N. Bell, *The Image and Likeness: The Augustinian Spirituality of William of St. Thierry* (Kalamazoo, MI: Cistercian Publications, 1984); and on the background to twelfth-century concepts of spir-

NOTES TO PAGES 113-114

itual change, see Gerhard Ladner, *The Idea of Reform: Its Impact on Christian Thought and Action in the Age of the Fathers* (Cambridge, MA: Harvard University Press, 1959). Scholars who emphasize the twelfth-century sense of a developing self often use "metamorphosis" to express this; see, for example, Marie-Magdeleine Davy, "Notion de l'homme et de l'univers au XIIe siècle," *Les Etudes philosophiques*, n.s., 16.1 (1961), pp. 31–38, esp. p. 38. In such analysis, metamorphosis tends to mean the development or unfolding of an essential self — exactly *not* what I mean by the term; see Introduction, pp. 28–33, and below, Chapter 4.

2. See André Vauchez, *Les Laïcs au moyen âge: Pratiques et expériences religieuses* (Paris: Editions du Cerf, 1987), esp. pp. 49–92; *idem*, "Saints admirables et saints imitables: Les Fonctions de l'hagiographie ont-elles changé aux derniers siècles du moyen âge?" in *Les Fonctions des saints dans le monde occidental (IIIe–XIIIe siècle)* (Rome: Ecole Française de Rome, 1991), pp. 161–72; and Chapter 1, n.39 above.

3. Marsha Dutton, "Eat, Drink, and Be Merry: The Eucharistic Spirituality of the Cistercian Fathers," and "Intimacy and Imitation: The Humanity of Christ in Cistercian Spirituality," in John R. Sommerfeldt (ed.), *Erudition at God's Service*, Studies in Medieval Cistercian History 11 (Kalamazoo, MI: Cistercian Publications, 1987), pp. 1–31 and 33–69, especially p. 60; Mary Carruthers, *The Craft of Thought: Meditations, Rhetoric, and the Making of Images, 400–1200* (Cambridge, UK: Cambridge University Press, 1998).

4. Bernard McGinn, *The Golden Chain: A Study in the Theological Anthropology of Isaac of Stella* (Washington, DC: Cistercian Publications, 1972); Jacques Le Goff, *The Birth of Purgatory*, trans. Arthur Goldhammer (Chicago: University of Chicago Press, 1984); Steven F. Kruger, *Dreaming in the Middle Ages* (Cambridge, UK: Cambridge University Press, 1992). On *imaginatio* as midpoint, see also Kathryn L. Lynch, *The High Medieval Dream Vision: Poetry, Philosophy and Literary Form* (Stanford, CA: Stanford University Press, 1988), p. 37. The twelfth-century idea of man as microcosm — midpoint in the chain of being — is not important in Bernard; on microcosm and macrocosm, see Marie-Dominique Chenu, *La Théologie au douzième siècle* (Paris: J. Vrin, 1957), pp. 34–43 and passim.

5. For the new work on "otherness," see Chapter 2, nn.64 and 67 above; also Michael Camille, *Image on the Edge: The Margins of Medieval Art* (Cambridge, MA: Harvard University Press, 1992), and Jeremy Cohen, *Of Giants: Sex, Monsters, and the Middle Ages* (Minneapolis: University of Minnesota Press, 1999).

6. On Bernard's sense of return as recovery of what is, see the works cited in n.1 above and Karl F. Morrison, *The Mimetic Tradition of Reform in the West* (Princeton, NJ: Princeton University Press, 1982), pp. 207–208. It is my point in this paper that, no matter how strong such ideas of return are in Bernard, they fit uncomfortably with his sense that return is also encounter with otherness; hence the centrality of the hybrid.

7. See, for example, M. André Fracheboud, "Je suis la chimère de mon siècle: Le Problème action-contemplation au coeur de saint Bernard," *Collectanea ordinis Cisterciensium Reformatorum* 16 (1954), pp. 45–52, 128–36, 183–91; E. Rozanne Elder and John R. Sommerfeldt (eds.), *The Chimaera of His Age: Studies on Bernard of Clairvaux* (Kalamazoo, MI: Cistercian Publications, 1980); John R. Sommerfeldt, "The Chimaera Revisited," *Cîteaux: Commentarii Cistercienses. Revue d'histoire cistercienne / A Journal of Historical Studies* 38 (1987), pp. 5–13; Christopher Holdsworth, "Bernard: Chimera of His Age?" in Robert G. Benson and Eric W. Naylor (eds.), *Essays in Honor of Edward B. King* (Sewanee, TN: University of the South, 1991), pp. 147–63. For much of the twentieth century, there has been attention to the ambiguities in Bernard's career; this reached a high point with Friedrich Heer's *Aufgang Europas* (1949), which saw Bernard as a sort of mean between extremes in a century of crisis. For a historiographical overview, see Adriaan H. Bredero, "St. Bernard and the Historians," in M. Basil Pennington (ed.), *Saint Bernard of Clairvaux: Studies Commemorating the Eighth Centenary of his Canonization* (Kalamazoo, MI: Cistercian Publications, 1977), pp. 27–62.

8. Conrad Rudolph, *The "Things of Greater Importance": Bernard of Clairvaux's Apologia and the Medieval Attitude Toward Art* (Philadelphia: University of Pennsylvania Press, 1990).

9. Elizabeth T. Kennan, "Antithesis and Argument in the *De consideratione*," in *Bernard of Clairvaux: Studies Presented to Dom Jean Leclercq*, Cistercian Studies

Series 23 (Washington, DC: Cistercian Publications, 1973), pp. 91–109; John R. Sommerfeldt, "Epistemology, Education, and Social Theory in the Thought of Bernard of Clairvaux," in Pennington (ed.), *Saint Bernard of Clairvaux*, pp. 169–79; *idem*, "Epistemological and Social Hierarchies: A Potential Reconciliation of Some Inconsistencies in Bernard's Thought," in Marion L. Kuntz and Paul G. Kuntz (eds.), *Jacob's Ladder and the Tree of Life: Concepts of Hierarchy and the Great Chain of Being* (New York: Peter Lang, 1987), pp. 141–51; Karl F. Morrison, "Hermeneutics and Enigma: Bernard of Clairvaux's *De consideratione*," *Viator: Medieval and Renaissance Studies* 19 (1988), pp. 129–51; Jeannine Quillet, "Saint Bernard et le pouvoir," in Coloman E. Viola (ed.), *Mediaevalia christiana XIe–XIIIe siècles: Hommage à Raymonde Foreville de ses amis, ses collègues et ses anciens élèves* (Tournai: Editions Universitaires, 1989), pp. 246–59.

10. Etienne Gilson, *The Mystical Theology of Saint Bernard*, trans. A.H.C. Downes (New York: Sheed and Ward, 1940), esp. pp. 119–52. And see J. Pépin, "'Stilla aquae modica multo infusa vino, ferrum ignitum, luce perfusus aer': L'Origine de trois comparisons familières à la théologie mystique médiévale," *Miscellanea André Combes*, 2 vols. (Paris: J. Vrin, 1977), vol. 1, pp. 331–75.

11. The standard interpretation of Bernard's mysticism sees it as Christocentric and incarnational. See, for example, Denis Farkasfalvy, "Use and Interpretation of St. John's Prologue in the Writings of St. Bernard," *Analecta Cisterciensia* 35 (1979), pp. 205–26; Dutton, "Intimacy and Imitation"; and Morrison, *Mimetic Tradition*, p. 207. My argument here makes the figure of Christ central too, but my interpretation of Bernard emphasizes not Christ or Christ's flesh as link or mediating point so much as the radical duality both of the human nature incorporated in Christ and of Christ himself.

12. For the theme of the complementarity of opposites in Gregory the Great, which is very different from Bernard's sense of radical doubleness, see Carole Straw, *Gregory the Great: Perfection in Imperfection* (Berkeley: University of California Press, 1988).

13. On *admiratio* and *stupor*, see Chapter 1, especially pp. 56–58, above. For the *admiratio/imitatio* contrast, see Chapter 1, pp. 51–53 and 72–73, and Bruce C. Brasington, "Non imitanda set veneranda: The Dilemma of Sacred Precedent

in Twelfth-Century Canon Law," *Viator: Medieval and Renaissance Studies* 23 (1992), pp. 135–52.

14. *Apologia*, 12.28–31, in Jean Leclercq, C.H. Talbot, and H.M. Rochais (eds.), *Sancti Bernardi opera*, 8 vols. (Rome: Editiones Cistercienses, 1957–1977) [hereafter OB], vol. 3: *Tractatus et opuscula*, pp. 104–107. (Numbers directly after titles to works edited in OB refer to sections and/or paragraphs.) The *Apologia* is also edited in Rudolph, "*Things of Greater Importance*," app. 2. The locus classicus on Bernard and Romanesque art is Meyer Schapiro, "On the Aesthetic Attitude in Romanesque Art," reprinted in Meyer Schapiro, *Romanesque Art* (New York: G. Braziller, 1977), pp. 1–27. Conrad Rudolph has revisited the topic in *Violence and Daily Life: Reading, Art, and Polemics in the Cîteaux Moralia in Job* (Princeton, NJ: Princeton University Press, 1997).

15. *Apologia*, 12.29, OB 3, p. 106. The Cluniac abbot Peter the Venerable, in a letter to Bernard, suggests that hilarious and undignified behavior on the part of monks is as if they are responding to images of centaurs and chimeras. See Peter the Venerable, letter 111, in Giles Constable (ed.), *The Letters of Peter the Venerable*, 2 vols. (Cambridge, MA: Harvard University Press, 1967), vol. 1, pp. 285–86.

16. See Thomas E.A. Dale, "*Deformis formositas ac formosa deformitas*: Monsters and Corporeal Deformity in the Romanesque Cloister Capitals of Saint-Michel de Cuxa," forthcoming. And see Bernard, sermon 7 on Psalm 90, discussed at n.27. I count thirteen types of monsters in Bernard's account whereas Rudolph counts fourteen, because I take the phrase "deformis formositas..." as a general heading, and Rudolph counts it as a specific figure.

17. See Richard Newhauser, "The Sin of Curiosity and the Cistercians," in Sommerfeldt (ed.), *Erudition*, pp. 71–95, and Javelet, *Image et ressemblance*.

18. See *Apologia*, 8.16–11.27, esp. 20, and 12.28, OB 3, pp. 95–103 and 104–105.

19. Letter 250, in J.-P. Migne (ed.), *Patrologiae cursus completus: series latina*, 221 vols. (Paris: J. P. Migne, 1841–1864) [hereafter PL], vol. 182, cols. 450–51: "Tempus est ut non obliviscar mei. Clamat ad vos mea monstruosa vita, mea aerumnosa conscientia. Ego enim quaedam chimaera mei saeculi, nec clericum

gero, nec laicum. Nam monachi jamdudum exui conversationem, non habitum. Nolo scribere de me quod vos per alios audisse existimo, quid actitem, quid studeam, per quae discrimina verser in mundo, imo per quae jacter praecipia." And see n.7 above.

20. Letters 195 and 196, PL 182, cols. 361–64, esp. letter 196, col. 363D: "Arnaldus de Brixia, cujus conversatio mel, et doctrina venenum: cui caput columbae, cauda scorpionis est." See also letter 1 to Robert, par. 4, for another wolf in sheep's clothing; OB 7, pp. 1–11, esp. p. 4. It is worth noting that another Cistercian, Walter Daniel, in his *Life of Aelred of Rievaulx*, trans. F.M. Powicke (London: Thomas Nelson and Sons, 1950), ch. 26, pp. 33–35, uses Ecclesiasticus 45.2 to refer to Aelred's "malignant and perverse" persecutors as "monsters" (*monstra*). Those who gossip against Aelred are not only perverse but also liars and hypocrites — hence double. Peter the Venerable, writing to Bernard, describes the dishonest man, in a phrase from Horace, as a monster in which a horse's neck and bird's feathers are joined to a human head. Peter the Venerable, letter 111, in Constable (ed.), *Letters of Peter the Venerable*, vol. 1, p. 297.

21. Letter 78 to Suger, 10–13, OB 7, pp. 201–10, esp. pp. 207–10. The letter to Suger is also an important text for understanding Bernard's conceptions of change and contradiction; see nn.55 and 68 below.

22. See n.221 to letter 78 in PL 182, col. 199D.

23. *De consideratione*, bk. 1, 4.5, bk. 2, 7.14, bk. 3, 4.17, in OB 3, pp. 393–493, esp. pp. 398, 422, 444. As I note below, Bernard moves to a miraculous sense of *mixtio* in book 5, where he speaks of *in utero Virginis... commixtio* and *fermentatio*. Bk. 5, 10.22, OB 3, p. 485. On Eugene as combination of opposites, see also letter 238, 3–4, PL 182, col. 429.

24. In *De consideratione*, bk. 5, 9.20, OB 3, p. 483, Bernard explicitly contrasts the *unitas* of soul and flesh in Christ, and to a lesser extent in us, a *unitas* that is a *sacramentum*, to other kinds of combinations that are *confusiones*. See below for Bernard's concept of *unitas*.

25. *De consideratione*, bk. 3, 4.17, OB 3, p. 444; trans. by John D. Anderson and Elizabeth T. Kennan in Bernard of Clairvaux, *Five Books on Consideration:*

Advice to a Pope, The Works of Bernard of Clairvaux 13 (Kalamazoo, MI: Cistercian Publications, 1976), pp. 101–102.

26. *De diligendo Deo*, 10.28, in OB 3, p. 143.

27. Sermon 7 *In Psalmum "Qui Habitat*," 8, OB 4, p. 417. As Thomas Dale reminds me, this psalm was sung at the evening office of Compline, when monks might well be especially aware of monsters that can come in dreams.

28. It is also important to note, however, that Bernard never quite says this. The closest to "us" that the word *mixtura* comes is the reference to our heroes and heroines, the martyrs, as mixed. Sermon 9 *In Psalmum "Qui Habitat*," OB 4, pp. 435–42, esp. p. 438.

29. See nn.23 and 24 above, and sermon 5 on the Song of Songs, 2.8–3, OB 1, pp. 24–25.

30. Sermon 3 for the Eve of the Nativity, 7–10, in OB 4, pp. 216–19. In its sense of opposites cohering, Bernard's text is reminiscent throughout of Augustine, *De civitate Dei*, 2 vols., ed. B. Dombart and A. Kalb, Corpus christianorum: series latina 47, 48 (Turnhout: Brepols, 1955), bk. 10, ch. 29, vol. 1, pp. 304–307. But Augustine does not speak of "mixture."

31. The sexual overtones of mortar and pestle may not be entirely unconscious; Bernard, after all, is referring to the act of conception. The image of the Holy Spirit as glue is also found in sermon 71 on the Song of Songs; see n.97 below.

32. On *admiratio* as non-appropriative, see Chapter 1, pp. 51–53 and 72–73.

33. Sermon 4 for the Eve of the Nativity, OB 4, pp. 220–28.

34. Bernard of Clairvaux, *De laude novae militiae*, in OB 3, pp. 213–39; and see also Bernard of Clairvaux, *Eloge de la nouvelle chevalerie, Vie de saint Malachie, Epitaphe, Hymne, Letters*, ed. Pierre-Yves Emery, Sources chrétiennes 367 (Paris: Editions du Cerf, 1990), pp. 48–133.

35. Isaac of Stella, sermon 48.8, in A. Hoste, G. Raciti, and G. Salet (eds.), *Sermons*, vol. 3, Sources chrétiennes 339 (Paris: Editions du Cerf, 1987), pp. 158–59; and see Emery, introduction to Bernard, *Eloge*, p. 23 n.1.

36. *De laude*, 1.1 and 4.8, OB 3, pp. 214–15 and 221; and *Eloge*, pp. 51–55 and 73. Even within the warrior role, Bernard emphasizes paradox and danger:

to seem less brutal, soldiers adorn their armor with "womanly fanciness," which adornment only makes it harder to fight; in killing the enemy, one can be killed or, in survival, kill one's soul; living or dead the soldier is a homicide; *De laude*, 2.3–3.4, OB 3, pp. 216–17; and *Eloge*, pp. 55–59.

37. *De laude*, 4.8, OB 3, p. 221; and *Eloge*, pp. 72–73.

38. *De laude*, 1.1, OB 3, p. 214; and *Eloge*, pp. 50–51.

39. *De laude*, 1 (*admiratione dignissimum*), 4.8 (*mirabile*), 5.10 (*duplex... bonum, ita duplicatur et gaudium*), OB 3, pp. 214, 221, 223; and *Eloge*, pp. 51, 73, 77.

40. Giles Constable, *Three Studies in Medieval Religious and Social Thought: The Interpretation of Mary and Martha, The Ideal of the Imitation of Christ, The Orders of Society* (Cambridge, UK: Cambridge University Press, 1995), pp. 3–141.

41. See, for example, the works by Sommerfeldt and Holdsworth cited in nn.7 and 9 above. I myself treated this theme in Caroline Walker Bynum, *Jesus as Mother: Studies in the Spirituality of the High Middle Ages* (Berkeley: University of California Press, 1982), pp. 110–69.

42. See the works by Sommerfeldt cited in n.9 above and Carruthers, *Craft of Thought*, p. 85.

43. Cf. sermon 18 on the Song of Songs, OB 1, pp. 103–108, with *De consideratione*, passim, in OB 3, pp. 393–493.

44. Sermon 12 on the Song of Songs, 6.9, OB 1, p. 66.

45. Bernard writes: "I rightly apply to myself those words of the Prophet: ... 'Play the mountebank I will... (2 Kings 6.22).' A good sort of playing this... by which we become an object of reproach to the rich and of ridicule to the proud. In fact what else do seculars think we are doing but playing when what they desire most on earth, we fly from; and what they fly from, we desire? [We are] like acrobats and jugglers, who with heads down and feet up, stand or walk on their hands.... And we too play this game that we may be ridiculed, discomfited, humbled, until he comes who puts down the mighty from their seats and exalts the humble." Letter 87, in OB 7, pp. 224–31, esp. p. 231; trans. Bruno Scott James in *The Letters of St. Bernard of Clairvaux*, intro. by Beverly M. Kien-

zle (Kalamazoo, MI: Cistercian Publications, 1998), as letter 90, p. 135. The passage makes it clear that Bernard sees himself and his monks more as grotesques, alternations, and reversals than as midpoints or resolutions. On symbolic reversal generally, see Caroline Walker Bynum, *Holy Feast and Holy Fast: The Religious Significance of Food to Medieval Women* (Berkeley: University of California Press, 1987), pp. 281–88.

46. Constable, *Three Studies*, pp. 27–28 and 110–13. It is worth noting that most thirteenth-century discussions argue for "both lives" rather than "a mixed life."

47. Sermon 2 on the Assumption, 9, in OB 5, pp. 236–37, esp. p. 237.

48. Sermon 3 on the Assumption, in OB 5, pp. 238–44.

49. Sermons 50, 51, and 57 on the Song of Songs, OB 2, pp. 78–89 and 119–26; quotation from sermon 40.3, OB 2, p. 26.

50. According to Constable, *Three Studies*, pp. 68–72, some twelfth-century thinkers, especially regular canons, had a real sense of a third life as a mean between the other two. Most Cistercians seem to have shared Bernard's sense of combination or alternation. William of St.-Thierry's concept of the "ambidextrous warrior," however, comes quite close to a concept of a mixed life; see *ibid.*, p. 67.

51. First Sermon for St. Victor, OB 6, pp. 30–31; see also Sermon for St. Martin, OB 5, p. 407. And see n.13 above.

52. Sermon 83 on the Song of Songs, 1.1–4, OB 2, pp. 298–301. For other examples of "with" words, see Bernard, *De gradibus humilitatis et superbiae*, 1.1–8.23, OB 3, pp. 15–35, esp. pp. 20–21, and sermons 8, 7.9; 21, 3.6; 27, 4.6–14; 71; and 80 on the Song of Songs, OB 1, pp. 41, 125, 185–92, and OB 2, pp. 214–24 and 277–83. And see P.M. Standaert, "La Doctrine de l'image chez saint Bernard," *Ephemerides theologicae Lovanienses* 23 (1947), pp. 70–129, and Etienne Gilson, "'Regio dissimilitudinis' de Platon à saint Bernard," *Mediaeval Studies* 9 (1947), pp. 108–30.

53. Sermon 5 on the Song of Songs, OB 1, pp. 21–26, esp. p. 25.

54. Javelet, *Image et ressemblance*, vol. 1, esp. pp. 169–97. See also Wilhelm Hiss, *Die Anthropologie Bernhards von Clairvaux*, Quellen und Studien zur

Geschichte der Philosophie 7 (Berlin: De Gruyter, 1964), pp. 66–89, and Bernard McGinn, "The Human Person as Image of God: II. Western Christianity," in Bernard McGinn and John Meyendorff (eds.), Christian Spirituality: Origins to Twelfth Century (New York: Crossroad, 1985), pp. 324–26.

55. See, for example, letter 78 to Suger, 5, OB 7, p. 204: "Similia ex similibus innotescunt, sed ex contrariis contraria aut placent amplius, aut displicent"; and sermon 82 on the Song of Songs, 3.7, OB 2, p. 297: "Et certe de ratione naturae, similis similem quaerit." See also sermon 27 on the Song of Songs, 4.6, OB 1, p. 183, and sermon 31, 1.2–3, OB 1, pp. 220–21.

56. Sermon 5 on the Song of Songs, OB 1, pp. 21–26. For other passages that stress likeness as movement toward God, see De gradibus, 3.6 and 4.13–18, OB 3, pp. 20–21 and 26–30; De diligendo Deo, 11.32, OB 3, p. 146; and sermons 21, 3.6; 31; and 81 on the Song of Songs, OB 1, pp. 125–26, 219–26, and OB 2, pp. 284–91. Sermon 74 on the Song of Songs, 2.5, OB 2, p. 243, stresses that God is deeper within us than we are to ourselves.

57. See n.9 above.

58. See Bernard McGinn (ed.), Three Treatises on Man: A Cistercian Anthropology (Kalamazoo, MI: Cistercian Publications, 1977), esp. pp. 164 and 253–55. Although two of the three treatises translated and studied by McGinn do, in a technical sense, see a third or median point at which soul and body join, all three treatises also treat the person as hybrid. William of St.-Thierry, for example, speaks explicitly of the person as a "mixture" of human and divine (p. 133). Isaac of Stella says: "soul, standing mid-way between [other] natures, is a mixture..." (p. 155). The anonymous De spiritu et anima says: "This fellowship between the flesh and the soul is indeed admirable; the breath of life is joined to the slime of earth. Marvelous, miraculous indeed it is that things so radically different from one another could be so intimately conjoined. And it is no less awesome that God united himself to the slime of our flesh so that God and slime should be joined, such sublimeness with such baseness" (p. 203). All three treatises stress movement of "like" (soul or person) toward "like" (God) and struggle, as does Bernard, to make such movement "change" but not "change of nature," unitas but not "identity"; see pp. 132–35, 164, 194–95.

59. *De conversione*, 8.14, OB 4, p. 88.

60. On likeness and contrast as ways of thinking, see the passage from letter 78 cited in n.55 above; also sermons 7 and 8 on Psalm 90, OB 4, pp. 412-35. For *glutinum*, see n.31 above and n.97 below.

61. For a brilliant study of Bernard's rhetoric in the *De consideratione*, which stresses this point, see Morrison, "Hermeneutics and Enigma," which should be understood in the context of his broader interpretation in *Mimetic Tradition*; see esp. pp. xiii-xiv. Morrison calls this strategy "enigma" and differentiates it from paradox or dilemma. I continue to call it "paradox," because I see Bernard's rhetoric moving so as to make opposites continuously confront each other; not the mystery but the confrontation of A and not-A, entirely incompatible with each other, seems to me central. On paradox in mystical thought generally, see J. Keller, "The Function of Paradox in Mystical Discourse," *Studia mystica* 6.3 (1983), pp. 3-19, and A.M. Haas, "Überlegungen zum mystischen Paradox," in Elenor Jain and Reinhard Margreiter (eds.), *Probleme philosophischer Mystik: Festschrift für Karl Albert zum siebzigsten Geburtstag* (Sankt Augustin: Academia Verlag, 1991), pp. 109-24. I do not mean quite what these theological interpretations mean, for I see in Bernard not just God's unknowability attested through the simultaneity of opposites but also a view of the world in which what *is* both cannot and must be sorted out in simultaneous and self-contradicting dichotomies.

62. *De conversione*, 3.4-4.5, OB 4, pp. 74-77. See also *ibid.*, 12.24, pp. 97-98. Trans. by G.R. Evans, *Bernard of Clairvaux: Selected Works* (New York: Paulist Press, 1987), pp. 69-70 and 84.

63. Paul's own usage varies; he sometimes uses *caro* as if it means the sinful part of the person but sometimes uses it to mean the body in a neutral sense. On Paul's ideas of the body generally, see Dale B. Martin, *The Corinthian Body* (New Haven, CT: Yale University Press, 1995).

64. *De conversione*, 4.6, OB 4, p. 77; and see the discussion of Christ knowing *per carnem* in *De gradibus*, 3.6-12, OB 3, pp. 20-26. Since modern readers are sometimes inclined to focus on Bernard's attitude toward the body at the expense of his more complex anthropology, it is important to note that, although

the senses are windows that let in "filth," the "dirty old woman" (in whom the "ulcers" of vice lodge) is the will; see *De conversione*, 6.10, pp. 82–84.

65. See *De diligendo Deo*, 11.30–31, OB 3, pp. 144–45: "It is not in dispute that [souls] want their bodies back.... Until death is swallowed up in victory... so that heavenly glory gleams even in bodies,... souls cannot wholly remove themselves [from worldly cares] and transport themselves to God."

66. Karl Morrison calls this rhetorical move "enigma"; see n.61 above.

67. Sermon 27 on the Song of Songs, 7.14, OB 1, p. 191. Bernard's sense of the disjunction of body and soul in man is sometimes called "anthropological dualism"; see Hiss, *Die Anthropologie Bernhards*, pp. 51–65, who sees the gulf between spirit and flesh as that between being and nonbeing and the basis for Bernard's concept of the salvation of the total man.

68. Likeness is also an epistemological principle to Bernard. See, for example, letter 78 (to Suger), where he remarks that we know by comparing like with like; contraries thus help us to understand difference by sharpening contrasts, as white appears whiter next to black. See nn.56 and 60 above.

69. *De conversione*, 4.6, OB 4, p. 77; *De diligendo Deo*, chs. 10–11, OB 3, pp. 143–47. See also Caroline Walker Bynum, *The Resurrection of the Body in Western Christianity, 200–1336* (New York: Columbia University Press, 1995), pp. 163–67.

70. See nn.84–85 below.

71. As Javelet explains (*Image et ressemblance*, vol. 1, pp. 169–97), the key texts on *imago* and *similitudo* differ. In the *De gratia*, Bernard locates free will in *mens* and sees it as *imago*, which is never lost, however much free counsel and compliance *are* lost. In sermons 80–83 on the Song of Songs, he treats soul not as *imago* but as *in* or *ad imaginem*. See at n.83 for a discussion of sermon 81 on the Song of Songs.

72. See nn.74–78 below.

73. See, for example, *De diligendo Deo*, 5.15, OB 3, p. 132; sermon 35 on the Song of Songs, 2.3–3.6, OB 1, pp. 251–53; and *De laude*, 6.12, OB 3, p.225 (discussed in n. 120 below). Since soul can never be lost and animals never have one, the slippage to beastliness is not really (even in metaphor) a metamorphosis; it is

257

more like putting on a (frightful) mask.

74. Yet Bernard also uses images of sin as ineradicable; see at n.78. In a profound contradiction, then, he sees sin both as never really added on and as never really removed. What is saved is the hybrid that we are — whether hybrid because body and soul or hybrid because self and sin. And, as I explain above, the two hybrids are not the same; see at nn.63 and 64. Bernard does not equate sin with body, although he sometimes makes use of the Pauline language that uses "flesh" for sin. But to Bernard sin is located primarily in the will, not the body. See *De conversione*, 6.8–7.10, OB 4, pp. 80–84.

75. Preface to *De consideratione*, OB 3, pp. 393–94.

76. Sermon 82 on the Song of Songs, 2.2, OB 2, p. 293.

77. *Ibid.* It is worth noting that Bernard here uses the verb *confusio* for such overclothing and also for the process of building an evil house on a good foundation.

78. *De conversione*, 15.28, OB 4, pp. 102–104; and see Carruthers, *Craft of Thought*, pp. 96–97. Twelfth-century scribes did, of course, often use knives to remove blots and mistakes without destroying the parchment.

79. First Sermon for St. Victor, OB 6, pp. 30–31.

80. See Chapter 1, nn. 25, 30–31 above.

81. On twelfth-century atomism, see Richard C. Dales, introduction to Marius, *On the Elements: A Critical Edition and Translation* (Berkeley: University of California Press, 1976), pp. 1–36. In connection with Bernard's use of atomism in this sermon, it is important to note that he frequently uses images from the science of his day, including the Galenic idea that contraries act on each other. See Morrison, "Hermeneutics and Enigma," p. 139.

82. Sermon 80 on the Song of Songs, 1.1–2.4, OB 2, pp. 277–80.

83. Sermon 81 on the Song of Songs, esp. 3.5, OB 2, pp. 284–91, esp. p. 287. It is important, of course, to Bernard to stress that God is immutable and that Christ is ever available to the soul; see sermon 74, 1.1, OB 2, p. 240: "Aut quem postremo vel cuiuscumque generis motum das illi, qui Deus est? Est quippe incommutabilis."

84. *De diligendo Deo*, 2.4–5.15, OB 3, pp. 122–32.

85. *De diligendo Deo*, OB 3, pp. 119–54; *De gradibus*, 1.1–8.23, OB 3, pp. 15–35.

86. See Javelet, *Image et ressemblance*, vol. 1, pp. 246–49 and 262–66.

87. *De diligendo Deo*, 10.27–28, OB 3, pp. 142–43.

88. To love God for God's sake is *gustare*. See *De diligendo Deo*, 9.26, OB 3, p. 141. See also at n.95 for eating imagery in sermon 71 on the Song of Songs.

89. *De diligendo Deo*, 10.28, OB 3, p. 143. My translation, but I have consulted *Bernard: Selected Works*, trans. Evans, p. 196. It is worth noting the eucharistic overtones; twelfth-century commentaries regularly speak of the water added to wine in the chalice at Mass as a symbol of the people joined to Christ; see Gary Macy, *The Theologies of the Eucharist in the Early Scholastic Period: A Study of the Salvific Function of the Sacrament According to the Theologians, c. 1080–c. 1220* (Oxford: Clarendon Press, 1984), p. 64.

90. See Gilson, *Mystical Theology*, pp. 119–32; and Javelet, *Image et ressemblance*, vol. 1, p. 443. We find the same sense of union in William of St.-Thierry, where language of transformation, of like knowing and seeing by becoming like, nonetheless retains elements of two-ness. See, for example, *Orationes meditativae* 8.5 (PL 180, col. 231), where William glosses the statement "she [soul] is made that which she eats [the sacrament]" with Genesis 2.23–24 "bone of your bone," suggesting that the *unitas* is that of marriage; see also *ibid.* 3.7–8 (col. 213), where William says that, as we become what we see in order to see, so we become what we love, but concludes: " ... quadam sui transformatione in id quod amat transmutatur; non quod idem sit in natura, sed affectu rei amatae conformatur...." Even on eucharistic change, where William wishes to assert real *transmutatio*, he nonetheless argues that there must be something in common, a sameness or continuity, underneath. Although he uses as a parallel to eucharistic change the image of a drop of wine being "changed in its nature" into the sea so that "nothing at all of it seems [*videatur*] to remain," he cites the maxim of Boethius "omnis mutatio fit secundum aliquid commune" and argues that eucharistic change occurs because "corpus autem Domini cum pane unius habet commune materiae subiectum." William, *De sacramento altaris*, ch. 4, PL

180, col. 350B and D. See Introduction n.7 above.

91. On the different understandings of body-soul union available in the twelfth-century, see the excellent discussion by McGinn in *Three Treatises*, pp. 86–92. See also Lars Thunberg and Bernard McGinn, "The Human Person as Image of God," in McGinn and Meyendorff (eds.), *Christian Spirituality*, pp. 291–330.

92. It is interesting to note that in the sermon for Benedict, ch. 5, he uses *una caro*, not *miscere*, for union of our flesh with swine; see OB 5, pp. 4–5, discussed at n.121.

93. R.W. Southern, *St. Anselm and His Biographer: A Study of Monastic Life and Thought, 1059–c. 1130* (Cambridge, UK: Cambridge University Press, 1963), pp. 21–25; Marcia L. Colish, *The Mirror of Language: A Study in the Medieval Theory of Knowledge* (New Haven, CT: Yale University Press, 1968), pp. 72–74.

94. Sermon 71 on the Song of Songs, 1.1–2, OB 2, pp. 214–15. In letter 78, Bernard says we need contradictions in order to understand; see n.68 above.

95. Sermon 71, 2.5, OB 2, p. 217. And see Dutton, "Eat, Drink, and Be Merry."

96. Sermon 71, 4.9, OB 2, p. 220, and see nn.107–108 below. For changes in the way theologians treated digestion, see Philip Lyndon Reynolds, *Food and the Body: Some Peculiar Questions in High Medieval Theology* (Leiden: Brill, 1999), passim. The changes in physiological assumptions Reynolds describes can be seen reflected in spiritual analogies and metaphors. Contrast, for example, Bernard's sense of "being eaten" as "joining with" to the later idea of "being eaten" as self-annihilation, which depends on a different physiological model of digestion. See, for example, the passage from Catherine of Genoa quoted in Bynum, *Holy Feast and Holy Fast*, pp. 184–85 n.206.

97. Sermon 71, 3.7–9, OB 2, pp. 219–20. For a parallel discussion in Arnold of Bonneval, see Macy, *Theologies of the Eucharist*, p. 124.

98. See n.9 above.

99. See esp. *De consideratione*, bk. 5, OB 3, pp. 467–93.

100. *Ibid.*, bk. 5, 9.21, OB 3, p. 484.

101. It is worth noting how similar Bernard is to Anselm of Canterbury. Although often mistranslated as "Why Did God Become Man?" Anselm's *Cur Deus homo* is of course an exploration of "Why the [hybrid] God-man?" And his *De conceptu virginali et de originali peccato*, like Bernard's letter on the Conception of the Virgin, deals with the question of the *unitas* of *humanitas* in the flesh of Mary and Christ. See Anselm, *Opera omnia*, ed. Francis S. Schmitt (Stuttgart: Frommann, 1984), vol. 1, pt. 2, pp. 139–73, and n.102 below.

102. Bernard, letter 174, OB 7, pp. 388–92; and see Carlo Balič, O.F.M., "The Medieval Controversy over the Immaculate Conception up to the Death of Scotus," in Edward Dennis O'Connor (ed.), *The Dogma of the Immaculate Conception: History and Significance* (Notre Dame, IN: University of Notre Dame Press, 1958), pp. 161–212.

103. See n.93 above and Introduction n.19 above.

104. See n.81 above.

105. See Bynum, *Resurrection of the Body*, pp. 163–76.

106. See Macy, *Theologies of the Eucharist*, pp. 28, 32, 40–41, 49–51, 72, 108, and Reynolds, *Food and the Body*, pp. 5–9, 56–59, passim.

107. Bynum, *Resurrection of the Body*, p. 125, Reynolds, *Food and the Body*, pp. 1–5, and Chapter 2, n.14 above. Theologians were aware that the natural philosophical tradition held growth to come via digestion and that Augustine could be cited as an authority for this position. Nonetheless they were, in the mid-twelfth century, virtually unanimous in rejecting this idea.

108. Reynolds, *Food and the Body*. See also Introduction nn.12 and 17 above; Chapter 2, nn.14 and 102, also Chapter 3 nn.23–25, 50, 52 above.

109. See nn.95–97 above.

110. Marius, *On the Elements*, ed. Dales.

111. Dales, introduction to *ibid.*, pp. 4–7 and 18–35.

112. Marius, *On the Elements*, bk. 1, pp. 62–76 and 98, bk. 2, pp. 164–66 and 174. And see Chapter 2, nn.22–23 above.

113. *Ibid.*, bk. 2, pp. 144–52 and 156–62. For Aristotle's concept of mixture, see *On Coming-to-Be and Passing-Away* (*On Generation and Corruption*), bk. 1, chs. 5 and 10, trans. E.S. Foster, Loeb Classical Library 194 (Cambridge, MA:

Harvard University Press, 1965), pp. 213–15 and 253–63. Scholars differ over how far, in Aristotle's concept, the mixture is really a new thing, supplanting the previous substances. This depends, in part, on what Aristotle meant by "each ingredient being still potentially what it was before they were mixed and not destroyed" (p. 257). See Robert P. Multhauf, "The Science of Matter," in David C. Lindberg (ed.), *Science in the Middle Ages* (Chicago: University of Chicago Press, 1978), p. 371, who finds Aristotle's concept inconclusive; Dales, introduction to Marius, *On the Elements*, pp. 13–14, who thinks Marius an advance on Aristotle because of his interest in the process of change; and Reynolds, *Food and the Body*, pp. 81, 224, 336, who seems to waver a bit in how he sees Aristotle.

114. Bynum, "Did the Twelfth Century Discover the Individual?" and "Jesus as Mother," in *Jesus as Mother*, pp. 82–109 and 110–69. The latter essay argues that the stern father and birthing/nursing mother Bernard saw himself to be reflected not merely an ambivalence about the authority he must exercise as abbot and the politicking he felt called upon to do in the world but also a spiritual response to the reversal required by the Sermon on the Mount.

115. See n.7 above. I tend to agree with Holdsworth that part of what Bernard understood by the active life was his writing, a possible source of pride.

I hope it is clear that I reject efforts, such as Heer's, to classify aspects of the twelfth century as "old" or "new" or to make Bernard paradigmatic for an entire age. I hope it is also clear that my stress on Bernard's sense of doubleness is not a criticism (or an approbation) of his spirituality launched from a twentieth-century standpoint but rather an effort to see the congruences between various aspects (theological, spiritual, natural philosophical, logical, and so on) of his thought. As I stress below, Bernard's ontological assumptions, in my view, empowered him to express certain aspects of the world and the divine with stunning clarity, while making other truths difficult to explain.

116. Bynum, "Did the Twelfth Century Discover the Individual?" and "Jesus as Mother."

117. It is important to note that contemporaries saw and commented on Bernard's ambivalence; for example, Hildebert of Lavardin and Peter of Celle

compared Bernard to Jacob with two wives. See Bredero, "St. Bernard and the Historians," p. 41 n.53.

118. Prologue to *De diligendo Deo*, OB 3, p. 120: "Verum illud indicit professio, etsi non ita conversatio"; trans. Evans, *Bernard: Selected Works*, p. 174. And sermon 30 on the Song of Songs, 3.6–7, OB 1, pp. 213–15. See also sermons 12 and 13 on the Song of Songs, OB 1, pp. 60–75; and *De conversione*, 21.38, OB 4, p. 114, where Bernard somewhat ambivalently explores various roles and warns against the desire to "walk in great and wonderful things that are beyond you." Sermons 51 and 57 on the Song of Songs clearly advocate alternation of roles.

119. Sermon 51 on the Song of Songs, 2.3, OB 2, p. 86.

120. See nn.18–20 above. Bernard's *In Praise of the New Army* provides another example. In the general context of discussing a new and hybrid role (and the specific exegetical context of the manger at Bethlehem), Bernard gives us a lengthy excursus on man's descent into beasts and return to the human (*ex pecore rursus conversus in hominem*); *De laude*, 6.12, OB 3, p. 225, and *Eloge*, p. 83.

121. Sermon for St. Benedict, OB 5, pp. 1–12.

122. On these figures in general, see Chapter 1, pp. 53–56, above. And see, for example, Walter Map's discussion of life at court in his *De nugis curialium: Courtier's Trifles*, ed. and trans. M.R. James, revised by C.N.L. Brooke amd R.A.B. Mynors (Oxford: Clarendon Press, 1983), dist. 1, ch. 1, and dist. 5, ch. 7, pp. 2–9 and 498–513. Walter says the court is a monstrous *centimanus gigas* . . . *ydra multorum capitum* (p. 2). It is suggestive that he wanders off from the question of identity into a discussion of alchemy and metallurgy and ends up in a description of the monstrous denizens of hell, all of whom *in curia nostra sunt* (p. 500). See also Chapter 2 n.17 above.

123. See Introduction n.1 and Chapter 2, pp. 92–97 and 105–109.

124. See Chapter 2, pp. 86–89, 98–101, and 146–147.

125. See n.5 above. An example of such overinterpretation is David Williams, *Deformed Discourse: The Function of the Monster in Mediaeval Thought and Literature* (Montreal: McGill-Queen's University Press, 1996). Although Williams has fascinating ideas (based on recent scholarship on Eriugena) about

what such monsters might have signified, he gives hardly any examples of their presence in twelfth- and thirteenth-century literature. Despite the emphasis of scholars such as Baltrušaitis, Kappler, and Lecouteux on hybrids and grotesques, it is worth noting that early bestiaries have few hybrids; see Lesley Kordecki, "Making Animals Mean: Speciest Hermeneutics in the *Physiologus* of Theobaldus," in Nona C. Flores (ed.), *Animals in the Middle Ages: A Book of Essays* (New York: Garland, 1996), p. 98, and Debra Hassig, *Medieval Bestiaries: Text, Image, Ideology* (Cambridge, UK: Cambridge University Press, 1995). See also Jurgis Baltrušaitis, *Le Moyen Âge fantastique: Antiquités et exotismes dans l'art gothique* (Paris: Armand Colin, 1955); Claude Kappler, *Monstres, demons et merveilles à la fin du moyen âge* (Paris: Payot, 1980); and Claude Lecouteux, *Les Monstres dans la pensée médiévale européenne: Essai de présentation* (Paris: Presses de l'Université de Paris-Sorbonne, 1993).

126. Camille, *Image on the Edge*; Janetta R. Benton, *The Medieval Menagerie: Animals in the Art of the Middle Ages* (New York: Abbeville, 1992); eadem, "Gargoyles: Animal Imagery and Artistic Individuality in Medieval Art," in Flores (ed.), *Animals in the Middle Ages*, pp. 147–65; Rudolph, *"Things of Greater Importance,"* pp. 117–25; and *idem, Violence and Daily Life*. It is moreover important that hybrids were used as memory figures: see Figure 11; Carruthers, *Craft of Thought*, pp. 140–42; and Michael Curschmann, "Imagined Exegesis: Text and Picture in the Exegetical Works of Rupert of Deutz, Honorious Augustodunensis, and Gerhoh of Reichersberg," *Traditio* 44 (1988), pp. 145–69.

127. Christine Ferlampin-Acher, "Le Monstre dans les romans des XIIIe et XIVe siècles," in Dominique Boutet and Laurence Harf-Lancner (eds.), *Ecriture et modes de pensée au moyen âge (VIIIe–XVe siècle)* (Paris: Ecole Normale Supérieure, 1993), pp. 69–87. See also Laurence Harf-Lancner (ed.), *Métamorphose et bestiare fantastique au moyen âge* (Paris: Ecole Normale Supérieure, 1985); Francis Dubost, *Aspects fantastiques de la littérature narrative médiévale (XIIe–XIIIe siècles): L'Autre, l'ailleurs l'autrefois* (Geneva: Slatkine, 1991); and Richard Bernheimer, *Wild Men in the Middle Ages: A Study in Art, Sentiment, and Demonology* (Cambridge, MA: Harvard University Press, 1952).

128. Sylvie Lefevre, "Polymorphisme et métamorphose: Les Mythes de la

naissance dans les bestiares," in Harf-Lancner (ed.), *Métamorphose et bestiare fantastique*, pp. 215–46.

129. See Jacques Le Goff, "The Marvelous in the Medieval West," in *The Medieval Imagination*, trans. Arthur Goldhammer (Chicago: University of Chicago Press, 1988), pp. 27–44, and chapter 1 n.8 and pp. 53–56 and 69–72 above.

130. See Chapter 2 above, and esp. nn.24 and 25 on alchemy. Many early alchemical texts held alchemical transformation to be impossible. As is well known, such caution gave way to enthusiasm in the fourteenth century.

131. See Bynum, *Resurrection of the Body*, pp. 165–67.

132. See *De diligendo Deo*, 11.30–31, OB 3, p. 145, and n.65 above. Because "we" are not truly "we" until soul and body are reassembled for Judgment, it is possible to argue that Bernard sees the period between death and resurrection as a period of development, because a period of longing (both for God and for body). One can therefore argue that Bernard in a sense introduces spiritual change and unfolding even into the afterlife. See Claude Carozzi, "Structure et fonction de la vision de Tnugdal," in *Faire croire: Modalités de la diffusion et de la réception des messages religieux du XIIe au XVe siècle: Table ronde . . .* (Rome: Ecole Française de Rome, 1981), pp. 223–34; see also *idem, Le Voyage de l'âme dans l'au-delà, d'après la littérature latine: Ve–XIIIe siècle*, Collection de l'Ecole française de Rome 189 (Rome: Ecole Française de Rome, 1994). Moreover, Javelet has argued that the Bernardian self is essentially developmental; to Bernard, I am what I become; I am what I love. See Javelet, *Image et ressemblance*, vol. 1, p. 458. The points are perceptive. But as this passage from *De diligendo Deo* suggests, the way Bernard writes about our need for resurrection also stresses the doubleness of the person unfolding toward God, awaiting resurrection.

133. *De conversione*, 3.4–4.5, OB 4, pp. 74–77.

134. Quoted at n.67 above and see Hiss, *Die Anthropologie Bernhards*, pp. 64–65.

135. On the Eucharist, see Introduction nn.5, 14, 17, 24, 36 and Chapter 2 nn.117–19 above. It is important to make clear that, after the controversy over

Berengar's ideas, most mainstream thinkers did not hold that the Eucharist was double in the sense in which the incarnate Christ was double. Consecration did not add Christ to bread; it changed bread into Christ. Exactly what this meant was, however, subject to a range of interpretation. In the years around 1200, a number of theories of eucharistic change saw "substance" or "substantial form" as in some sense existing after the consecration; and even in the early thirteenth century, views close to consubstantiation were sympathetically discussed (although ultimately rejected) among the Schoolmen. See, for example, Jaroslav Pelikan, *The Christian Tradition: A History of the Development of Doctrine*, vol. 3: *The Growth of Medieval Theology (600–1300)* (Chicago: University of Chicago Press, 1978), pp. 199ff.; Hans Jorissen, *Die Entfaltung der Transsubstantiationslehre bis zum Beginn der Hochscholastik* (Münster: Aschendorf, 1965), esp. pp. 1–50, 87–95, 117–19; and Gary Macy, "The Dogma of Transubstantiation in the Middle Ages," *The Journal of Ecclesiastical History* 45.1 (1994), pp. 11–41. As Dutton makes clear, Bernard is actually less eucharistic in his thought and imagery than his contemporary Cistercians; see "Eat, Drink, and Be Merry," pp. 11–12.

136. See passages cited at nn.89 and 95 above.

137. What I am identifying here as a sense of hybridity in anthropology is also characteristic of writings from the School of Laon in the earlier twelfth century. See, for example, the sentence fragment edited by Lottin that asserts that soul and body, "diverse, even opposite in nature," are joined into one person by "miraculous *unitas*" in a "secret and ineffable nexus"; Odon Lottin, *Psychologie et morale aux XIIe et XIIIe siècles*, vol. 5: *Problèmes d'histoire littéraire: L'Ecole d'Anselme de Laon et de Guillaume de Champeaux* (Gembloux: J. Duculot, 1959), no. 523, p. 345; and see the work being done by Susan Kramer on the School of Laon in her Columbia University dissertation, "Secret Sin and the Privacy of Interior Homo."

138. See Introduction, p. 30, above, and M.M. Bakhtin, *The Dialogic Imagination: Four Essays*, ed. Michael Holquist, trans. Caryl Emerson and Michael Holquist (Austin: University of Texas Press, 1981), pp. 70–82 and 111–18.

139. For Arnold, see at n.20 above. In the *Life of Malachy*, ch. 41, OB 3,

pp. 346–47, Bernard tells of a woman saved from rape when an "abominable monster" crawls from between her legs and frightens the rapist. The monster is literally, in this case, a visualization of sin. In a similar visualization (the first sermon for Lent, ch. 2), Bernard writes of the hypocritical faster as a monster (*horrendum monstrum*), a hybrid with the body of a man and the head of the devil (*corpus quidem hominis, caput autem daemonis habens*); OB 4, pp. 354–55.

140. See nn.1 and 6 above.

141. Morrison has remarked in "Hermeneutics and Enigma," pp. 145–47, that Bernard has no sense of history. We see this when we contrast his discussions of Church and religious roles with those of Anselm of Havelberg or Gerhoh of Reichersberg, for example. We also note it when we compare his spirituality with that of, for example, Hugh of St. Victor or Peter Lombard, both of whom put theological matters in a "salvation history" perspective.

CHAPTER FOUR: SHAPE AND STORY

1. This essay was delivered as the National Endowment for the Humanities Jefferson Lecture on March 22, 1999, in Washington, DC. I am grateful to the staff of the National Endowment for the Humanities, especially Joy Evans, and to NEH director William Ferris for their assistance. Because the Jefferson Lectures are intended for a broad national audience of supporters of the humanities, this essay was planned to stand alone without footnotes. I have altered the text somewhat and added a few references but have let the original character remain. I am grateful to Bruce Altshuler, Teodolinda Barolini, Kathy Eden, Martha Howell, Dorothea von Mücke, Ramona Naddaff, and Guenther Roth for ideas.

2. Adrienne Rich, "Meditations for a Savage Child," in *Diving into the Wreck: Poems 1971–1972* (New York: W.W. Norton, 1973), p. 58.

3. For bibliography on the question of identity, especially the third sense discussed here, see Caroline Walker Bynum, *Fragmentation and Redemption: Essays on Gender and the Human Body in Medieval Religion* (New York: Zone Books, 1991), pp. 398–400 nn.22–34; on identity position, see *eadem*, "Why All the Fuss About the Body? A Medievalist's Perspective," *Critical Inquiry* 22 (Autumn 1995), pp. 1–33, esp. nn.85–91.

NOTES TO PAGES 164-169

4. Oliver Sacks, *The Man Who Mistook His Wife for a Hat and Other Clinical Tales* (New York: Summit Books, 1985).

5. For recent literature on the werewolf, see Chapter 2 nn.76–80 above. For medieval resistance to metamorphosis, see Chapter 2 passim and esp. nn.20–25, 35, 50–52.

6. See the now-classic work by Keith Thomas, *Religion and the Decline of Magic: Studies in Popular Beliefs in Sixteenth and Seventeenth Century England* (London: Weidenfeld and Nicolson, 1971).

7. On allegorical exegesis, see Beryl Smalley, *The Study of the Bible in the Middle Ages* (Notre Dame, IN: University of Notre Dame Press, 1964). As I explain in Chapter 2, pp. 86–89 and 98–101, Ovid was not moralized in the earliest stage of his reception; the "moralized Ovid" is a fourteenth-century phenomenon.

8. Tzvetan Todorov, *Introduction à la littérature fantastique* (Paris: Editions du Seuil, 1970), pp. 28–62.

9. Ovid, *Metamorphoses*, 2 vols., 3rd ed., trans. F.J. Miller, revised by G.P. Goold, The Loeb Classical Library, 42–43 (Cambridge, MA: Harvard University Press, 1977), vol. 1, pp. 16–19. The version by Ted Hughes, *Tales from Ovid* (New York: Farrar, Straus, Giroux, 1997), p. 17, has it:

> He has become a wolf.
> But still his humanity clings to him
> And suffers in him.
> The same grizzly mane,
> The same black-ringed, yellow,
> Pinpoint-pupilled eyes, the same
> Demented grimace. His every movement possessed
> By the same rabid self.

10. See William S. Anderson, "Multiple Change in the *Metamorphoses*," *Transactions of the American Philological Association* 94 (1963), pp. 1–27; and Leo C. Curran, "Transformation and Anti-Augustanism in Ovid's *Metamorphoses*," *Arethusa* 5.1 (1972), pp. 71–91. Among recent work on Ovid, I have found especially helpful Leonard Barkan, *The Gods Made Flesh: Metamorphosis and the Pursuit*

of Paganism (New Haven, CT: Yale University Press, 1986), Warren Ginsberg, "Ovid and the Problem of Gender," in Marilynn R. Desmond (ed.), *Mediaevalia: A Journal of Medieval Studies* 13 (1989, for 1987): *Ovid in Medieval Culture: A Special Issue*, pp. 9–28, and Charles Segal, "Ovid's Metamorphic Bodies: Art, Gender, and Violence in the *Metamorphoses*," *Arion* 5 (1997), pp. 9–41.

11. Marie de France, *Bisclavret*, in Jean Rychner (ed.), *Les Lais de Marie de France* (Paris: Honoré Champion, 1966), pp. 61–71; trans. by Joan Ferrante and Robert Hanning, *The Lais of Marie de France* (Durham, NC: Labyrinth Press, 1978), pp. 92–100. See also the commentary by Ferrante and Hanning in *ibid.*, pp. 100–104.

12. *Bisclavret,* v. 154, in Rychner (ed.), *Lais de Marie de France*, p. 66.

13. See, for example, William Sayers, "*Bisclavret* in Marie de France: A Reply," *Cambridge Medieval Celtic Studies* 4 (1982), pp. 77–82, Kathryn I. Holten, "Metamorphosis and Language in the Lay of *Bisclavret*," in Chantal E. Maréchal (ed.), *In Quest of Marie de France, a Twelfth-Century Poet* (Lewiston, NY: Edwin Mellen Press, 1992), pp. 192–211, and the articles by Bruckner and Dunton-Downer cited in n.15 below. For an interesting reading that de-emphasizes the narrative elements in Marie, see Evelyn Birge Vitz, *Medieval Narrative and Modern Narratology: Subjects and Objects of Desire* (New York: New York University Press, 1989), pp. 149–75.

14. See *Bisclavret,* v. 157, in Rychner (ed.), *Lais de Marie de France*, p. 66. See also *ibid.*, vv. 154 and 208, pp. 66–67.

15. Although, as Matilda Bruckner points out, there is nothing intrinsic to who the wife is (that is, nothing about her femaleness) that makes it impossible for her to learn; see Matilda T. Bruckner, "Of Men and Beasts in *Bisclavret*," *Romanic Review* 81.3 (1991), pp. 251–69; see also Leslie Dunton-Downer, "Wolf Man," in J. J. Cohen and B. Wheeler (ed.), *Becoming Male in the Middle Ages* (New York: Garland, 1997), pp. 203–18.

16. Salman Rushdie, introduction to Angela Carter, *Burning Your Boats: The Collected Short Stories* (London and New York: Penguin Books, 1995), p. xii. Rushdie is speaking of Carter's use of the "Beauty and the Beast" fable, but the remark seems to me to apply to all her animal fables. On Carter, see also Wendy

Steiner's review of *Shaking a Leg*, in *New York Times Book Review*, December 27, 1998, pp. 6–7.

17. See the works cited in Chapter 2 nn.77 and 78 above, and J.A. MacCulloch, "Lycanthropy," in James Hastings (ed.), *Encyclopedia of Religion and Ethics* (New York: Charles Scribner's Sons, 1916), vol. 8 pp. 206–20. For an example, see Gervais of Tilbury, *Otia imperialia*, in G.W. Leibniz (ed.), *Scriptores rerum Brunvicensium*, 3 vols. (Hanover: N. Foerster, 1701–1711), decisio 3, ch. 120, vol. 1, p. 1003.

18. The stories relevant to my discussion are "The Bloody Chamber," "The Courtship of Mr. Lyon," "The Tiger's Bride," "Puss-in-Boots," "The Erl-King," "The Snow Child," "The Werewolf," "The Company of Wolves," "Wolf-Alice," and "Peter and the Wolf," in Carter, *Burning Your Boats*, pp. 111–94, 210–28, 284–91.

19. The parallel of werewolf and Christ is old; see Gerald of Wales, *Topographia Hibernica*, dist. 2, ch. 19, in J.S. Brewer, J.F. Dimock, and G.F. Warner (ed.), *Giraldi Cambrensis opera*, 8 vols., Rerum Britannicarum medii aevi scriptores 21 (London: Longman, 1861–1891; Kraus reprint, 1964–1966), vol. 5, p. 104 (not in the first recension).

20. "The Company of Wolves," p. 219. On integument, see Marie-Dominique Chenu, "*Involucrum*: Le Mythe selon les thélogiens médiévaux," *Archives d'histoire doctrinale et littéraire du moyen âge* 30 (1955), pp. 75–79.

21. A point made by Jasper Griffin, in "Cosmic Leg-Pull," *New York Review of Books*, April 20, 1995, pp. 10–14.

22. John J. Fitzgerald, "'Matter' in Nature and the Knowledge of the World: Aristotle and the Aristotelian Tradition," in Ernan McMullin (ed.), *The Concept of Matter in Greek and Medieval Philosophy* (Notre Dame, IN: University of Notre Dame Press, 1965), p. 59, and Sarah Waterlow, *Nature, Change, and Agency in Aristotle's Physics: A Philosophical Study* (Oxford: Clarendon Press, 1982), ch. 1, esp. pp. 1 and 15. For Platonic resistance to real change, see, for example, Plato, *The Republic* 2.380d–381b, 2 vols., trans. Paul Shorey, Loeb Classical Library 382–83 (Cambridge, MA: Harvard University Press, 1969–1980), pp. 188–91, where Socrates and Glaucon discuss whether the gods change form. Socrates says:

"Do you think god is … capable of … changing and altering his shape in many transformations …? Is it not true that to be altered and moved by something else happens least to things that are in the best condition, as, for example, a body by food … and plants by the heat of the sun … — is it not true that the healthiest and strongest is least altered? … and is it not the soul that is bravest and most intelligent, that would be least disturbed …? It is universally true, then, that that which is in the best state by nature or art or both admits least alteration by something else … [and] it is impossible then … for a god to wish to alter himself. …"

23. Aristotle, *On Coming-to-Be and Passing-Away* (*On Generation and Corruption*), trans. E.S. Foster, Loeb Classical Library 194 (Cambridge, MA: Harvard University Press, 1965), pp. 162–329, and Aristotle, *Poetics*, ed. and trans. Stephen Halliwell, Loeb Classical Library 199, 2nd ed. (Cambridge, MA: Harvard University Press, 1995), pp. 28–141, esp. ch. 10, pp. 62–65, which discusses different sorts of change in tragic plots. And see Introduction nn.6, 7, 19 above.

24. H.H. Munro (Saki), "The She-Wolf," in *The Penguin Complete Saki*, intro. by Noel Coward (London: Penguin Books, 1976), pp. 235–41. See also his stories "Laura," "Gabriel-Ernest," and "The Wolves of Cernogratz," in *ibid.*, pp. 241–45, 63–69, 410–14. For another modern retelling of the werewolf story that plays radically with the tradition, see Ursula K. Le Guin, "The Wife's Story," in *The Compass Rose* (New York: Harper and Row, 1982), pp. 245–49. Charlotte Otten mentions a number of recent werewolf stories and films in Charlotte Otten (ed.), *A Lycanthropy Reader: Werewolves in Western Culture* (Syracuse, NY: Syracuse University Press, 1986), pp. 1–2.

25. See the wonderful elaboration of this point in Ginsberg, "Ovid and the Problem of Gender." In a sense, of course, the same concern lies behind twelfth- and thirteenth-century theological efforts to apply the Boethian maxim that change requires something in common (*aliquid commune*). See Introduction n.7 above.

26. See Introduction nn.32 and 33 above.

27. Ovid, *Metamorphoses*, bks. 1 and 15, vol. 1, pp. 2–57, and vol. 2, pp. 364–427.

28. See Chapter 2 nn.35 and 99 above.

29. See Joyce E. Salisbury, *The Beast Within: Animals in the Middle Ages* (New York and London: Routledge, 1994), and Caroline Walker Bynum, *The Resurrection of the Body in Western Christianity, 200–1336* (New York: Columbia University Press, 1995), pp. 214–20.

30. Although we should not forget Christian fundamentalist opposition to such stories.

31. See, for example, *Yonec*, in Rychner (ed.), *Lais de Marie de France*, pp. 102–19, in which the bird-shape allows for freedom and self-realization, although the outcome is sad.

32. Carter, "Peter and the Wolf," p. 291.

33. For some remarks on this point, see Wendy Doniger O'Flaherty, *Other People's Myths: The Cave of Echoes* (New York: Macmillan, 1988), pp. 1–5.

34. See Bynum, "Why All the Fuss?" pp. 1–12 and 27–33.

35. See the works cited in n.43 below.

36. For recent controversy in feminist and queer theory over essentialism, see Bynum, "Why All the Fuss?" nn.1–19, esp. n.3.

37. Barkan, *Gods Made Flesh*, pp. 87–91.

38. On body as performance, see the works of feminist philosopher Judith Butler, *Gender Trouble: Feminism and the Subversion of Identity* (New York: Routledge, 1990) and *Bodies That Matter: On the Discursive Limits of "Sex"* (New York: Routledge, 1993).

39. Two modern examples of this sense that shape, especially in the form of scars, carries story and therefore identity are the lines from Adrienne Rich I quote as epigraph above (at n.2) and the novel *Beloved* by Toni Morrison. For a medieval example, see the obscure Middle Irish text "Tidings of Resurrection," which insists on the resurrection of the martyrs *with their scars*: "Tidings," ch. 11, ed. Whitley Stokes, in *Revue celtique* 25 (1904), pp. 240–41.

40. Ovid, *Metamorphoses*, bk. 3, v. 345–510, pp. 148–61.

41. On Dante, I have found especially helpful Teodolinda Barolini, *The Undivine Comedy: Detheologizing Dante* (Princeton, NJ: Princeton University Press, 1992), and Warren Ginsberg, "Dante, Ovid, and the Transformation of

Metamorphosis," *Traditio* 46 (1991), pp. 205–33. On Dante's conflation of himself as poet with the project of Ovid's great poem, see Kevin Brownlee, "Pauline Vision and Ovidian Speech in *Paradiso* I," in Rachel Jacoff and Jeffrey T. Schnapp (eds.), *The Poetry of Allusion: Virgil and Ovid in Dante's Commedia* (Stanford, CA: Stanford University Press, 1991), pp. 202–13, esp. p. 206.

42. For text and translation, I have used Dante, *The Divine Comedy*, trans. Charles S. Singleton, Bollingen Series 80, 6 vols. (Princeton, NJ: Princeton University Press, 2nd printing with corrections, 1977).

43. For the technical notion of body and soul in Dante, see Etienne Gilson, "Dante's Notion of a Shade: *Purgatorio* XXV," *Medieval Studies* 29 (1967), pp. 124–42, Bynum, *Resurrection of the Body*, pp. 295–305, Ginsberg, "Dante, Ovid, and the Transformation of Metamorphosis," and Manuele Gragnolati, "Identity, Pain, and Resurrection: Body and Soul in Bonvesin da la Riva's *Book of the Three Scriptures* and Dante's *Commedia*" (Ph.D. diss., Columbia University, 1999). Necessary as background is Philip Lyndon Reynolds, *Food and the Body: Some Peculiar Questions in High Medieval Theology* (Leiden: Brill, 1999), pp. 396–440.

44. On the tradition of representing souls with bodies, see Carol Zaleski, *Otherworld Journeys: Accounts of Near-Death Experiences in Medieval and Modern Times* (New York: Oxford University Press, 1987), and Eileen Gardiner (ed.), *Visions of Heaven and Hell Before Dante* (New York: Italica Press, 1989).

45. Unless, of course, we can find a way of thinking with the sense of paradox found in Bernard of Clairvaux. See Chapter 3 above.

46. See Kathy Eden, "Great Books in the Undergraduate Curriculum," *Literary Imagination: The Review of the Association of Literary Scholars and Critics* 2.2 (2000), pp. 125–33.

AFTERWORD

1. As Sarah Waterlow says of the paradox of becoming: "[O]rdinary discourse shows it up in all its force;... the paradox is all the more unnerving now it is found to lie at the heart of our untutored responses to the world. The philosopher who sees this will not stop at wondering how *change* is possible: for the incoherence of a notion so central to the human picture of the world casts

doubt on all our claims to knowledge." See Sarah Waterlow, *Nature, Change, and Agency in Aristotle's Physics: A Philosophical Study* (Oxford: Clarendon Press, 1982), p. 15.

Photo Credits:

Figure 1.
Réunion des musées nationaux/Art Resource, NY.

Figure 2.
Plate 7 from Charles Darwin, *The Expression of the Emotions in Man and Animals* (1892).

Figure 3.
Herzog August Bibliothek, Wolfenbüttel.

Figure 4.
Giraudon/Art Resource, NY.

Figure 5.
Conrad Kyeser, *Bellifortis*, fol. 85v.

Figure 6.
Kyeser, *Bellifortis*, fol. 105r.

Figure 7.
Plate 73, fig. 242 from Joseph Braun, *Die Reliquiare des christlichen Kultes und ihre Entwicklung* (Freiburg: Herder, 1940).

Figure 8.
By Permission of The British Library, London.

Figure 9.
Bibliothèque nationale, Paris.

Figure 10.
Bibliothèque nationale, Paris.

Figure 11.
Mary Carruthers, *The Craft of Thought* (Cambridge: Cambridge University Press, 1998), p. 141. Reprinted with the permission of Cambridge University Press.

Figure 12.
Courtesy of Thomas E. A. Dale.

Figure 13.
Bibliothèque municipale, Dijon.

Figure 14.
Plate 26 from Marcel Durliat, *La Sculpture romane en Roussillon*, vol. 1 (Perpignan: Tramontane, 1952), p. 35.

Figure 15.
Photo by Achim Bednorz, from Rolf Toman, *Romanesque: Architecture, Sculpture, Painting* (Cologne: Könemann, 1997), p. 335.

Index

Designed by Bruce Mau with Barr Gilmore and Michael Barker
Typeset by Archetype
Printed and bound by Maple-Vail on Sebago acid-free paper